The Centre of Thing

to Cicely
with best wishes
from Chris.
27. 3. 91.

TITLES OF RELATED INTEREST

Burke's Reflections on the Revolution in France
F. P. Lock

Locke's Two Treatises of Government
Richard Ashcraft

Gender, Genre and Narrative Pleasure
edited by Derek Longhurst

The Centre of Things

Political Fiction in Britain from Disraeli to the Present

CHRISTOPHER HARVIE
Universität Tübingen

London
UNWIN HYMAN
Boston Sydney Wellington

Published by the Academic Division of
Unwin Hyman Ltd
15/17 Broadwick Street, London W1V 1FP, UK

Unwin Hyman Inc.
955 Massachusetts Avenue, Cambridge, MA 02139, USA

Allen & Unwin (Australia) Ltd
8 Napier Street, North Sydney, NSW 2060, Australia

Allen & Unwin (New Zealand) Ltd
in association with the Port Nicholson Press Ltd
Compusales Building, 75 Ghuznee Street, Wellington 1, New Zealand

First published in 1991

British Library Cataloguing in Publication Data

Harvie, Christopher
   The centre of things : political fiction from Disraeli to the present
   1. Fiction. Special subjects. Politics. Critical studies
  I. Title
809.39358

ISBN 0–04–445593–3
ISBN 0–04–445592–5 pbk

Library of Congress Cataloging in Publication Data

Harvie, Christopher T.
   The centre of things : political fiction from Disraeli to the present
 / Christopher Harvie.
     p. cm.
   Includes bibliographical references and index.
   ISBN 0–04–445593–3. — ISBN 0–04–445592–5 (pbk.)
   1. Political fiction. English—History and criticism. 2. English
fiction—19th century—History and criticism. 3. English fiction
—20th century—History and criticism. I. Title.
PR830.P6H37 1991
823.009′358—dc20   90–46071
                                            CIP

Typeset in 10 on 12 point Bembo
Printed in Great Britain by
Billing and Sons, Ltd., London and Worcester

Contents

To Margot,
and in memory of
Arnold

Preface

This book was originally commissioned as part of a polemical series whose writers ended up orphaned in the storm which descended on British publishing in the mid-1980s. This in itself was a commentary on the break-up of the conventions it records, and the basic argument of the ill-mannered early draft I find still holds good. It took time to rewrite it, partly because much more reading was necessary, partly because of my own involvement in Scottish affairs as a broadcaster, consultant and journalist. I hope that both experiences have added depth to my analysis.

I have continually been indebted to students too numerous to mention who have participated in my seminars at Tübingen. Their enthusiasm and energy in reading and discussing texts have been a continual stimulus. Carola Ehrlich, Helmut Schröder and Paddy Bort have, besides their own research, also acted as my assistants and helped word-process the text. Among my academic colleagues I am particularly grateful to Hans Schwarze, Walter Greiner, and Martyn Thompson for their expertise in different areas, and to my former colleagues at the Open University, Clive Emsley, Anne Laurence, Tony Aldgate, Graham Martin, Henry Cowper, Angus Calder and Arthur Marwick. I have benefited during the course of writing from many conversations with, among others, Neal Ascherson, Tom Nairn, James Naughtie, Owen and Ruth Dudley Edwards, Alasdair Gray, Rory Watson, John McGrath, Bernard Crick, Catherine Hall, Anthony Barnett, John Osmond, John Milne, John Mackenzie, Jeff Richards, Douglas Gifford, David Daniell, Colin MacArthur, Paul Addison, Victor Kiernan, Roy Foster, David Wright, Kenneth Morgan, George Cubie, Colin Matthew and Michael Brock. I am also grateful to the editors of *The Scotsman*, *The Times Higher Education Supplement*, the *New Statesman*, and *Cencrastus*, in whose columns early versions of some sections appeared, and to the Librarians of the London Library and of the National Libraries of Scotland and Wales. My parents, brother and sister, and my Aunt Jessie have been endlessly hospitable to a wandering scholar, and besides coping with the aforesaid wandering scholar my wife Virginia's knowledge of the Victorian novel, and stamina for 'close reading' – of these and various drafts – was enormously valuable. My daughter Alison's demand for fairy stories has been put to uses she can't at the moment imagine. Whether it's a Good Thing for a historian to rush into literary affairs

I leave to the reader to judge. I was stimulated into this by my work at the Open University and years of friendship with Margot and Arnold Kettle. I dedicate this book to them.

Tübingen
24 January 1990

1

The Conversation of People Who Counted

TOWARDS THE END of Trollope's novel *The Prime Minister* (1876) the Duke of Omnium takes his cabinet colleague Phineas Finn to his favourite view on his estate of Matching. Omnium's coalition government is falling apart; he is alienated from his ambitious and tactless wife; he will never be prime minister again. As they walk, the Duke haltingly explains his political philosophy to the young Irishman, who doesn't much like it. The Duke talks about equality. He envisages a time when the condition of a future duke and that of his coachman will converge. Finn implies his dissent. 'By equality?' he asks. 'The millennium', answers the Duke, '. . . is so distant we need not even think of it as possible'; and Finn, who has painfully pulled himself up over six volumes from the doctor's surgery of Killaloe, in the west of Ireland, to the Cabinet and marriage with a wealthy widow, can draw breath. 'Equality would be a heaven, if we could obtain it', the Duke continues, 'How can you look at the bowed back and bent legs and abject face of that poor ploughman, who winter and summer has to drag his rheumatic limbs to his work, while you go a-hunting or sit in pride of place among the foremost few of the country, and say that it is all as it ought to be?' The Duke looks up into the clouds and, lost for words, sits down. 'Equality is a dream. But sometimes one likes to dream – especially as there is no danger that Matching will fly away from me in a dream . . .'[1]

I quote this episode because, although it's a discussion of political ideology – and, indeed, an expertly 'composed' view of the well-heeled humanitarianism of the English ruling class, from Gladstone to Prince Charles – it can only be conveyed by fiction. The fumbling, fudging discourse of the Duke, the setting and the metaphors both for morally necessary social change and the possessions on which Omnium's power depends, the scepticism of the younger career politician: all give a density and solidity far beyond conventional political writing. If we want to understand why the political theme has been so strong in English literature, this is the obvious place to start.

But is there a proper genre to be investigated? If there is, what does it consist of? Why is it important? Is this for intrinsic reasons, or because of the politics of its own production and reception? I believe the importance of the genre lies in its *praxis*: it merged 'entertainment' and ideology to produce a useful political discourse for a traditional society intent on social and economic change, and then, more capriciously, it commented on and provoked its increasingly eccentric development in the twentieth century. The genre's success also depended on its being as complex as the social reality it had to explain; in other words, its apparent equipoise has stemmed from internal tensions being debated and, at least in earlier days, worked out.

The political novel was more than a commentary on the politics of its golden age, the epoch of Trollope and Disraeli; it was an important part of them. This duality has continued, in step with the decline of British civil society. In the 1980s, as imports from Europe, America and Japan decimated British manufacturing, and trade unions and Celtic nationalism threatened to pull the State apart, the weakness of British political imagination seemed basic to the failure to cope with new situations and problems.[2] The conventions which had once made for stability seemed now only capable of producing stasis.

At the same time this imperilment focused attention on what, precisely, those conventions had been. What codifications of political custom and usage had held the State together? And where did political fiction fit in? H. A. L. Fisher, historian, education minister under Lloyd George, and Virginia Woolf's cousin, defined the political novel in 1928 as 'the novel which chiefly concerns itself with men and women engaged in contemporary political life and discussing contemporary political ideas'.[3] Obviously this meant something more than political ideas or metaphors: a realistic treatment of parties, Parliament, the work of government – and the relationship of this to less overtly political things like religious and economic conflicts, public opinion and the media, industry, war and foreign policy. Even in Britain the occasional abstract idea, conveyed by treatise or by non-naturalistic fiction – Orwell's *Nineteen Eighty-Four*, for example – might have to be admitted. Political fiction is a literary artefact, which deals with historical events and ethical quandaries, but a mirror in the Whitehall roadway cannot reflect a simple scene.

The British political novel has only incidentally been about the relationship of ideals to personal life and psychology, as in the great European novels of society from *Le Rouge et le Noir* to *Anna Karenina* or *The Man without Qualities*. When Doris Lessing complained in 1973 that

'There isn't one [British] novel that has the vigour and conflict of ideas in action that is in a good biography of William Morris',[4] she highlighted the importance in Britain of 'institutional' novels – political novels, university novels, spy novels – not of low quality but necessarily restricted in scope. E. M. Forster in *Aspects of the Novel* rejected such themes as a means of categorizing – denouncing this as 'pseudo-criticism' – but the existence of these genres also seems to account for what he regarded as the marginality of the nineteenth-century English novel, when confronted with the monuments of Balzac, Turgenev or Tolstoy.[5]

Yet fiction was taken seriously by the political intelligentsia of Trollope's day. Men such as Frederic Harrison, John Morley or James Bryce, who as reviewers, editors and publishers' readers – a small élite linked by family relationship, profession and education – mediated between the legislature and law-courts and the 'upper ten thousand': the guardians of convention in a constitution-less state.[6] This makes disentangling the significance of the corpus complex: relating the novels, their plots, characterization, and symbolism, not only to the biography of their creators, but also to their publication and reception and thus to their function in society. What follows is an attempt at a general topography whose major source cannot, alas, be reproduced here: a bibliography of political fiction that I started in 1984 and which had accumulated some 600 titles at the last count - ranging from classics to pulp, and at least indicating when activity in this area was particularly noticeable, and what sort of themes were being stressed at any given time.

II

The standard account of political fiction sees it evolving in the 1840s, and the central figure is Benjamin Disraeli, spelling out his political creed in the trilogy of *Coningsby*, *Sybil* and *Tancred* in 1844–7, and then dominating the Conservative Party for a further thirty-three years.[7] Although Trollope hated him, Disraeli made relevant, in George Watson's words, 'a corpus of fiction unique in the world . . . in the simple prominence it confers on the parliamentary idea'.[8] Watson was following the American scholar Maurice Edmund Speare who had published *The Political Novel: Its Development in England and America* in 1924, taking the political novel from the 1840s to H. G. Wells's *The New Machiavelli* of 1911.[9] According to Watson, such novels thrived only in a particular epoch:

> Most of the novels considered here are about a parliamentary state . . .
> perhaps one-sixth of male adults had the right to vote . . . Democracy
> is among the issues raised . . . but it is not itself the background of

assumption, and this fiction concerns itself rather with an elective and deliberative process for which 'parliamentary' seems the only name.[10]

Yet in 1973, while parliamentarianism was less than thriving, political fiction was pouring out, as novels, plays, films and television series. By 1984 the commemoration of George Orwell's dystopia had to share publicity with Jeffrey Archer's lucrative Westminster soap-opera *First among Equals*.

Whether Archer's commercial success showed the health of the genre was another matter. It could be argued that in the 1980s there re-emerged a much more intimate and critical idea of politics, not just region- but class- or sex-specific. This could be linked to a parallel political culture which reflected more of a European bourgeois cast of mind, originating in the 'Jacobin novelists' of the 1790s and the 'theoretical histories' of the Scotsman John Galt, who applied Machiavelli's 'civic humanism' to the parliamentary life in the first political novel *tout court*: *The Member* of 1832.[11] At no point did the 'parliamentary novel' totally supplant this 'civic humanist' tradition in political fiction. Indeed, the high Victorian period, Trollope's epoch, substantially integrates it.

So we can say that: first, for over a century political fiction - from Galt and Disraeli via George Eliot's *Felix Holt* and Trollope's Palliser novels to Meredith's *Beauchamp's Career* and H. G. Wells's *The New Machiavelli* – was an important component in a constitution which, being unwritten, was peculiarly dependent on its political culture; second – and much less positively – the failure of these conventions to solve the economic and structural problems of British society after the First World War – the period in which Arnold Bennett's *Lord Raingo* and Joyce Cary's *To Be a Pilgrim* and Chester Nimmo trilogy are set – has been reflected in the dissolution of the genre: not a total collapse, but an eviction of those 'considered' and subtle literary treatments which once endorsed the general political structure.

Why, then, has political fiction been neglected? One problem is that the range and importance of the ideas and activities covered - controversial almost by definition – go beyond the novel to tap all sorts of literary communication: plays, short stories, dramatic poems, films, television and radio dramas. One story can appear in two or three modes, in different contexts, and with different results. Take Trollope's *Can You Forgive Her?* This started out as a play, became a novel, was broadcast and ultimately televised in 1973. Its setting changed from the French Revolution to the Victorian ruling class; but after a period when the notion 'Trollope' embodied a bluff confidence in the resilience of 'the British way' it made its greatest impact in the 1970s, when its solidity stood in stark contrast to a Britain riven by industrial action and chronic inflation – not all that far from what Trollope originally wanted to convey, back in 1850.

Is politics not also the wrong classifying factor in novels still dominated by the sequences of love, 'from the first meeting of the eyes to bed'? Love-interest, Trollope for one continually tells us, is what makes the world of his novels go round. Yet all aspects of relationships between the sexes, from physical desire through idealistic inspiration to the ensnaring of heiresses and inheritances, play particular political rôles. The same could be said for 'action', dominant in one kind of political novel, the thriller, which has in fact been an ingredient from the earliest days.

This opaqueness has given us a fairly exiguous critical tradition. There is a recognizable 'English novel of manners', a 'novel of religion', a 'socialist novel', and so on, each genre with its recognized custodians, but surveys of political fiction – though they exist – are episodic and, with only a couple of exceptions, lightweight. Effectively, they boil down to the monograph by Speare, Watson's essay of 1973, and a lengthy piece by Roy Foster, written in 1981 and buried in a rather obscure learned journal.[12] Speare's book is mainly an apologia for Disraeli; Watson's is similar in time-scale but somewhat broader in scope; Foster's is a perceptive study of Victorian political novels by one of the few historians who can tackle literature. All three have been of value to the present study, but none goes beyond the First World War, although the genre palpably does, nor do they treat the genre as a social, as well as a literary and political phenomenon: something which has perforce to include Jeffrey Archer as well as Joyce Cary.

The problem is partly one of refereeing between incompatible methodologies. *Littérateurs* see principle and consistency break down into an almost existential struggle which defies moral, let alone literary-theoretical, appraisal; historians see incomprehensible theories imposed on situations which make sense only in terms of 'the rules of the game'. Both are terrified of straying into each other's territory. So historians fail to examine the imaginative lives of politicians, or account for why a particular fictional treatment carries weight, while literary scholars all too often erect their theories on out-of-date or simplistic historical models. Influential political fiction may not be, in any sense, 'good' fiction. It may succeed, like so many politicians, by endlessly repeating some proposition in 'graspable' terms. But its existence will inevitably affect any 'serious' writer who chooses a political theme.

This is not to enforce some determinist pattern as a criterion of literary – or for that matter political – worth. Political fiction itself stresses that culture, ritual, individual psychology and self-awareness have all at critical times cut across economic pressures and class-formation. But to isolate the genre's influence we need to know how its components have been produced, distributed and absorbed by society, even if this means charting the sociological shallows of popular fiction and its marketing as well as the 'moments of vision' that great literature can provide. The second needs, and indeed can scarcely exist without, the first.

Forster insisted that the strength of English fiction lay in its cultivation of psychological self-examination on a domestic scale. But Virginia Woolf (the most private of novelists, but also a typical volunteer in the army of left-wing progress, married to a leading figure in the Labour Party) was conscious of that other, debatable land. She wrote in her diary for 18 October 1918, after talking to H. A. L. Fisher:

> It's quite obvious of course that for some reason perhaps not creditable to me I think HF worth many more words than Ka, say or Saxon . . . My theory is that for some reason the human mind is always seeking what it conceives to be the centre of things; sometimes one may call it reality, again truth, again life – I don't know what I call it; but I distinctly visualise it as a possession rather more in HF's hands than in other people's. For the moment he makes all the rest of the world's activities appear as ramifications radiating from him. But this is roughly stated –.[13]

Woolf recognized this, and although she did not follow her cousin into his 'centre of things' there is irony and honesty in her appreciation. There is none in Fisher's self-absorption, although his position was contingent on a shifting political scene, whose ramifications ultimately trapped him rather than radiated from him. Richard Crossman would see Warden Fisher of New College, fifteen years later, still in thrall to 'the charm of politics'.[14]

Other writers took up the challenge and tried to understand the actions and thoughts of people faced with the ambiguous morality of politics, important in the context of any governing élite like the British, educated 'humanistically' rather than – in the German sense – 'scientifically'. Yet 'the centre of things', like Peer Gynt's onion, diminishes as each layer of mystification is peeled off. Understanding it involves taking on the cash-nexus of the literary-economic structure and the glue which fastens the genre on to the British consciousness – cliché, stereotype, perhaps even archetype:

'Does your novel have a title?' Llewellyn asked.

'Something like, "Whatever happened to Jerusalem", with an exclamation mark.'

'You don't mean that, of course.'

'All right, what about "Arrows of Desire"?'

'So it's all about the crumbling of ideals. The young hero seduced by fame and the good life, abandoning responsibilities. Meanwhile back in his home town the pinched faces of the unemployed hang over their bowls of thin gruel in the soup kitchens. He's a poor lost soul, the tiresome git, and makes a pilgrimage of rediscovery - self-regeneration by sharing the poverty of the noble proles he left behind. But it's too late. He forgot the golden rule. Never Go Back. They shun him in the streets. They *stone* him in the streets. But there's this old flame he put in the family way when he was the hope of the valley – it's got to be set in Wales, this – and now she's grey and withered. She alone befriends him and takes him to her bed. The roof falls in just as he's giving her one.'[15]

Such plots recur in scores of novels, films and plays: idealism tarnishes, London illusion prevails over provincial reality, sexual betrayal follows political deceit. Sure as fate. When the serious novel about politics has long been in abeyance, and a television comedy about government, Anthony Jay and Jonathan Lynn's 'Yes, Minister', has become an ideological oracle, despite its aggravated cynicism, are the last layers being peeled off the onion?

The British genre had no consistent equivalent in any major European country. Clemenceau and Goebbels may have written novels, and plays and operas also served political ends – Verdi and Manzoni being particularly important in the Italian Risorgimento; but the great discontinuities – revolutions, wars and dictators - cast long shadows over Stendhal, Zola and Sartre.[16] German writers produced perceptive novels about constitutional politics – Theodor Fontane's *Der Stechlin* (1898) or Heinrich Mann's *Der Untertan* (*Man of Straw*) (1918) – and cabaret provided a satiric, sometimes surreal, commentary, yet only in the last decade has a genre akin to the British begun to emerge. When Gisela Elsner published a novel about the 1976 election, *Der Punktsieg* (*Win on Points*), this was regarded as an original idea. Elsewhere there is no established tradition. Masterpieces such as Giuseppe di Lampedusa's *The Leopard* (1958) stand isolated, coexisting rather strangely with some impressive and influential interpretations of European politics from British authors: George Meredith, E. L. Voynich, Richard Hughes, Sybille Bedford and John Berger.

There have been enough American political novels for Joseph Blotner's *The Modern American Political Novel* (1966) to identify 138 such between 1900 and 1960. Particularly prolific during the 'muckraking' 1900s and the New Deal era, these were derived from 'lobby' novels about the notoriously corrupt Grant administration, whose authors included, among others, Mark Twain and Henry Adams.[17] Later on, Hollywood films like *Mr Deeds Goes to Town* (1939) continued to contrast rural virtue with political chicanery. The rate increased sharply after 1961–5, reflecting the Kennedy years, the industry of Gore Vidal and the scandal of

Watergate, but Blotner's judgement seems fair: American fiction, lacking the 'British' qualities of institutional familiarity and what Lukacs called 'composure', took a disturbingly Manichaean view: '. . . the forces of evil are ever present . . . even when the forces of right triumph, the triumph is but one engagement in a most uncertain conflict.'[18] Ultimately, he finds only four novels – by Robert Penn Warren, John Dos Passos and Lionel Trilling – which can bear comparison with a 'typical' British equivalent: Joyce Cary's *To Be a Pilgrim* (1942).[19]

III

If the political novel is defined, as G. M. Young described history, as 'the conversation of the people who counted',[20] then Disraeli originated the genre, and we must start with him. It's difficult to tackle basic questions of definition completely in the abstract, and the story has to begin somewhere. So let's take *Sybil* (1845) and compare it with Balzac's *The Member for Arcis* (1847).

Plots first (I don't intend to make a habit of summarizing plots, but here it's unavoidable). One: *The Member for Arcis*. Balzac deals with the 1839 election in Arcis-sur-Aube, birthplace of Danton. The republicans are putting up a candidate to oppose the aristocratic nominee, only to hear that he has been killed in a colonial war. The centre-right government sends down a failing roué, Maxime de Trailles, to infiltrate a government placeman. But the mayor, a hosier and successful speculator, outmanoeuvres both and claims the seat.

Two: *Sybil*. Lord Egremont is elbowed out of his rights by his elder brother Lord Marney. In the ruined Marney Abbey he meets a beautiful girl, Sybil, along with her father Walter Gerard, a Chartist leader, and his friend Morley, a socialist journalist. Egremont falls in love with Sybil, whose father believes himself to be the heir of Mowbray Castle, and shows sympathy to the Chartists. But while preparing a Chartist rising Gerard contacts the antiquary Baptist Hatton (whose brother 'Bishop' Hatton heads a 'physical force' rabble in Wodgate, a Black Country town), who tells him that the documents proving his claim are in the keep of Mowbray Castle. Morley, out to win these and Sybil, leads an attack with Bishop Hatton on the Castle. Gerard is cut down by Lord Marney, leading the yeomanry, who is then stoned to death by the mob. Troops led by Egremont kill Morley, and Mowbray Castle, along with Bishop Hatton, is burned down, but not before the papers have been found. Sybil, now an heiress, marries Egremont, now Lord Marney, and everyone still alive lives happily ever after.

Both writers were disciples of Walter Scott and even of overcharged romantics like Charles Maturin and 'Monk' Lewis. Both were critics of the new manufacturing order acute enough to win the respect of Karl Marx, still obscure, whose *Communist Manifesto* was being drafted in 1847, and both were *au fond* shrewd students of the machinery of politics. That said, their two books – in plot, characterization, intention and the treatment of actuality – could scarcely be more different. The plot-summaries speak for themselves: Balzac's sober realism against Disraeli's wild melodrama. Both authors were, however, specific about their political intentions: *Sybil* 'would now draw public thought to the state of the people'; Balzac published in an opposition newspaper supporting the exiled Bourbons. Balzac implied his criticisms of the July monarchy when he had the local capitalist thrust aside revolutionary and aristocrat alike, and when he made the far-from-sympathetic Eugène de Rastignac criticize the instability of the system in the prescient tones of an English Tory, seeing in the ambitions of the Chamber of Deputies the threat of a new Napoleon:

> The representative is called the Cabinet, and in France there is no Cabinet – only a Will for life. In France only those who govern can blunder, the opposition can never blunder; it may lose every battle and be none the worse; it is enough if, like the Allies in 1814, it wins but one victory. With 'three glorious days' it could destroy everything. Hence not to govern, but to sit and wait, is to be the next heir to power.[21]

Where Disraeli painted his political colours with a broad brush and simply wiped out all opposition to his cardboard hero and heroine, Balzac's chief characters, notably Rastignac, had matured before his readers over several books of *The Human Comedy*. Both writers attempted to present a panorama of their societies, but *The Member for Arcis* could depict only a small part of the France of the late 1830s. Balzac wrote within the English realist tradition, rejecting universals and myths in favour of 'the individualisation of . . . characters and . . . the detailed presentation of their environment'.[22] Disraeli used extracts from government reports on public health and employment to punch home his message, but the overall result was best described in Q. D. Leavis's recipe for bestseller literature: 'Bad writing, false sentiment, sheer silliness and a preposterous narrative are all carried along by the magnificent vitality of the author.'[23] That said, Disraeli's blend of action, incident and romance was what, every year, English families went in their thousands to see in the theatre or the pantomime. Balzac's sobriety appealed to a small-circulation novel-reading public of educated conservatives and (as it turned out) 'scientific socialists', for whom he could, instead, have written an article.[24] Disraeli existed *within* that wider public, roughly co-terminous with the electorate, which was beginning to read novels and was as enthusiastic about Dickens as it had earlier been about Paine (probably) and Bunyan (almost certainly). It wanted entertainment, thrills and some instruction besides; it got them from Disraeli, who used fiction as, literally, the only way he could put his ideas across.

Disraeli and Balzac both appreciated the impact of history, and admired Scott as its great actualizer. Yet while Balzac saw the uniqueness of historic events disrupting attempts to unify the novel of politics and the novel of manners, Disraeli capitalized on his readers' appetite for grand ideas, romance and sensation.[25] Balzac writes in the context of 1789. None of his characters dies violently, but the guillotine and Napoleon's battlefields are always audible, influencing their loyalties and behaviour, while they operate in the complicated structure of post-revolutionary French administration. *Préfets* and *Contrôleurs-Générals*, newspapers and their journalists, the venerable-sounding titles of the *nouveaux riches*, all hold together a complex European politico-literary scene, fissured by revolution, difficult to visualize, or to explain to the inexpert.

In both writers the State is present. But, while Balzac has to document it, Disraeli merely hints. As power was derived from social status, and not vice-versa, his definitions and characters could be simple, and arranged in convenient pairs: aristocracy and middle class, churchman and dissenter, industry and land, capital and labour. Apprehension existed: Disraeli had a thing about conspiracies run by secret societies. But politician as well as storyteller kept this under control through the game of politics and the rules its players, the parties, drafted. While Balzac's Rastignac calculated apprehensively in his ministry, Disraeli had already pronounced with supreme confidence: '. . . the foundation of civil polity is Convention . . . everything and every person that springs from that foundation must partake of that primary character.'[26] For Disraeli political fiction became as much part of that convention as party. With reason, for the eccentricities of *Sybil* still contain some of the most resilient of British political concepts, as regularly exercised on platforms in the 1980s as at any time in their history:

'Two nations; between whom there is no intercourse and no sympa-thy; who are as ignorant of each other's habits, thoughts and feelings, as if they were dwellers in different zones, or inhabitants of different planets; who are formed by a different breeding, are fed by a different food, are ordered by different manners, and are not governed by the same laws.'
'You speak of — ' said Egremont hesitatingly.
'THE RICH AND THE POOR.'[27]

Disraeli's achievement was profound, complex, and deeply contra-dictory. His literary vehicle combined social realism with adventure and romance, but the fuel that powered it was a combination of complacency and menace, of politics as sport and politics as chaos, from Egremont at the Derby to the holocaust of Mowbray Castle. *Sybil* differs radically from the Balzacian novel in being a *thriller*, with the basic requirements of the genre – a society regarded as at least potentially perfect, a conspiracy, a dynamic hero (or, rather, hero and heroine), and a violent denouement in which all is resolved.[28]

The essentially 'paranoid' structure of the Establishment novel of politics – the preservation of the system – was Disraeli's main bequest. *The Two Nations* was *Sybil's* subtitle, but by the 1870s 'one nation' had become a Conservative theme, successfully deployed for over thirty years.[29] Disraeli's discourse provided a *myth* convenient to the practices of the party system. He was not the last prime minister to write a novel (Ramsay MacDonald and Winston Churchill both did) or to behave as if he were a character out of one (Arthur Balfour, Lloyd George or Harold Macmillan would qualify here), but his career made the genre something to be respected.[30] Second, he gave British political fiction the *range* of its appeal: drama, intrigue, romance, realism and comedy – the stock-in-trade of traditional, and enduring, popular entertainment.

IV

British political fiction is older than Disraeli, but he acquired for it its oracular reputation. 'The whole programme of the Labour Party is contained in its pages', wrote Fisher of *Sybil* in 1928.[31] It is still, a century and a half later, sufficiently alive for Thatcherite Conservatives to feel they have to fight it, or for a contemporary novelist, Piers Paul Read, to put this in the mouths of his characters:

'And in a more general sense,' he asked, 'can anything be done?'
'I think it can.'
'How?'
'Have you read *Sybil* by Disraeli?'
'Some time ago.'
'Do you remember the "two nations"? The rich and the poor? How they should be one?'
'Yes.'
'They aren't, are they? Despite the Welfare State.'[32]

Disraeli's novels attracted attention because he was an unmistakable political presence, who had rallied the protectionists and the country gentry against Sir Robert Peel, driven him from the party, and taken over the leadership of the Commons. *Coningsby* and *Sybil* could be quarried by those who wished to divine his intentions. But, though he claimed a coherent logic in 1849 for his use 'of a method which, in the temper of the times, offered the best chance of influencing opinion',[33] as little coherence attended the trilogy as success attended Disraeli's leadership of the Tories. 'Young England' was in ruins before *Sybil* was published.[34] Yet, as the fiction of the next thirty years would show, Disraeli had pushed the genre to the centre of the stage, and this parliamentary ethos was ingested into literary culture, helping create the idea of 'Britishness': a complex product of social ritual, political and publishing organization, during the decade in which British political evolution radically – and unexpectedly – diverged from that of its continental neighbours.

To understand why this happened we have to grasp both the extent of the crisis of the 1840s and the rôle of literature in it, as estimated at the time and subsequently. We can thus set the various literary responses to the British predicament against the traditions and sources on which Disraeli himself drew. In so doing we can incidentally trace the evolution of the genre before Disraeli, and the nature of his contribution to it. This enterprise is unwieldy – first crisis, then literary response, then politico-literary tradition – but it seems unavoidable. We need to consider all three.

NOTES

1   Anthony Trollope, *The Prime Minister* [1876] (London: Oxford University Press, 1938), vol. 2, pp. 320–1.
2   The literature of self-laceration recurs throughout this book. A representative selection of the more recent examples could start with Tom Nairn, *The Break-Up of Britain* (London: New Left Books, 1977), and include Martin Wiener, *English Culture and the Decline of the Industrial Spirit, 1850–1980* (Cambridge: Cambridge University Press, 1981), and Ralf Dahrendorf, *On Britain* (London: BBC, 1982). I have tried to sum up the whole enterprise in 'Liturgies of national decadence', *Cencrastus*, Summer 1985; while Neal Ascherson has addressed its political implications in 'Ancient Britons and the republican dream', in *Games with Shadows* (London: Radius, 1988).
3   H. A. L. Fisher, 'The political novel', *Cornhill Magazine*, vol. 64 (1928), p. 25.
4   Doris Lessing, introduction to *The Golden Notebook* (1962; reissued London: Granada, 1973), pp. 10–11.
5   E. M. Forster, *Aspects of the Novel* (London: Arnold, 1927), p. 22.
6   See the present author's *The Lights of Liberalism: University Liberals and the Challenge of Democracy, 1860–86* (London: Allen Lane, 1976).
7   See Robert Blake, *Disraeli* (London: Eyre & Spottiswoode, 1966), pp. 193ff.
8   George Watson, *The English Ideology: Studies in the Language of Victorian Politics* (London: Allen Lane, 1973), p. 133.
9   M. E. Speare, *The Political Novel: Its Development in England and America* (New York: Oxford University Press, 1924), pp. 74ff.
10 Watson, *English Ideology*, p. 135.
11 Gary Kelly, *The English Jacobin Novelists, 1780–1805* (London: Oxford University Press, 1976); and P. H. Scott, *John Galt* (Edinburgh: Scottish

Academic Press, 1985); and see J. G. A. Pocock, *The Machiavellian Moment* (Princeton: Princeton University Press, 1975).

12 Roy Foster, 'Political novels and nineteenth century history', *Winchester Research Papers in the Humanities* (1981).

13 See *The Diary of Virginia Woolf*, ed. Ann Olivier Bell, Vol. 1, *1915–1918*, (Harmondsworth: Penguin, 1977), p. 205.

14 Richard Crossman, 'H. A. L. Fisher', in *The Charm of Politics* (London: Hamish Hamilton, 1958).

15 This example is taken from Arthur Hopcraft, *Mid-Century Men* (London: Hamish Hamilton, 1982), p. 224. Not a bad novel, but evidently owing its origins to an abortive television script.

16 The 'craving for excitement' that characterized French fiction was attributed by a censorious but perceptive critic to 'two generations of ceaseless revolution, of dazzling conquests and bewildering defeats'. See W. R. Greg, 'French fiction: the lowest deep', originally in *Edinburgh Review*, 1855, reprinted in *Literary and Social Judgements* (London: Trübner, 1877), p. 190.

17 cf. Mark Twain and Charles Dudley Warner's *The Gilded Age* (1873), Frances Hodgson Burnett's *From One Administration to Another* (1878) and Henry Adams's (anonymously written) *Democracy* (1880).

18 Joseph Blotner, *The Modern American Political Novel* (Austin: University of Texas Press, 1966), p. 358.

19 Robert Penn Warren's *All the King's Men* (1946), John Dos Passos' *Adventures of a Young Man* (1939) and *The Grand Design* (1949), and Lionel Trilling's *The Middle of the Journey* (1947).

20 G. M. Young, *Victorian England: The Portrait of an Age*, [1936] (London: Oxford University Press, 1953), p. vi.

21 Honoré de Balzac, *Le Député d'Arcis* in *La Comédie humaine* (Paris: Gallimard, 1977), vol. VIII, p. 810.

22 Ian Watt, *The Rise of the Novel* (Harmondsworth: Penguin, 1963), p. 19.

23 Q. D. Leavis, *Fiction and the Reading Public* (London: Chatto & Windus, 1932), p. 62.

24 Marx intended to follow *Capital* with a book on Balzac; see Edmund Wilson, *To the Finland Station* [1940] (London: Fontana, 1960), p. 332.

25 See F. W. J. Hemmings, *The Age of Realism* (Harmondsworth: Penguin, 1974), pp. 36–67. In France most MPs were landowners, while most ministers were officials or professional politicians; see W. L. Langer, *Political and Social Upheaval* (New York: Harper, 1969), p. 2.

26 Benjamin Disraeli, *A Vindication of the English Constitution* (1835), ch. 5.

27 Benjamin Disraeli, *Sybil* (Harmondsworth: Penguin, 1954), p. 73.

28 See Jerry Palmer, *Thrillers* (London: Edward Arnold, 1978), p. 38; and Christopher Harvie, 'Political thrillers and the Condition of England', in Arthur Marwick (ed.), *Literature and Society* (London: Routledge, 1990).

29 Foster, 'Political novels', p. 18.

30 For MacDonald's novel (never published), see David Marquand, *Ramsay MacDonald* (London: Cape, 1977), pp. 28–9; for Churchill's *Savrola* (Macmillan, 1897), see W. D. Norwood, 'Sir Winston Churchill as a novelist', *Bulletin of the New York Public Library*, vol. 66 (1962), pp. 539–46.

31 Fisher, 'Political novel' p. 28.

32 Piers Paul Read, *A Married Man* (London: Secker & Warburg, 1979), p. 116 (subsequently paperbacked and produced as a television serial, 1983).

33 Preface to fifth edition of *Coningsby*, 1849.

34 Sarah Bradford, *Disraeli* (London: Weidenfeld & Nicolson, 1982), p. 139.

2
The Literature of Crisis

I

IN THE 1840s an economic catastrophe seemed imminent. Cyclic slumps had been getting worse since 1815; the population, particularly in Ireland, was soaring, and an overcapitalized industrial sector, narrowly based on textiles, was being battered by bad harvests and the failure of the new elixir – railway construction – to work. In 1842 (the year in which *Sybil* is set) the economy touched a level which, if repeated, would cause a revolt, much to the satisfaction of Friedrich Engels, in 1844, who wrote of 'slight impulses' setting 'the avalanche in motion'. Only Tennyson's metaphor and mood were different:

Slowly comes a hungry people, as a lion, creeping nigher.
Glares at one that nods and winks besides a slowly-dying fire.[1]

The British working class had organized itself into Chartism between 1839 and 1842, and both knew it could do so again, in a movement without European parallel which tapped a tradition of plebeian radicalism antedating 1789 and, according to E. P. Thompson, turned 'everything, from their schools to their shops, their chapels and their amusements . . . into a battleground of class'.[2]

Differences with Europe were also political and demographic. In 1841, Britain was a multi-national state. Over 42 per cent of its population lived in Scotland, Wales and Ireland; many of these spoke languages other than English. (By 1891 the non-English quotient was less than 25 per cent and non-English speakers were a tiny minority.) The State lacked legitimacy among many of its inhabitants. Most Irish wanted Repeal of the Union, and had organized under Daniel O'Connell to this end. Scotland and Wales, under-represented in Parliament, their electorates skewed in favour of the propertied, had religious inclinations quite opposed to the English establishment. But one force was lacking in Britain: the radical middle class, the 'National Guards' who (with bayonets fixed against marauding proles) were to sweep the despots from power in March 1848.

Britain's decentralization meant that the 'commanding heights' of the State were not – as in Paris or Berlin – staffed by professional bureaucrats, and prone to be grabbed by those - students, journalists, and so on – who were aspirant bureaucrats. Apart from some wavering in 1842, the middle class had different goals even from the 'labour aristocracy', and much in common with the traditional élite. If revolution threatened, it would neither show 'democratic' solidarity, nor directly confront, but 'incorporate' enough leading cadres of the working classes to diffuse the threat they posed. The Bradford woollen manufacturer W. E. Forster, Carlyle's and later Trollope's friend and Matthew Arnold's brother-in-law, wrote to his mother in April 1848:

> Unless some concessions be made to those masses, and unless all classes strive earnestly to keep them better fed, first or last there will be a convulsion; but I believe the best political method of preventing it is by the middle class sympathising with the operatives, and giving themselves power to oppose their unjust claims by helping them in those which are reasonable.[3]

With free trade gained in 1846, and the major conflict with the ruling élite settled, the discontent which made Richard Cobden the hero of European liberals on his Continental tour was dissolved. Philanthropy and literary fellow-feeling could now be a definitive – and safe – middle-class response.

This applied even to literary 'radicals'. In 1842 Dickens published the first of his Christmas Stories, *A Christmas Carol*. When an economist attacked the benevolence of the reformed Scrooge as mindless, he determined to make his next 'little book', of 1843, 'a blow for the poor' (and also to improve on the £500 royalty he had got from Chapman & Hall for the *Carol*). But after Julian Harney of the *Northern Star* begged him to 'throw the weight of his great name into the scale on poverty's side' he backed off.[4] He was not to be the last. Literary responses to the 'Condition of England' in the 1840s – from Mrs Gaskell, Charlotte Brontë, Disraeli and Kingsley as well as Dickens – still stock the university syllabuses. But was this substitution of sympathy for a democratic polity the only – or even, in the long term, the most successful – approach?

The 'literary view' of British industrialization dates from the 1890s and was part of a masterful – and largely French – inquest on Victorian Britain: Mantoux, Boutmy, Halévy, Ostrogorski. Louis Cazamian wrote in 1903 that

. . . the *roman à thèse* was the outstandingly influential didactic literary genre of the period . . . Literary realism was the best weapon social idealists could have wielded against the attitude of mind that they opposed. Utilitarianism and political economy were alike abstract. The idealist reaction was able to castigate individualism for its failure to appreciate the real and concrete . . . The social novel implanted realism in English thinking.[5]

He was following Arnold Toynbee's argument in his 'industrial revolution' lectures that the novelists had educated the middle classes in their new responsibilities, through *Mary Barton, Alton Locke, Sybil,* and so on. This was part of the same anti-Marxian reaction which produced French sociology – an élite enlightenment dissolving dogmatism and mutual ignorance, and restoring social solidarity. But this point was made by selection, discarding the literature of radicalism and incorporating Disraeli in the ranks of the concerned middle class. I want to argue instead that there were three possible literary interventions: radical didactic fiction, the middle-class humanist novel, and the embryo political novel. All had their limitations, but the last won. By borrowing from all three types, Disraeli both succeeded in his own political ploys and launched the novel of party and parliament.

II

Engels saw the British workers in 1844 as men 'possessed of a will as well as of working-power' and forecast that 'the whole Political Economy of today is at an end'.[6] Yet radical fiction, although part of a culture ranging from broadsheet ballads to Cobbett's polemic, Hazlitt's criticism and Owen's social schemes, has suffered acutely from the 'monstrous condescension of posterity'. Martha Vicinus talks of the 'speeches, essays, prison letters, dialogues, short stories, lyrical poems, epics' issuing in periodicals, of which the *Northern Star* had in the 1830s and early 1840s one of the biggest circulations of any English weekly.[7] These, moreover, were not half-digested importations from the Continent but came from a tradition of radical dissent running back to the the Civil War – of Hampden, Milton, Harrington and Bunyan.

But many of the masters of pamphlet-literature regarded fiction as evil. Cobbett wrote in his *Advice to Young Men* in 1830: 'I deprecate *romances* of every description. It is impossible that they can do any *good,* and they may do a great deal of harm. They excite passions that ought to lie dormant.'[8] Fiction was as pernicious as organized religion, while poetry could ennoble and inspire. However, the frontier between the acceptable 'moral fable' such as W. J. Linton's 'Records of the World's

Justice, by a Hardwareman' and didactic romances like those of Bunyan was conveniently uncertain. *The Pilgrim's Progress* was inevitably much adapted. In 1839, Thomas Doubleday, a Quaker soap-manufacturer in Newcastle and a Cobbettite, produced 'A Political Pilgrim's Progress' in the *Northern Liberator*. 'Vanity Fair' is, not surprisingly, Whitehall; an election for the 'City of Plunder' is predictable: 'Hundreds of houses were opened for eating and drinking and the electors were reeling about in the streets in a state of savage and beastly intoxication.'9 Doubleday followed his Bunyan up with an adaptation from Swift, 'The Political Tale of a Tub'. This linked the Chartist cause with Tory pamphleteers of the early eighteenth century, the age of Pope and Bolingbroke, who assaulted the Whigs' alienation of the Church to their own purposes, a theme, common to radicals and high churchmen, which Disraeli was to use in *Sybil*.

By the late 1830s Chartist papers recognized how popular novels were among working people and filled up spare columns more with extracts looted from current novels, even by Tories like Captain Marryat, than original writings by workers and radicals.10 Even the latter deferred to literary eminence; the engraver Linton revered Walter Scott for portraying working people 'struggling against illegitimate power',11 while Mrs Trollope found her factory novel championed by the *Northern Star*, somewhat to her embarrassment: 'I don't think anyone cares very much for *Michael Armstrong* – except the Chartists. A new kind of patrons for me!'12

By the 1840s Chartist publicists had become even more positive. Ernest Jones wrote of the novel in the *Labourer* in 1847 that there was 'not a more powerful medium through which to indoctrinate the general mind – it has access where a sterner style of writing would never gain admittance. It leads the reader, as it were in chains of wild flowers, to the harvest field of truth';13 and in 1849 Thomas William Wheeler wrote in the *Northern Star* that 'the opponents of our principles' had been allowed to colonize the novel, 'to wield the power of the imagination over the youth of our party, without any effect on our part to occupy this wide and fruitful plain'.14 Both Wheeler and Jones later wrote serial melodramas. Wheeler's *Sunshine and Shadow* ran for thirty-seven issues of the *Northern Star* in 1849–50, and Ernest Jones's *De Brassier: A Democratic Romance* ran in his *Notes to the People* in 1851–2. Even if the *Northern Star* was past its peak, over 100,000 bought, let alone read, it; and Jones, the Welsh-German gentleman-radical, was probably the most popular poet of his day.15

Such serials had one crude advantage for radical editors: their episodes could be expanded or contracted as a makeweight to news stories or other articles. But this meant that they lost the great compulsion that 'every week thousands of readers were delivered to the same point in the narrative, collectively conscious of one another in a way unattainable in modern fiction'.[16] Moreover, Chartist politics could never rival the satisfactions of the commercial melodrama. The latter depended on a grand-slam denouement with virtue rewarded and vice punished. Didactic serial novels like *Sunshine and Shadow* and *De Brassier* could not escape from an atmosphere of continuing, not to say dispiriting, struggle. De Brassier, speculator and demagogue, is, because of his wealth and energy, more interesting than Jones's working-class martyrs. The latter have to resemble the readers, while De Brassier *is* the system, realized in stage-villain terms. The good are imprisoned within the moral fable; the bad, with their illegitimate but enduring allure, gain the liberty of romance.[17]

The enthusiasm of Chartists for 'bourgeois' literature – their faith in Dickens, for example – reflected their fundamental commitment to parliamentary democracy. So why did middle-class writers respond so negatively? 'Novelists – even the most liberal', Wheeler wrote, 'can never draw a democrat save in warpaint.'[18] They regarded Chartism as Jacobin *and* anarchic, although even deeper than the split between Chartists and middle-class free traders were the differences between the national programme – the 'Six Points' – and Chartism's provincial variety: nonconformists like Edmund Gosse's father, who rejected all but scriptural inspiration; Irish and Welsh and Highland workpeople whose English, if it existed, was primitive; Owenites seeking a remodelled industrial community; O'Connorites wanting to do away with industry altogether. Moreover the middle class seemed to underestimate the strength of its own system of cultural communication. Just as Lord John Russell's government responded to the last great Chartist demonstration – on 10 April 1848 on Kennington Common – by buying over the private telegraphs for a week, so 'print-capitalism', in the shape of the publishing industry, could, if challenged, mediate a concerned but fundamentally conservative social philosophy.[19]

III

The sense of 'crisis' in the late 1830s forced itself on the comfortably off and the economically inexpert in terms which interdicted the cross-class alliance which had extorted Reform in 1832. The middle class, embodied in the Anti-Corn Law League, aimed at different goals from those of plebeian radicals; but at the same time – partly because of the urgency of its own agenda - it feared that events might engulf it. This apprehension – unlikely to be encountered among Continental intelligentsias at the time of the *Vormärz* – achieved peculiarly effective literary embodiment in Thomas Carlyle who, despite his contempt for its 'long ear', helped the novel 'to a status in literature and life which it has hardly yet lost'.[20] His persona still resounded in D. H. Lawrence a century later, having figured in Disraeli, Trollope, Kingsley, Dickens, George Eliot and Meredith.[21]

Meredith defined the Carlyle problem when he wrote of him inducing 'an electrical agitation in the mind and joints',[22] but of being in matters of legislation 'no more sagacious nor useful nor temperate than a flash of lightning in a grocer's shop . . . Read The French Revolution and you listen to a seer: the recent pamphlets, and he is a drunken country squire of superordinary ability.'[23] Carlyle's contribution was both personal – despite his Dumfries-shire seclusion he had become by 1834 perhaps the best-read man in Britain – and the result of a peculiar national predicament. One of a talented generation which had matured during the post-1815 upheavals and the decline of Scottish autonomy, he struggled to impose an intellectual *approach*, rather than an order, on what he saw as chaos. His remarkable prose was a sort of choric mosaic of excerpts from Scots Calvinism and Common Sense, German idealism and French Saint-Simonianism, thrown together as an existential 'gospel of work' which many besides the liberal John Morley used as a route out of the 'great gulf which is fixed round our faculty and existence'.

Carlyle's quest for a *polis* contributed something fundamentally disquieting to British political culture.[24] Struggling from the ruin of Adam Ferguson's 'civic humanist' Scots community, Carlyle appropriated from idealism – Schiller and Goethe in particular - the relativizing of facts within a *Weltanschauung*; from Saint-Simon he acquired the division of historical development into 'organic' and critical periods, which the years since the French Revolution obviously seemed to be. The result – 'the world as text' – was neither pulpit nor laboratory, but a replication of conflict. In 'Characteristics' (1831) he attacked the 'system-making' that climaxed in the French Revolution, while insisting on the physical roots of discontent: 'It is not by Mechanism but by Religion; not by Self-interest but by Loyalty, that men are governed or governable.'[25] Carlyle not only shows the power of imaginative language to articulate a critical theory when more logical systems break down; he capitalized on the traumas which political collapses visit on the individual psyche. To say that menaces threaten mankind, but the real illness is spiritual – materialism and 'dryasdust' specialization which prevents material discontent from being perceived – is both portentous and universal. A declining Scottish nationalism is neither.

D. H. Lawrence talked of Carlyle's philosophical mania – something which implied an exploding galaxy of radical ideas, kept together by sheer energy and viscerally appealing to a readership which was cosmopolitan – Scots, German, American: Jeffrey, Goethe, Emerson – rather than metropolitan English. This dynamism persisted in his first London years, when his friends the Bullers and John Stuart Mill aligned him with the philosophical radicals, and attracted to him nationalists like Mazzini and the future Young Irelanders Charles Gavan Duffy and John Mitchel.[26] Erudite, friendly, and brilliant in conversation – Dr Johnson a century on – his reaction to the denationalized mechanism of the Scottish enlightenment, that 'flat continuous threshing floor for logic', his search for a new national identity, could only be contagious.[27]

Disraeli was infected – and could also turn in a passable imitation, as in the series of letters from 'Coeur de Lion' to *The Times* in 1837.[28] Many of his profundities are Carlyle's. When Eva instructs Tancred in Jerusalem about the ills of civilization – 'Europe is too proud, with its command over nature, to listen even to prophets. Levelling mountains, riding without horses, sailing without winds, how can these men believe that there is any power, human or divine, superior to themselves?'[29] – she repeats almost word for word what the young unknown had told the readers of the *Edinburgh Review* in 1829: 'We remove mountains, and make seas our smooth highway; nothing can resist us. We war with rude Nature; and by our resistless engines, come off always victorious, and loaded with spoils.'[30] Carlyle offered imaginative writers a secularized religious impulse; in 1800 perhaps two-thirds of books published were religious; evangelical fervour had to be maintained even if the agenda changed.[31] After a period when Britain had been cut off from Europe, he was cosmopolitan. He insisted in 1837 on the irreversible impact of the French Revolution, and in *Oliver Cromwell* (1845) he equated Britain's own civil war with it, something which also stressed the 'industrial revolution' whose consequences had still to be faced.[32] Finally, he used the spirit and language of the dialectic in a therapeutic way, institutionalizing contradiction in society and politics. He attacked individualism but preached the sanctity of the individual soul; his violent, millenarian, 'revolutionary' prose (something he shared with his compatriots Thomas Chalmers and Edward Irving) rejected radical mechanism for tradition and hierarchy; his cosmopolitanism and Scottish nationalism articulated the 'Condition of England' question.[33]

Heroes and Hero-Worship (1840), at which lectures Dickens met Carlyle, is explicitly élitist and anti-liberal, anticipating Weber, Pareto and Mosca and the emphasis of their generation on myth and folklore in creating social doctrine. Where economic liberals like Ricardo, Malthus and Sismondi got more pessimistic as the problems of industrialism increased, Carlyle insisted that the hero, not least 'the hero as man of letters', ought still to inspire and reform.[34] This scornful rhetoric ended in inaction in a way that Bentham, say, would never have done. Engels, developing the radical element in Benthamism, later condemned Carlyle's 'sullen Philistine grumbling at the tide of history that cast him ashore', but in 1844 he praised him for prescience: '. . . he has sounded the social disorder more deeply than any other English bourgeois, and demands the organisation of Labour.'[35] Engels had read *Chartism*, but the Chartists, or at least the *Northern Star*, did not recognize themselves in Carlyle's book: respectable carpenters, dissenting ministers and compositors, who had been talking politics for decades were no hunger-maddened Jacquerie. Although Carlyle disliked parliamentarians, Disraeli – 'that superlative Hebrew conjurer' – more than most, his influence on them was profound. His radical critique of industrialization ended with *Latter-Day Pamphlets* (1850), but as a communicator he experimented with the secular sermon, the moral fable, and even, in 'The Diamond Necklace', with the conspiracy mystery. He gave to middle-class individualists a best self, a *soul*, to strive towards.

Carlyle was what imperial Germany called a *Kulturpessimist*, convinced that materialistic rationalism would cause cultural and community decay. He drew on Ferguson as well as on Schiller's *Letters on Aesthetic Education* (1794), in which he, like Herder, had offered the nation as the reconciler of this atomism. Carlyle, profound in his Scottish nationalism in his essays on Burns and Scott, followed the Germans, but housed his dilemmas in 'Britain'. His later rhetoric supported the existing order, and placed its faith in that same Platonic élite prescribed by such Victorian oracles as Jowett and the Positivists,[36] but in the 1830s and 1840s what mattered was his portrayal of history as a contemporary drama to which the participants would write their own conclusion.

IV

No one more so than the novelists of the 1840s. Both Cazamian and Kathleen Tillotson, in *Novels of the 1840s* (1954), saw them expand the novel's social range until it became *the* literary commodity of middle-class Britain: 'scouts who had crossed the frontier (or penetrated the iron curtain) and brought back their reports'.[37] The thriller metaphor, even at this early stage, is intriguing. But she also notes that prudishness and insularity were waiting in the wings.[38] If 'the novel has entered on that career of thoughtfulness which, crude, chaotic, unbalanced as its early stages may be, leads to *Middlemarch*',[39] a lot of places don't get reached: in particular the home, work, love and politics of the mass of the population. More recently Sheila Smith has argued that the novelists doctored and diluted the – frequently scandalous – reports of others, and prescribed from their own ideological pharmacopoeia: 'The Romantic artist's "vision" ceases to proceed from the substance of the Other Nation's life, imaginatively apprehended; rather, a spurious "vision" of the future has been mechanically imposed upon it.'[40] Considering fiction apart from novels, the 1840s seem even more conservative. In the 1830s politicians were bombarded with literary polemic.[41] Galt's and Disraeli's satires came on top of Ebenezer Elliott's *Corn Law Rhymes* (1831) and the factory plays of Thomas Walker and Douglas Jerrold, whose *Factory Girl* (1832) was attacked for turning Drury Lane into 'a *scenic rotunda* for the promulgation of republican principles'.[42] These were followed by *Oliver Twist* (1838) with its assault on the Poor Law, Frances Trollope's *Michael Armstrong* (1840), also staged, and Bulwer's radical, though safely historical, dramas. Before *Coningsby* was published, *Punch* (then distinctly radical, publishing Thomas Hood's 'The Song of the Shirt' in 1843) and George Reynolds's 'Salisbury Square school' of sensationalist radical writers were going full blast.[43] This sort of public pressure had already forced governments to undertake factory inspection (1833), mitigated the rigours of the Poor Law, sanctioned Edwin Chadwick's inquiry into public health and begun the regulation of coal-mines. The authors of this literature ranged from Tories like Frances Trollope to utilitarians like Harriet Martineau, but their centre of gravity lay in the provinces or London bohemia.

This reformism lasted until 1842; thereafter a new, more literary wave seems to take over.[44] Disraeli belonged to it. *Coningsby* came out in May 1844 and *Sybil* in May 1845. Although Winifred Gerin denies it, Mrs Gaskell must have read him, or at least a review, as there are similarities in plot and symbolism between *Sybil* and *Mary Barton* (1848).[45] More positively, *Sybil*'s combination of crisis, Carlyleianism and the chivalric ideal of an 'organic society' - out of German historical writing and neo-medievalism à la Kenelm Digby – imprinted itself on the writers who came to maturity in 1848.[46] Yet the latter were neither positive nor illuminating in Cazamian's sense, but deeply pessimistic and almost brutal in fighting fire with fire.

Mrs Gaskell confessedly tried to avoid politics in *Mary Barton*[47] but she regarded even Chartist parliamentarianism, rather orthodox after the experiments of Owenism, as the fuse on a social powder-keg. Although a conservative critic, the former factory-owner W. R. Greg, saw the social novels as unfair to working-class politicians, the prevailing image was Carlyle's, of a coming Irish-engendered poverty which would awake the 'Berserkir rage' in the heart of the English workers.[48] Against them, the novelists showed collective fear, not sympathy. Cazamian was right to contrast their solid decriptions with the thin didactics of Martineau and Frances Trollope.[49] But while they quarried personal experience and public documents – the Blue Books and newspaper reports – with the energy of Scott they made individual fates emblematic of the dangers of democracy. Theoretical reformers, however admirable, get carried into a vortex of violence: John Barton becomes involved in the same sort of murderous conspiracy that threatens Gerard Moore in *Shirley* (1849), Alton Locke is swept off by a rural Jacquerie; Stephen Morley and Walter Gerard, in *Sybil*, are dragged at the heels of 'Bishop' Hatton to the sack of Mowbray Castle.

Where does violence come from? Chorus, from the delusions of radical politics. Kingsley began his Christian Socialist involvement with the Chartists by denouncing their political goals, their demand for (quoting Carlyle) 'a fifty-thousandth share in a Talker in the National Palaver at Westminster',[50] and he sets out to prove this in *Alton Locke* (1850) with examples of incompetence and division shading into mania. Disraeli depicts Morley and Gerard as confused idealists in the grip of the trade unions, sinister masonic-like secret societies. When John Barton sets out for London as a delegate to the National Convention in 1839, this is not seen as a challenge to Parliament, but as an act of supplication: 'So a petition was framed, and signed by thousands in the bright spring days of 1839, imploring Parliament to hear witnesses who could testify to the unparalleled destitution of the manufacturing districts.'[51] Barton is lobbied by representative locals. One asks for machines to be broken up, another 'would like thee to tell 'em to pass the short hours bill'; a neighbour presents Barton with a shirt, but complains 'what a sore trial it is, this law o' theirs, keeping childer fra' factory work'; a 'pompous, carefully-speaking man' wants all MPs to be made to wear calico shirts; Job Legh, the artisan-intellectual, ends by articulating the 'sensible' orthodoxy of the Anti-Corn Law League '. . . ask parliament to set trade free, so as workmen can earn a decent wage, and buy their two, ay and three, shirts a year; that would make weaving brisk.'[52]

'Aw a muddle', as Stephen Blackpool put it in *Hard Times*. Just as Dickens changed the erudite Ernest Jones into the loutish Slackbridge, Mrs Gaskell's Manchester artisans appear never to have heard of Carlyle and Hetherington, or read *Twopenny Trash* or the *Monstrous Black Book*. Think of Jedediah Coleman in Mark Rutherford's *The Revolution in Tanner's Lane* (which, although published in 1887, was based on Rutherford's knowledge of such old Chartists as Linton) and this sort of thing becomes frankly incredible. Moreover, the theme of violence doesn't, historically, fit. *Mary Barton* takes place in the first phase of Chartism, 1838–42, but John Barton's murder of young Carson was based on an incident of 1832. *Shirley* is explicitly historical, set in the Luddite troubles of 1811, but into *Sybil*, set in the same period as *Mary Barton*, Disraeli cheerfully throws every riot he could think of. Kingsley's *Alton Locke* actually tries to tackle the 1848 period, but his climax, Locke's arrest for inciting a rural riot, is more typical of the Swing risings of 1831.

The resolution of the real conflicts was beyond the humanitarianism of the novelists. They could produce civic equity only by falsifying the scale of exploitation: one contrite capitalist equalling one errant labourer. But the true proportion created differences in life-chances which made it impossible for anyone but the besotted enthusiast for some monocausal explanation of human distress – like temperance or sanitary reform – to convince even himself. Carlyle's characterization of the English response to the Irish was, for most people, closer to the truth: 'The wild Milesian features, looking false ingenuity, restlessness, unreason, misery and mockery, salute you on all highways and byways. The English coachman, as he whirls past, lashes the Milesian with his whip, curses him with his tongue; the Milesian is holding out his hat to beg.'[53] You either fell in with what the Milesians wanted – Carlyle nearly did, through his influence on Young Ireland – or you reached for the whip. One Irish observer, Maria Edgeworth, noted astutely the desolation of the irresolute: despite the 'happy' ending, *Mary Barton* 'leaves a melancholy, I almost feel a hopeless, impression'.[54]

The heroes of the social novelists emigrate or die, suggesting that any sort of humane existence in Britain was impossible. This pessimism reaches an extremity in *Alton Locke*, which was too much even for Carlyle: '. . . while welcoming a new explosion of red-hot shot against the Devil's Dung-heap', he wrote to Kingsley, 'I must admit your book is definable as crude. The impression is of a fervid creation, left half chaotic.'[55] *Alton Locke*'s horrific pictures of misery and insecurity, among tailors, in London slums and on the land, had no rival until Robert Tressell; and, though he borrowed heavily from Henry Mayhew, Kingsley obviously *felt* his convictions; he may have regarded violence as mistaken, but not as unjustifiable.[56]

But, since he had to put over his religious line and please the publishing establishment, *Alton Locke* ends truly bizarrely. Coming back from a forlorn attempt to redeem an Irish Chartist, Locke falls into a delirium in which he relives man's evolution, a strange mixture of sex, violence and pre-Wellsian science fiction. From this it appears that revolution – conveyed by a symbolism both Mosaic and phallic (Locke leads his tribe in an effort to tunnel through a mountain to the promised land) – is both imminent and inevitable. Locke's tribe overthrows the rich, and follows him to the tunnel to break through to the 'good land and large'. Only then does a Christian Socialist titled lady appear to Locke to urge him to claim the new commonwealth for God. This slams the theological brakes on something which, for all Christian Socialism's defensive meliorism, was looking dangerous. Kingsley's outcome – the example of Bunyan flashes to mind – *ought* to have been unambiguously revolutionary, as the author was dreaming, according to his brother-in-law J. A. Froude, 'of nothing but barricades and provisional governments and grand Smithfield bonfires where the landlords are all roasting in the fat of their own prize oxen'.[57] Sheila Smith writes that the social novelists 'represent the reactionary religious heart protesting against the progressive Utilitarian head',[58] yet Kingsley, the most religious, was also the most radical, producing a melodrama of ideas perhaps without parallel until Orwell's *Nineteen Eighty-Four*. *Alton Locke* was also explicitly 'British' in that its leading figures are English, Irish and Scots. Yet that impatience with consistency and logic that the critic W. R. Greg noted as common to Kingsley and Carlyle (who made an all but personal appearance in *Alton Locke*) enabled Kingsley to check an argument grown dangerous.[59] For good. The 1850s saw 'Parson Lot' as muscular as ever, but now a Christian imperialist, wielding the whip.

V

The social novel was pervaded less by liberal philanthropy than by the threat of revolution – through the influence of Carlyle, the 1842 economic crisis, and the redirection of religious millenarianism. Although by the late 1840s economic improvements – free trade and the railway boom – had removed any immediate threat of breakdown, the *literati* ended in stasis. When confronted with a polite radical political movement, they recoiled into metaphors of moral collapse. Carlyle's 'revolutionism' proved, by 1850, no less metaphysical. The result was a decade, the 1850s, when literary meliorism ought to have been evident, but was not. Instead, there was a retreat to the domestic and the parochial, to *Cranford* and *Adam Bede* and the Barchester of *The Warden*.

Social fiction *had* become more sophisticated at the expense of confidence. It echoed the middle-class *malaise* patent in the division over the Crimean War, the subsequent collapse of political radicalism and supremacy of Palmerston, from whose bombast intellectuals withdrew into private life. Leslie Stephen credited Thackeray in *Vanity Fair* (1847–8) with measuring the level of the upper-class society which fought elections and was at home in Parliament;[60] but Thackeray, though recognizing Disraeli's skill,[61] proved incapable of developing this – as was indicated by his one disastrous election campaign in Oxford in 1857.[62] Trollope, in his first 'social problem' novel, *The MacDermots of Ballycloran*, recognized the crisis of legitimacy afflicting English government in Ireland, but thereafter deserted an evidently unpopular theme.

What is lacking in all these cases is any concept of the state and of the rôle of a clerisy – an official intelligentsia – in winning legitimacy for it. Carlyle knew this, and his authoritarianism reflected the strategies which brought about national unity in much of Europe. But if he recognized the peculiarity of Britain – the fact that a multi-national society complicated the 'Condition of England Question' – he remained eccentric to English intellectual development and, as it proved, too deeply pessimistic to engage with it. The same could also be said of Christian Socialism. The theology of Liberal Anglicanism which underpinned the efforts of Maurice, Ludlow, Neale and Kingsley in 1848 was based on the equation of individual self-development with the State articulated by German idealist historiography, transmitted via Coleridge and Thomas Arnold.[63] Its political projects, although successful within limits, had scarcely any impact on Parliament, but through the public schools and working-class education they continued to influence a liberal but still rather authoritarian upper-class view of national politics. The achievements of J. M. Ludlow in trade union reform and E. V. Neale in consumer co-operation were considerable, and Maurice's own monument was the Working Men's College in St Pancras, of which A. V. Dicey was later director.[64] Christian Socialism was the nearest that was to be achieved to an 'English nationalism', but it still partook of the hysterical quality that afflicted post-Carlyleian fiction. Marx and Engels saw the fluctuating political alliances of the 1850s as a long-drawn-out transfer of power from the Whigs to the bourgeoisie, and were disappointed when the two apparently confirmed an alliance. The social novels would have enlightened them about the deep lack of middle-class confidence in its ability to govern on its own.

The one person whose notions seemed to be borne out was Disraeli, a figure certainly affected by the ideologies of the time, but capable of qualifying these with the *praxis* of parliamentary politics and the long literary view of their rôle in British history. To study this implies surveying the evolution of a hitherto absent component: the political theme in English fiction after the French Revolution. But it will also be – not fortuitously – a study of Disraeli's own ideological formation.

NOTES

1   F. Engels, *The Condition of the Working Class in England* [1844] (London: Panther, 1969), p. 322; Tennyson, 'Locksley Hall' (1842) pp. 137–8; and see Asa Briggs, *The Age of Improvement* (London: Longman, 1959), pp. 295 ff.

2   E. P. Thompson, *The Making of The English Working Class* (London: Gollancz, 1963), p. 832.

3   Quoted in T. Wemyss Reid, *Life of William Edward Forster* (London: Chapman & Hall, 1888), Vol. I, p. 233.

4   Quoted in Horst Rössler, *Literatur und Arbeiterbewegung: Studien zur Literaturkritik und Frühen Prosa des Chartismus* (Frankfurt: Peter Lang, 1985), p. 68.

5   Louis Cazamian, *The Social Novel in England: Dickens, Disraeli, Mrs Gaskell, Kingsley* [1903], trans. Martin Fido (London: Routledge, 1973), pp. 2–3; and see Arnold Toynbee, *The Industrial Revolution* (London: Rivington, 1884), p. 85–93.

6   Engels, *Condition*, p. 245.

7   Martha Vicinus, *The Industrial Muse* (London: Croom Helm, 1974), p. 94.

8   Quoted in Rössler, *Literatur*, p. 54.
9   Quoted in ibid., p. 165.
10 Ibid., p. 58.
11 See F. B. Smith, *Radical Artisan: William James Linton, 1812–97* (Manchester: Manchester University Press, 1973), p. 7.
12 Quoted in W. H. Chaloner, 'Mrs Trollope and the early factory system', *Victorian Studies*, vol. 4, no. 2 (December, 1960), pp. 160, 164.
13 Quoted in Rössler, *Literatur*, p. 64.
14 *Northern Star*, 31 March 1849.
15 Vicinus, *Industrial Muse*, pp. 125–35; and see John Saville, *Ernest Jones, Chartist* (London: Lawrence & Wishart, 1952), p. 20 ff.
16 William Donaldson, *Popular Literature in Victorian Scotland: Language, Fiction and the Press* (Aberdeen: Aberdeen University Press, 1986), p. 85.
17 In *Except the Lord* (1954) Joyce Cary made Chester Nimmo both perceive the element of social protest within the nineteenth-century melodrama – in this case *The Murder in the Red Barn* – and identify with the superhuman qualities of the villain, Corder.
18 Quoted in Rössler, *Literatur*, p. 70.
19 Vicinus, *Industrial Muse* p. 22; F. C. Mather, 'The Railways, the Electric Telegraph and public order during the Chartist period, 1837–48', *History*, vol. 38 (1953).
20 Tillotson, *Novels of the Eighteen-Forties* (London: Oxford University Press, 1954), p. 155.
21 For Disraeli, see M. E. Speare, *The Political Novel: Its Development in England and America* (New York: Oxford University Press, 1924) p. 164; for Trollope, George Eliot and Meredith, see John Clubbe (ed.), *Carlyle and his Contemporaries* (Durham, NC: Duke University Press, 1976), passim; for Kingsley, see Susan Chitty, *The Beast and the Monk*, pp. 61, 133; for Lawrence, see Keith Sagar (ed.), *A D. H. Lawrence Handbook* (Manchester: Manchester University Press, 1982), pp. 67, 72.
22 George Meredith, *Beauchamp's Career* (London: Chapman & Hall, 1876), p. 22.
23 Quoted in Michael Goldberg, '"A universal howl of execration": Carlyle's *Latter-Day Pamphlets* and their critical reception', in Clubbe, *Carlyle*, p. 128.
24 John Morley, 'Carlyle', *Fortnightly Review*, July 1870.
25 Thomas Carlyle, 'Characteristics', reprinted in *Scottish and Other Miscellanies* (London: Dent, n.d.), p. 221.
26 See Owen Dudley Edwards, 'Ireland', in *Celtic Nationalism* (London: Routledge, 1968), pp. 122-5.
27 Thomas Carlyle, 'Burns', in *Miscellanies*, p. 28.
28 Fred Kaplan, *Thomas Carlyle: A Biography* (Cambridge: Cambridge University Press, 1983), esp. chs 9–11.
29 Benjamin Disraeli, *Tancred* [1847] (London: Longman, 1900), p. 309.
30 Thomas Carlyle, 'Signs of the times', *Edinburgh Review*, vol. 93 (1829), reprinted in *Miscellanies* p. 226.
31 Ian Watt, *The Rise of the Novel* (Harmondsworth: Penguin, 1963), p. 55.
32 See Victor Kiernan, 'Class and ideology: the bourgeoisie and its historians', *History of European Ideas*, vol. 6, no. 3 (1985), pp. 271–4.
33 Una Pope-Hennessy, *Charles Dickens* [1945] (Harmondsworth: Penguin, 1970), p. 172.
34 Thomas Carlyle, *Heroes and Hero-Worship*, Tauchnitz, [1840] (Leipzig:

1916), p. 195; and see H. Stuart Hughes, *Consciousness and Society* (London: MacGibbon & Kee, 1959).

35   Engels, *Condition*, pp. 184, 317.

36   Goldberg, '"Universal howl"' p. 141; and compare Fritz Stern, *The Politics of Cultural Despair: A Study in the Rise of the Germanic Ideology* (Berkeley: University of California Press, 1961).

37   Tillotson, *Novels of the Eighteen-Forties*, p. 80.

38   ibid., pp. 8, 63.

39   ibid., p. 123.

40   Sheila M. Smith, *The Other Nation: The Poor in English Novels of the 1840s and 1850s* (London: Oxford University Press, 1980), p. 204.

41   Tillotson, *Novels of the Eighteen-Forties*, p. 124.

42   J. F. Stephens, *The Censorship of Drama in England* (Cambridge: Cambridge University Press, 1979), p. 54.

43   Tillotson, *Novels of the Eighteen-Forties*, p. 27.

44   See E. P. Thompson and Eileen Yeo (eds), *The Unknown Mayhew* (Harmondsworth: Penguin, 1974).

45   See R. W. Stewart, *Benjamin Disraeli: A List of Writings by Him. . .* (n.p.: Scarecrow Press, 1979), pp. 63–7; Winifred Gerin, *Elizabeth Gaskell*, (London: Oxford University Press, 1976), p. 85.

46   See Mark Girouard, *The Return to Camelot* (New Haven, Conn.: Yale University Press, 1981), p. 54.

47   Smith, *Other Nation*, p. 189.

48   Thomas Carlyle, *Chartism*, [1839], in *Critical and Miscellaneous Essays*, vol. IV (London: Chapman & Hall, 1899), p. 140.

49   Cazamian, *Social Novel*, pp. 58, 235–7.

50   Quoted in Susan Chitty, *The Beast and the Monk* (London: Hodder & Stoughton, 1974), p. 109.

51   Elizabeth Gaskell, *Mary Barton* (London: Chapman & Hall, 1848), ch. 8.

52   ibid.

53   Carlyle, *Chartism*, p. 28; for Carlyle's relations to the Irish, see Kaplan, *Carlyle*, pp. 334–46.

54   Easson, 'Elizabeth Gaskell and the novel of local pride', *Bulletin of the John Rylands Library*, vol. 67, no. 2, (1985), p. 695.

55   Quoted in Chitty, *Beast and the Monk*, p. 133.

56   See E. P. Thompson and Eileen Yeo (eds), *The Unknown Mayhew*, (London: Merlin, 1971), pp. 30–1.

57   Chitty, *Beast and the Monk*, p. 121.

58   Smith, *Other Nation*, p. 211.

59   Greg, 'Kingsley and Carlyle' [1860], *Literary and Social Judgements* (London: Trubner, 1877), vol. 1, pp. 143 ff.

60   Leslie Stephen, 'Mr Disraeli's novels' [1876] in *Hours in a Library* (London: Smith Elder, 1892), vol. 2, p. 117.

61   *Morning Chronicle*, 13 May 1844.

62   Gordon Ray, *Thackeray* (London: Oxford University Press, 1958), Vol. 2, pp. 268–71.

63   Duncan Forbes, *The Liberal Anglican Idea of History* (Cambridge: Cambridge University Press, 1952), pp. 101 ff. Despite the fact that he was a renegade utilitarian, Mrs Gaskell regarded F. D. Maurice with 'great and lasting admiration'. Gerin, *Gaskell*, p. 98.

64   See Asa Briggs, 'Thomas Hughes and the public schools' in *Victorian People* (Harmondsworth: Penguin, 1965), pp. 148 ff.

3

The Triumph of Disraeli

I

DISRAELI STOOD right outside the classical tradition of élite education, but he was from the start marinated in Eng. Lit. His father Isaac had moved from orthodox Jewry to become a literary historian and even – some have claimed – a sociologist of an erudite and unsystematic sort, and young Benjamin was let loose in his 25,000 volume library.[1] Isaac was a Tory, and contributed to the anti-Jacobin cause a novel, *Vaurien*, 'a smart and libellous Invective on the Leaders of the Democratick and Philosophick Partys' which has some of the marks of his son's style – mysterious revolutionists, ramifying conspiracies, and so on – but as a friend of Godwin and Blake he was less a Burkian 'organic conservate', than a remnant of Enlightenment intellectualism.[2]

This distance from the political establishment is important. There was no tradition of political entertainment within metropolitan society. Although many of the pioneers of the eighteenth-century realist novel – notably Defoe, Richardson and Fielding – were drawn from the political class, Walpole's government had choked politics on the London stage in 1737 by imposing rigid theatre licensing. This sensitivity and the absence of a local political tradition from which readers could be drawn meant that the realist novel swore off politics, although in many ways fitted to deal with it.[3] The sort of artisan or shopkeeper likely to back reform was still likely to take his, largely religious, politics from *The Pilgrim's Progress*, the continuing bestseller of the century, with 160 editions by 1792.[4]

Fiction did not appeal to radicals. 'The pestilential breath of Fiction poisons the sense of every instrument it comes near.'[5] Yet Jeremy Bentham, assaulting the 'legal fictions' of Blackstone's Tory jurisprudence, came close to Isaac's illuminism and to the first experiments in political fiction, by writers provoked by the French Revolution into a radical critique of British politics, through the novel and the 'Modern Jacobinical drama'. Coleridge's *Osorio* (1797) and Wordsworth's *The*

Borderers (1802) were unpublished and unperformed, but the 'Jacobin novelists' – Robert Bage, Thomas Holcroft, and above all William Godwin – though misnamed by a hostile government (they were closer to the moderate Girondins in the French Assembly), voiced the critical bourgeois culture of provincial scientists and entrepreneurs like the Birmingham Lunar Society – Watt, Boulton, Erasmus Darwin, Joseph Priestley and their friends.[6]

Godwin's *Enquiry Concerning Political Justice* (1793) asserted the capacity of free men and women to create a political society through contract, and thus demolish the tyranny of the State, which he saw as the instrument of former, and now decaying, privilege. *Things as They Are* was written in the following year, to show the falseness of existing society, and the same programme was pursued by Robert Bage's *Man as He Is; or, Hermsprong* (1793), and Thomas Holcroft's *Hugh Trevor* (1794). These aimed 'to depict, somewhat hopefully, the struggle and eventual triumph of reason over l'infâme'.[7] Their weapon was knowledge. 'The rich excel the poor', says a character in *Hugh Trevor*, 'not in their greater store of wealth, which is but a source of vice, disease and death; but in a little superiority of knowledge, a trifling advance towards truth.'[8] All three applied the same root-and-branch critique to British institutions as Bentham, dramatizing this into psychological experience through the same intimacy of observation as Richardson and Fielding. But when all structures, whether those of established churches or governments, are called in question writing realistically about social behaviour becomes difficult. Arnold Kettle observed that the results were, as literature, 'disastrously and often ludicrously abstract. Again and again . . . one has the sense that what is being written about is not life but ideas about life. Even when they become involved with a specific social situation . . . they manage to dehydrate the reality into an abstract generalisation.'[9] Godwin realized this peril and tried to carry the reader along with a 'fictitious adventure, that should in some way be distinguished by a very powerful interest'.[10] To this end he constructed *Things as They Are*, later titled *Caleb Williams*, round a plot of murder and persecution in a way that anticipates the thriller: a strategy not lost on the younger Disraeli.

II

This problem was not just ideological or artistic. Agricultural and industrial changes had been unparalleled in Europe, shifting the population about 'so that', as Carlyle later wrote, 'no man knows his whereabouts'. The Napoleonic Wars provoked an unprecedented centralism, at its most dramatic in the Irish union of 1800, but also stimulated, in reaction to

Jacobinism, a conservative culture of regionalism. Several writers tried to mediate between both forces. Isaac D'Israeli and Godwin reanimated the 'country party' politics of Viscount Bolingbroke (1678–1751), whose cult Benjamin was to make a central feature of Young England.[11] Maria Edgeworth, out of the same provincial enlightenment as Robert Bage, gave voice to Irish feelings on the eve of the Union.[12] Although London was the largest European city, areas could easily be reached where an oral, or non-English, culture still persisted. One of the tasks of the élite was to co-ordinate these potentially fissile cultures into 'Britain'.

Edgeworth did this effectively because she commanded two vocabularies: the metropolitan mode and the vivid speech, legend and imagery of the Irish people. *Castle Rackrent*'s (1800) Godwinian theme – the decline of a feckless family of the *ancien régime* – is firmly grounded in popular memory, through the steward Thady Quinn, who personifies the social processes he describes. In her later novels Edgeworth's didacticism could (though not always) be qualified by her sense of *Gemeinschaft*, as in *Ormond* (1817) where 'King' Corny McShane's country of the Black Islands is invoked to condemn the metropolitan place-hunting of Sir Ulick McShane.[13] Edgeworth was agnostic about 'Britain', given the deterioration in the condition of Ireland between 1789 and 1815, but her self-confessed disciple Walter Scott not only seemed enthusiasm personified, but also created a provincial literary capitalism to back his judgement.

Scott's career, in this respect, was ambiguous. *Marmion* (1808), mourning both the breakdown of the 'Union of Hearts' between Scotland and England, culminating in the battle of Flodden, and the Younger Pitt, who had just died, seemed to apply the Enlightenment capacity for inquiry and generalization to the idea of Britain, as did the sequence of the Waverley novels.[14] But in the 1820s Scott's emotional commitment to an older Scotland, to Jacobitism, and the continuity of the oral tradition reacted with the threat of reform, assimilation and his own financial collapse to foster a pessimistic conservative nationalism.[15] By reviving the novel's demotic roots, its links to epic and romance, he created an implement for those eager to rediscover or fabricate a 'people's history' directed *against* authority – in much of Europe, and in Ireland where the work of the Banim brothers and William Carleton inspired both Young Ireland and young Trollope.[16]

Similar in range, although not in mood, was Thomas Love Peacock, on the fringe of the Godwin group, whose blend of *causerie* and knockabout was very apt for politics. In the contest for the borough of Onevote in *Melincourt* (1817) the victor is that strongest and most silent of heroes, Sir Oran Haut-ton, Bart.[17] Peacock's stories often had their roots in the folk-tales which still maintained a political rôle on the Celtic fringe, such as *The Misfortunes of Elphin* (1829), a miniature Arthurian epic.[18]

Seithenyn ap Seithyn Saithi, Lord High Commissioner of the Royal Embankment, possibly Peacock's greatest comic creation, transforms a High Tory speech by George Canning into an apotheosis of boneheaded boozy reaction:

> There is nothing so dangerous as innovation. See the waves in the equinoctial storms, dashing and clashing, roaring and pouring, spattering and battering, rattling and battling against it. I would not be so presumptious as to say, I could build any thing that could stand against them half an hour; and here this immortal old work, which God forbid the finger of modern mason should bring into jeopardy, this immortal work has stood for centuries, and will stand for centuries more, if we let it alone. It is well: it works well: let well alone. Cupbearer fill. It was half-rotten when I was born, and that is a conclusive reason why it should be three parts rotten when I die.[19]

The embankment promptly collapses into Cardigan Bay. Peacock combined his folklorism with total cynicism about Parliament, seen as just another watering-hole for the corrupt which his courtly simian would positively grace.

Disraeli was unusually aware of Britain beyond England. He recommended Crofton Croker's pioneering *Fairy Legends of Ireland* to John Murray in 1825, and praised the Scots Covenanters in *Tancred*. Scott's influence was patent throughout his works, and he greeted Peacock as his 'master' when he met him in 1848. He has plenty of Seithenyns; echoes of the epic and the folk-tale in most of his plots.[20] Disraeli's image of power is the cosmopolitan super-intellectual Sidonia – the Carlyleian 'hero as empire-builder' – yet he saw that he stood at a transition between two types of nationalism. Young England aped the liberal 'nationalism as mission' of Mazzini's 'Young Italy' founded in 1831 and Thomas Davis's 'Young Ireland' of 1842;[21] yet there was also a conservative internalized nationalism, associated with the Grimm brothers and their patron Karl von Savigny, Prussian Justice-Minister, concerned to refine substantive law out of folk-consciousness and custom, which would later be encountered in revolt against the multi-national empires.[22] To Disraeli democratic nationalism led to republicanism; conservative folklorism to localism: both would threaten the multi-national state – *polis* would be too specific a word – in which he intended to make his career.

III

Disraeli could radiate an existential optimism, whereas the provincials were fundamentally pessimistic about their own communities. Nor was the mood of the first political novel *tout court*, John Galt's *The Member* (1832), at all supportive of the parliamentarianism it described. Augustus Jobbry is a Scots nabob who buys himself an English borough, Frailtown, to steer patronage in the direction of his gannet-like family. His subsequent embroilment in parliamentary and constituency conflicts gives him an enforced education in the evils of the system which sustains him. When Jobbry meets Mr Selby, a colonial proprietor ruined (like Galt) by government default, he realizes that his own affability and accessibility mask impotence and indifference. Selby's ideas of reform, on the other hand, promise to destroy the very basis of parliamentary sovereignty:

> Till Governments, and Houses of Commons, and those institutions which the sinful condition of man renders necessary, are made responsible to a tribunal of appeal, whose decisions shall control them, there can be no effectual reform. The first step is to take away all will of its own from Government – for statesmen are but mere men, rarely in talent above the average of their species, from what I have seen – and oblige it to consider itself no better than an individual, even with respect to its own individual subjects. Let the Law in all aspects be paramount, and it will matter little whether the lords or the vagabonds send members to Parliament . . .[23]

In due course officialism strikes at Jobbry himself, when he is caught up in a farm labourers' riot, taken for Captain Swing himself, and dragged off to gaol. The experience almost moralizes him, but after a shuddering glance at Reform he ends unregenerate: 'I had indeed a sore heart when I saw the Whigs and Whiglings coming louping, like the puddocks of Egypt, over among the right hand benches of the House of Commons, greedy as corbies and chattering like pyets.'[24] He retreats to his estate and dedicates his memoirs to the Tory whip.

The Member is the cumulation of a sequence of 'theoretical histories' which started with *Annals of the Parish* in 1821. In these Galt shows us politics – decision-making and power-broking – integrated into a society in process of industrial and urban development. Directly influenced by Dugald Stewart and Adam Ferguson, he applied 'the general principles of the philosophy of history', derived from the Scottish enlightenment, to 'the West' – that area of Scotland bounded by Glasgow, Greenock and Ayr – and took it from rural tranquillity to the vertiginous industrial insecurity that succeeded the Napoleonic Wars.[25] In *Annals of the Parish* a Scots minister doucely records the history of 'Dalmailing' from 1760 to 1810. Roads are improved, fields enclosed, factories built; contract takes over from status. *The Provost* (1822) is set in more debatable land. The 'autobiography' of James Pawkie, thrice provost of the burgh of

Gudetown, whose council still elected itself, and appointed a delegate to choose an MP, as part of the most restricted franchise in Britain, shows some development in Gudetown from the American War to 1815, but more in Pawkie's fortunes. Gudetown is prospering, on his authority; near-bankrupt, by his implicit admissions. 'Improvement' is a second-order goal in the manoeuvres whereby he 'got the cart up the brae, and the whole council reduced to the will and pleasure of his majesty, whose deputies and agents I have considered all inferior magistrates to be, administering and exercising, as they do, their power and authority in his royal name.'[26] The absolute bourgeois, in his materialism and opportunism, Pawkie is also one of nature's crawlers, whose manoeuvres destroy local self-government, and whose type multiplied in Metternich's Austria or Bomba's Naples. Galt relied on the minutes of Irvine town council, but his scope was anything but parochial; Pawkie fitted into the strategies discussed in *The Prince*, as the negation of the principles Machiavelli stood for. As P. H. Scott has written, it was, in a grim sense, 'a treatise on the realities of politics'.[27] But in 1822 it sold 'like snaw off a dyke', adding Canning to Scott, Jeffrey, Byron and Coleridge as Galt's admirers.

Between then and writing *The Member*, Galt experienced the lobbies of St Stephen's, administration in Ontario, a debtor's prison in Liverpool, and work as a hack for Blackwood's. He used *The Member* as a vehicle for reforming ideas – its sequel, *The Radical*, is little more than a didactic pamphlet – but his irony cut these down to size. As shrewd as Peacock but, no secure civil servant, Galt knew what it was to be the victim of government. Meeting him at Fraser's, Carlyle liked him but consigned him to the past, with the 'Scotch novel': the end of the 'auld sang' of a semi-independent Scotland.[28] Yet Galt's wit works because it *is* provincial. Jobbry has the pungent vernacular of one of nature's back benchers, which deflates both his own ambitions and Parliament:

> It is a place not just like the world, but it is in fact a community made up of peculiar people, and the members are more unlike to one another than the generality of mankind, and have upon them besides, a stamp and impress of character that makes them as visibly a distinct race in the world, as the marking of sheep distinguishes one flock from another at tryst or market.[29]

Did Disraeli read Galt? Isaac certainly knew him, and Benjamin could have met him in the Lobby in the boom of 1825. There are one or two traces in *Coningsby*. Taper's 'sound Conservative government . . . Tory men and Whig measures' is close to Jobbry's 'a Tory is but a Whig in office, and a Whig but a Tory in opposition'.[30] The transformation of the waiter Warren into the nobleman Fitzwarene in *Sybil* has the right ring of 'theoretical history'. But Galt would never be inspiriting; no one was going to lay down *The Member* exclaiming, as George Smythe is said to have done on finishing *Coningsby*: 'Thank God! I have a faith at last!'[31]

IV

There is a solid moral centre to Galt quite lacking in the *milieu* in which Disraeli published *Vivian Grey* in 1825. The centralization of authority, the expansion of the National Debt, and the luxurious ambience of the Court – Cobbett's 'Thing' - conjured up the lightweight fiction of such as Lady Morgan and Theodore Hook.[32] Satirized by Carlyle in *Sartor Resartus* and crushed by Thackeray in *Vanity Fair*, this 'silver fork' ambience forced some writers into moral concern, particularly over the issue of authority. The landed aristocracy was in decline relative to the new wealth derived from banking and trade. Its Burkeian conservatism had failed to dam social change; even government was notoriously plebeian; and both were under threat from industrialization, population-growth, and revolt in Ireland. In this rootless society 'prestige', 'fashion' and 'tone' replaced the old securities of landed power, and Byronism – something Disraeli never altogether escaped from – wandered Europe, unconstrained by any credible religious or social affections.[33]

Silver-forkery produced some experiment, at least in themes and literary organization. Edward Bulwer-Lytton, whom Disraeli first met in 1829, had a success which G. M. Young reckoned as meteoric as Kipling's, and Q. D. Leavis has seen him as the first of modern bestseller writers, churning out novels to order.[34] But, although Bulwer-Lytton did a lot of hackwork, he took politics and ideas seriously. His reforming views won him the support of Bentham and Godwin, whom he followed in rehabilitating Bolingbroke and, in *Paul Clifford* (1829), in turning his political critique into a crime-story. His historical dramas were regarded as radical; he led campaigns against press and theatre control, and in favour of copyright protection, public libraries and cheap books, and in his quasi-sociological *England and the English* (1833) he began the documentary investigation in which many subsequent writers were to 'bottom' their political fiction.[35]

The increasing politicization of the novel of fashion – 'its Victorian heir was less Thackeray than Trollope' – also invokes Robert Plumer Ward, a retired Tory politician who achieved great success with *Tremaine; or, The Man of Refinement* in 1825, and *De Vere; or, The Man of Independence* in 1827, and was for a time suspected – amazingly – of writing *Vivian Grey*.[36] Ward (who was half-Jewish) was certainly part of Isaac's circle, but while he had, as a law officer, tracked down Jacobin plots in the

1790s there is, as T. H. S. Escott tactfully put it, 'more of philosophy and theology than of politics' in his novels. They are, in title and mood, an intriguing throwback to Henry Mackenzie's *Man of Feeling* of 1771, which has been seen as the point at which the social 'sympathy' of the Enlightenment decayed into the cultivation of a private sensibility and left Adam Smith's 'invisible hand' to its own devices.[37] Ward set out solemnly to remind his class of its ethical standards – 'I hope to make Wentworth, and, by implication, our modern ministers, redeem all those of the old Walpole and Newcastle school' – with indifferent results; Canning, who was supposed to be Wentworth, saying that Ward's law-books were more exciting than his novels.[38]

With reason. The most that *Tremaine* and *De Vere* show is that there must have been a demand for novels about politics. De Vere is a fastidious aristocrat isolated and nearly destroyed by an ambitious careerist, Clayton. De Vere's scruples bring him deliverance and an admirable wife, Clayton is packed off to count fish-boxes in Wick. Despite an invocation of the Bolingbroke cult – Wentworth and De Vere going on a lengthy pilgrimage to Bolingbroke's place of exile in France – when Wentworth forms a government De Vere retires from public life. The time appears to be the 1770s. There is no hint that the author was living in the decade of O'Connell and Cobbett, nor is there any relish in the political life, seen as 'a kind of demoniacal magic, poisoning and corroding everything it touches'.[39] The impression conveyed is one of a small and rather bewildered élite, worried about the corrupting power of government – hence the appeal to Bolingbroke – but equally uncertain about the scope of mass politics.

If there are similarities between the 1820s and the 1920s, then Disraeli, who told Ward he had read a dialogue in *Tremaine* thirty times, anticipates Waugh's Basil Seal.[40] Impudent and unscrupulous, Vivian Grey was another of Disraeli's borrowings from the fairy-story. But although the name of his master, the Marquis of Carabas, suggests *Puss in Boots*, his obscure political conspiracy was modelled on Disraeli's own involvement in an attempt in 1824 to set up a Tory paper, *The Representative*. The novel breaks down in melodrama when Vivian shoots his colleague Cleveland (supposedly J. G. Lockhart) in a duel, and sudden death also terminated Disraeli's first proper political novel, *A Year at Hartlebury; or, The Election*. Written with his sister as 'Cherry and Fair Star', this produced the piquant effect of a Jane Austen vicarage invaded by Byron, in the person of the fabulously wealthy and talented radical Aubrey Bohun who returns from banditry in the Levant to contest the local borough, get in by one vote, and be murdered by the son of a local landowner, his companion in the East. Bohun hints at the 'imperium et libertas' of later Toryism; and much of the pace and excitement of the election scenes – based on Disraeli's second contest for High Wycombe in December 1832 – was carried into *Coningsby*: not enough, alas, to overcome the ludicrous plot. Published in April 1834, it was then forgotten about by everyone concerned.[41]

The 1830s were a false dawn. Galt's novels were well reviewed but badly marketed, and fell out of print, Disraeli's simply vanished. But, while Galt's failing health drove him back to Scotland, Disraeli began the affair with Henrietta Sykes which brought him to the attention of Lord Lyndhurst, and by 1835 gave him a patron at the heart of the Tory Party. *Hartlebury* would not have been useful, although Bohun is authentically self-flattering:

> He was fully master of his subject – he abounded in facts, and each fact was an epigram. The Treasury Bench writhed. It was not only the most successful debut ever made in that House, but the most brilliant oration that had for years been held within its walls. And from this night he spoke in all great debates, and ever with the same success, for he was equally powerful in attack or defence.[42]

The Treasury Bench would indeed writhe a decade later, when Disraeli lacerated Peel. Yet Bohun was an aristocrat, while Disraeli, as bourgeois as Galt, regarded the aristocracy as a failing class. The gentry in *Hartlebury* are politically as incapable as Mrs Gaskell's Chartists. Disraeli and Galt are, however, more than bourgeois; they are what F. W. Bateson, following Maurice Barres, called 'métèques' – writers with the exotically enlarged style – and perhaps vision – of the alien. Galt's strange but resonant ∟owland Scots political slang – 'propugnacious', 'notandums', 'clishmaclavers', 'perjink' – bears comparison with Coningsby bludgeoning a dim MP with his even odder constitutional theory:

> 'We should have had the Venetian Republic in 1640,' said Coningsby, 'had it not been for the Puritans. Geneva beat Venice.'
>
> 'I am sure these ideas are not very generally known,' said Sir Joseph, bewildered.
>
> 'Because you have had your history written by the Venetian party,' said Coningsby, 'and it has been their interest to conceal them.'[43]

Both could be classed with Carlyle for audacity, but while Carlyle and Disraeli represented the shift to London, Galt's province would shrivel with the Disruption of 1843. Disraeli promised to raise the theatre of electoral politics to new and more exciting – but still safe – levels than the dreary and predictable contests that actually happened. The people were to be admitted to the political process, even if only as an audience.

Both, too, dramatized historical change. Debt-ridden Gudetown was like many Scottish burghs (Edinburgh, the jewel of 'improvement', went bankrupt in 1833), and emblematic of Britain after the Napoleonic Wars; when Gerard in *Sybil* flourishes the population-returns before Egremont he touches the raw nerve of the 1840s.[44] Galt's response to the challenge is ironic and pessimistic. Pawkie puts down riots, Jobbry gets dragged into one – and is only too relieved to get out of politics. But with Disraeli consistency always took second place to manoeuvre.

V

Britain in the 1840s required a theory of the State. Macaulay had bruited the notion of a minimal 'policeman' order in 1830 in his essay on Southey:

> Our rulers will best promote the improvement of the nation by strictly confirming themselves to their own legitimate duties . . . by maintaining peace, by diminishing the price of law, and by observing strict economy in every department of the state. Let the Government do this: the people will assuredly do the rest.[45]

But this faltered in the face of deepening depressions. 'Classic' economics either became tentative, in Mill and Sismondi, or apocalyptic, in Marx. The 'crowning discovery' of the bourgeois seemed at once the culmination and the collapse of their order.[46] Wagner's metaphor, Bernard Shaw would later insist, was the *Ring of the Nibelungs*: capitalism as the bearer both of power and destruction.[47] Apprehension drove Europe's bourgeoisie to compromise with the old order, reordering history to justify this. Against an industrial proletariat, the State was to be armed with nationalist aims and charismatic leaders – Bismarck, Cavour, Napoleon III.

In Britain, where state power was minimal, and national unity already 'achieved', the risks ought to have been greatest. Yet as Britain remained a multi-national society the élite had one particular resource to hand: the intelligentsia. 'A section of the ruling class who have comprehended the movement of history'[48] – a somewhat Carlyleian definition – the intellectuals were nominated by Marx and Engels as the organizers of revolution. An ambiguous status: if they had this thaumaturgic power, could they not, equally effectively, *prevent* revolution? By 1848 this 'section' was putatively in being as 'Bohemia': writers, artists and publicists both sustained by and alienated from print-capitalism, usually excluded from official life either through their own principle or state hostility. These ranged from the *flâneurs* of Flaubert's *L'Education Sentimentale* (1869) to Marx, Engels and their associates; and Belinski, Heine, George Sand,

Hugo, Nestroy in literature. Their humanist 'socialism' spread itself widely over popular fiction and the weekly press, persisting through Garibaldianism and the Commune to the founding of mass socialist parties in the 1870s.

In Britain, however, Bohemia split in the 1840s between 'gentleman journalists' of the Pendennis sort – satirists of and for the middle class – and a 'graver and more deeply committed camp' around Douglas Jerrold and Henry Mayhew, which retained connections with the radical movement.[49] When, for instance, a 'Society of British Authors' was projected in 1843, aimed at protecting them in dealings with publishers and cheapening the cost of books, it was headed mainly by Benthamite radicals from the *Westminster Review*, but flopped when big names like Carlyle and Dickens pulled out. They were able to make their own terms with publishers; the rest of Grub Street had to manage as it could.[50]

European states were vulnerable to revolution because power was over-concentrated. In Britain not only was it diffused, but their distinct cultures also gave the nations their own chronologies of crisis. Wales blazed up with the Newport Rising in 1839, the North with the Plug Plot in 1842, Scotland (for quite different, religious, reasons) in 1843, Ireland thereafter. This diffusion was maintained, and the threat of a concerted assault neutralized, through the new, 'industrialized' print culture. The metropolis could co-opt intelligentsias conscious of historical crisis from the periphery. These couldn't charm away the central economic crisis but they could ensure that, defined as 'the condition of *England*', it was manageable.

This strategy was most logically expounded by the Christian Socialists, but their millenarianism did not square with the post-1847 economic upswing caused by railway construction, and their Anglicanism isolated them from the mass of the population.[51] 'National' solutions had to acquire the mechanism of 'national' promotion: a theatre, personalities, gossip, recognition. During the 1840s Britain got these: the new Palace of Westminster (whose House of Commons opened in 1847); *Punch*, founded in 1842; Disraeli's political trilogy, with *Coningsby* and *Sybil* being reprinted in a cheap edition in 1852. By the time Walter Bagehot, himself an outsider as a Unitarian banker from Somerset, published his *English Constitution* serially in the *Fortnightly Review* in 1865, parliamentarianism had emerged as the distinctive British version of the conservative settlement.

VI

Disraeli's 'trilogy' of 1844–7 is a basic document of parliamentarianism, although without the programme he later claimed for it. There is no link between the plots of *Coningsby* and *Sybil*, and the characters of all three only encounter one another at a dinner-party at the beginning of *Tancred*. 'Young England' collapsed in May 1844, just as *Coningsby* appeared; after this, *Sybil* was, not surprisingly, less successful and *Tancred*, which sold only 2,300 copies, was not reprinted until 1870.[52] But Young England was *British*: its aristocrats, 'representing' England (Manners), Ireland (Smythe) and Scotland (Baillie-Cochrane), re-creating Kenelm Digby's chivalric ideal, recently boosted by the High Tory Eglinton Tournament (1838). Lord Coningsby had been one of the first feudal revivalists, and Digby's *Tancredus* (1828) lauded 'the religion and the discipline which belonged to chivalry in the heroic age of Christianity', enabling Anglo-Normanism to compete with the Anglo-Saxonism – Norman Yoke and all – which still flourished on many a radical platform.[53] Anglo-Saxonism was *English* to the point of sheer racism, while Anglo-Normanism – in the manner of Scott's *Ivanhoe* – offered both a link between the separate kingdoms and enough 'cosmopolitanism' to include an alien figure like Disraeli.[54]

Disraeli assaulted the Tories' Burkeian self-esteem with his version of Bolingbroke's 'Patriot King', but his exaltation of ideology in *Coningsby* plainly owes more to Carlyle and the Oxford Movement: less in such explicit references as Sidonia's praise of the heroic in politics, or Eustace Lyle's neo-medieval almsgiving, as in his destructive satire, which paralleled Carlyle's stress on intellectual unsettlement in an 'epoch of transition' (derived from Saint-Simon) and Newman's assault on the Anglican compromise.[55] Disraeli complained, while writing *Coningsby*, that 'action and speculation will never blend', and the novel is a political cabaret in which his earlier *personae* do their turns: Coningsby's introduction to his wicked old grandfather, Lord Monmouth, and his *demi-mondain* entourage, is out of *Vivian Grey*, the Eton scenes recall Disraeli's *Bildungsroman*, *Contarini Fleming* (1832), and the political polemic is rehashed from *A Vindication of the English Constitution* or the *Times* articles of 'Coeur de Lion'.

What is new is the pace of the narrative, the magus figure of Sidonia, and – in almost total contrast – the immediacy and common sense of its political business. Coningsby is whisked from post-Regency London to Eton, to Gothic country houses, to Manchester. His surroundings fall into position like theatre sets: in a dozen pages he is on his way again, the reader (trying to make sense of the tortuous inheritance-plot which runs through the novel) on his heels. Sidonia, in age and opinions close to Disraeli himself, is both a sort of Master of Ceremonies and the imaginative antithesis of the pettiness of the Tadpoles and Tapers and their world. Yet he is, like Goethe's Faust, symbolically maimed, incapable of emotional life or of national attachment.

As if unconvinced about Young England and his hero (whose model, Smythe, switched to Peel over Free Trade in 1846), Disraeli doesn't give *Coningsby* the positive direction we expect. Coningsby marries the daughter of the industrialist Millbank, and regains his inheritance through the kindness he has shown Monmouth's illegitimate frail daughter. Beyond stating that youth is better than age, that most politics is humbug, and that women matter more politically than their rights would suggest, no great message has been conveyed. But to say this would be to miss the main point, the author's political *nous*:

> No government can be long secure without a formidable opposition. It reduces their supporters to that tractable number which can be managed by the joint influences of fruition and of hope. It offers vengeance to the discontented, and distinction to the ambitious; and employs the energies of aspiring spirits, who otherwise may prove traitors in a division or assassins in a debate.[56]

Not only is this a shrewd statement of parliamentary conservatism – what separated Disraeli from Bismarck – but *Coningsby* also conveys the vitality of politics, in London clubs, in country houses, in decrepit inns in remote boroughs: at a whole range of levels, somehow being drawn together around Whitehall. In this sense Disraeli's trilogy is the literary analogue to Barry and Pugin's huge gothic palace, then rising beside Westminster Hall.

How serious was Disraeli about his heroes? Or was his real hero the author *as character*, taking his dolls out of their box and setting them up on the stage? Leslie Stephen's point, that one never knew when Disraeli was being ironic, and doubted whether he knew himself, is both perceptive and misleading.[57] It indicates the gifts that a novelist ought to have – but Disraeli never set out to write realist novels. As a politician he was a cross between the epic narrator and the entertainer, and both are callings which demand a belief – however fleeting – in what's being said. *Sybil*, which Stephen dismissed by marvelling that it could prove possible to transmute Blue Books into melodrama, is a case in point.

After 1870 regarded as Disraeli's chief contribution to the 'Condition of England' debate, *Sybil* is *not* about the social problem in the way the famous 'Two Nations' quotation leads us to expect. These words are Stephen Morley's – an Owenite socialist – which *Sybil* does not endorse, but test. Disraeli does not see the classes as polarized. Morley is a journalist. Sybil's father, Walter Gerard, for all his radical politics and noble expectations, is a factory manager. Of the workers, Dandy Mick and Devilsdust and their girlfriends represent well-off factory workers; 'Bishop' Hatton and his Wodgate tribe are prosperous anarchic drunks; only the hand-loom weavers are really poverty-stricken. An extreme crisis, Disraeli seems to be arguing, *might* cause these to coalesce – but then their values would not be those of Morley but the atavistic violence of the Hellcats.

Disraeli is selective about his 'poor'. No mention of agricultural labourers, whom radicals regarded as the Tories' victims, or of the Irish, the staple bogymen of working-class Tory propaganda. Disraeli could be shrewd and sympathetic about Ireland but he couldn't logically have played a Protestant card and had a Catholic heroine.[58] This had its logic. Disraeli's 'continental, revolutionary mind' eliminated Irish awkwardnesses to manufacture an English identity. Bolingbrokian Toryism, moreover, could end up as the boozy ineffective Jacobitism of Scots like W. E. Aytoun or 'Christopher North' or the crypto-Chartism of the Yorkshire Tory radicals, so Disraeli discovered 'enemies within'. He revived the international plot of quasi-masonic secret societies, propounded in Isaac's day by the Scots academic John Robison, and used it to exorcize Jacobin and Jacobite alike.[59]

The alternative is a 'humane' politics of personality, something borne on Sybil as she flees from the Chartist conspirators in London, and just before (as luck would have it) she runs into Egremont:

> She had seen enough to suspect that the world was a more complicated system than she had preconceived. There was not that strong and rude simplicity in its organisation which she had supposed. The characters were more various, the motives more mixed, the classes more blended, the elements of each more subtle and diversified than she had imagined.[60]

This solution is achieved in English 'national' terms, completely rejecting the regionalism of the 1840s novel. Mowbray could be Manchester, Trafford's mill village could be Styal, but Marney could be anywhere and Wodgate was out of a Blue Book. Disraeli deliberately disregarded the *Gemeinschaft* prop that Mrs Gaskell and Charlotte Brontë would later use against the threat of class confrontation. What he put in its place is shown when Egremont ends up as Sybil's husband, the new Lord Marney and a Palmerstonian Whig. Neither Sybil's Catholicism nor Morley's Owenism, not even positive legislation, but the party system is necessary to divide élites whose natural – and in troubled times fatal – tendency is to coalesce as an upper-class interest. 'Real' politics marries party to day-to-day existence, as he was to remind the Commons in his final and successful assault on Peel.

Sybil's most suggestive episode is chapter 10 of book I, in which Morley visits the 'Temple of the Muses' in Mowbray, an early but large and definitely classy music-hall above a pub, catering for affluent mill-workers:

The room was very full; some three or four hundred persons were seated in different groups at different tables, eating, drinking, talking, laughing or even smoking . . . Nothing, however, could be more decorous than the general conduct of the company, though they consisted principally of factory people. The waiters flew about with as much agility as if they were serving nobles . . . Some nights there was music on the stage; a young lady in a white robe with a golden harp, and attended by a gentleman in black moustachios. This was when the principal harpist of the King of Saxony and his first fiddler happened to be passing through Mowbray, merely by accident, or on a tour of pleasure and instruction, to witness the famous scenes of British industry. Otherwise the audience . . . were fain to be content with four Bohemian brothers, or an equal number of Swiss sisters.[61]

While Speare, comically, sees these as 'hectic and immoral pleasures', to Sheila Smith it is an optimistic picture, based on an actual Manchester music-hall which Disraeli visited in 1844.[62] Disraeli implies that freedom, hierarchy and idealism can all co-exist; and, rightly handled, the workers are deferential. They don't want Morley's severe co-operative enterprises; they want a good time and to feel themselves respected. Matters in Mowbray turn ugly only when economic depression closes the Temple of the Muses down.

'Temple of the Muses': 'Palace of Enchantments'? It's tempting to see Disraeli's politics as a type of theatre, Bagehot's 'dignified' part of the constitution – a lavish production in which even the most obscure MP could carry off a minor colourful rôle – masking its 'efficient part . . . decidedly simple and rather modern': the Cabinet.[63] But Disraeli's theatricality ends when he deals with the actual institutions of politics. The Temple of the Muses, like by-elections or Commons tactics, is described straight: as if the dialectic he set up between extremes purged itself of its rhetoric to reach its practical conclusions. Whether or not Disraeli read Hegel, he formulated an élitism with an 'absolute' comprehension which probed the weakest point of dialectical materialism: the intellectual as *reinforcement* of established society. Marx could be perceptive about Disraeli's immediate background, recognizing that the Conservatives had a predilection for *parvenus* as leaders; he also observed that ordinary readers were still drawn to epic and romance rather than to the realist novel of print-capitalism.[64] But, although he could crush the 'socialist' sensationalism of Eugène Sue , he never coped with Disraeli's blending of parliamentarianism with epic to create a political 'myth' resilient enough to frustrate his own forecasts.[65]

VII

Disraeli's rapid rise in the Tory Party, after Peel's secession and the death of Lord George Bentinck, gave *Coningsby* and *Sybil* importance as the testament of a leader otherwise given to hooded-eyed impassivity. Disraeli can still charm, as an ideal dinner-companion: Wilde without the sodomy and Waugh without the temper. Yet Anthony Trollope, a clubbable man, hated him for corrupting youth: 'He has struck them with astonishment and aroused in their imagination ideas of a world more glorious, more rich, more witty, more enterprising than their own. But the glory has ever been the glory of pasteboard, and the wealth has been a wealth of tinsel.'[66] This late judgement was also ungrateful. Without Disraeli's trilogy, would Trollope have written the Palliser novels? Yet it pointed up the moral relativism of political novels. Victorians could appreciate their realistic social landscape, their close engagement with the life of the politico-literary élite, yet still find their moral stance suspect.

Particularly if they were among the few who read *Tancred*, Disraeli's own favourite but, at first glance, even weirder than *Sybil*. Tancred, Marquis of Montacute, sets off from London and boring Young Englanders for the Holy Land, to gain a religious revelation. Like Scott's Waverley in the Highlands, he is then captured by the locals and plunged into a sequence of Levantine intrigues, chiefly directed by the devious Christian chief, Emir Fakredeen. These become ever more complex, until Disraeli, having got Tancred out of an attempt to become ruler of the Near East and into the arms of a beautiful Jewess, Eva, simply slams the book shut in mid-chapter, with the unexplained arrival of Tancred's parents, the Duke and Duchess of Bellamont, in Jerusalem.

Tancred the man is even duller than Coningsby; and English society gossip vanishes at the end of book II. What then takes over is an intriguing mixture of documentary on Near East politics and heterodox religion. Disraeli had travelled via Albania, Greece and Turkey to Cairo in 1831, there encountering the Italian archaeologist Botta, who had gone native in Syria; later he read through government reports on the crisis of 1841 caused by the rising of Mehmet Ali, governor-general of Egypt.[67] The result is a subtle understanding of the complexity of Lebanese politics – painfully apparent in the 1980s – and an argument for the supra-national authority provided by the Turkish empire. Thus *Tancred* anticipates both Disraeli's 'finest hour' in the 1870s – the Congress of Berlin and the purchase of the Suez Canal – which established British supremacy in the Near East, and that curious Tory obsession with the Arabs, from Wilfred Scawen Blunt, C. M. Doughty and Mark Sykes to T. E. Lawrence and St John Philby.

But the ethos of *Tancred* is even more ambitious than Disraeli's usual philo-Semitism. Disraeli is not, in fact, very Jewish. Sidonia is remote from the ghettos of Europe and the discipline of Mosaic law. Kipling, of all people, got that atmosphere better. *Tancred*'s 'Semitism' instead conflates Judaic, Christian and Muhammadan into a synoptic 'Arabism' floating alarmingly free of all Western nationalisms. This has its moments. Tancred (playing Moses) is granted an interview on Mount Sinai by the Angel of Arabia:

> 'Child of Christendom' said the mighty form, as he seemed slowly to wave a sceptre fashioned like a palm; 'I am the angel of Arabia, the guardian spirit of that land which governs the world; for power is neither the sword nor the shield, for these pass away, but ideas, which are divine!'[68]

If the Angel of Arabia is nigh, Aladdin is nigher still. But the end result of *Tancred is* disconcerting: a real sense of statecraft and a sort of non-national Napoleonism. Ideas being greater than states, Disraeli rejects the Graeco-Roman–Christian tradition, blaming on it the intrigue of Fakredeen and the vengeful nationalism of his ally Queen Astarte. The claim that pure intellect is, instead, found in the mobile world of the Arabs – 'the Jews on horseback' – expresses, more than anything else, the alien quality which Gladstone detected in his enemy. Yet romanticism is balanced by common sense. There are worse vade-mecums to British foreign policy in one of its most important areas. And foreign policy was what 'high' parliamentary politics was about.

The Victorians subscribed to enlightened self-interest but worried about the pressures that society, reflecting aggregated individual desires, could exert on personal identity. Thus Mill, Meredith, Trollope and George Eliot – but not Sidonia:

> 'The age does not believe in great men, because it does not possess any,' replied the stranger. 'The Spirit of the Age is the very thing that a great man changes.'
>
> 'But does he not rather avail himself of it?' inquired Coningsby.
>
> 'Parvenus do,' rejoined his companion; 'but not prophets, great legislators, great conquerors. They destroy and they create.'
>
> 'But are these times for great legislators and great conquerors?' urged Coningsby. 'When were they wanted more?'[69]

The influence of Carlyle is patent here, though not as a prophylactic against the depersonalizing influence of industry and mass society. Disraeli used him to reinforce his ambition in the party system. In a perceptive essay, James Bryce remarked that Disraeli's egoism was constrained by a parliamentary environment which 'edited' the information it was presented with:

Men who enter Parliament soon begin to forget that it is not, in the last resort, Parliament that governs, but the people. Absorbed in the daily contests of their Chamber, they over-estimate the importance of those contests. They come to think that Parliament is in fact what it is in theory, a microcosm of the nation, and that opinion inside is sure to reflect the opinion outside.[70]

What Bryce saw as a disadvantage was exactly what Disraeli set out to exploit, while his writing (he was no more given to public speaking than his other contemporaries) kept up links of a sort with the public. Broad in scope, Disraeli's conspectus was also, at its most tactically acute, focused through Westminster.

Did Disraeli's novels help his career? He spent over thirty years on the Opposition benches, which suggests that they had little effect in reconciling his party – Bagehot's 'best brute vote' – to his exotic personality. Indeed, it was only after he had carried the Second Reform Act in 1867, become Prime Minister in 1868, and published *Lothair* in 1870 that reprints of his works became frequent. Disraeli's literary fame – if useful in his relations with the Queen – depended on a political success which took impossibly long by twentieth-century standards, but it justified the novel of politics – particularly at a time when the greatest Victorian author, whose attitudes to Parliament were quite different, bowed out.

VIII

Charles Dickens had visited Manchester with Disraeli in 1844. Eight years younger, he had been part of Disraeli's *milieu* in the 1830s, aped his dandy style, and also encountered Thomas Carlyle, though not until 1839 when he read *Chartism*.[71] But he never reconciled himself to the Parliament he had spent dispiriting years (1832–6) reporting. More than any of his contemporaries, Dickens maintained Hazlitt's and Cobbett's assault on 'old corruption'. He did not mellow with age, as *Hard Times*, his most 'political' novel, showed.

Hard Times was dedicated to Carlyle, and the idea seems to have matured for several years before it 'laid hold of me by the throat' in late 1853. Dickens started writing weekly instalments for *Household Words* in January 1854, and finished in July. Carlyle obviously lay behind the savagely comic description of the 'cottonopolis', Coketown:

The jail might have been the infirmary, the infirmary might have been the jail, the town hall might have been either, or both, or anything else, for anything which appeared to the contrary in the graces of their construction. Fact, fact, fact, everywhere in the material aspect of the town; fact, fact, fact, everywhere in the immaterial.[72]

At the beginning of the novel, Dickens seems to be attacking the Liberal–utilitarian manufacturing class, personified by the ironmonger MP Gradgrind and his banker friend Bounderby. Dickens mocks Gradgrind's 'Society for the Diffusion of Useful Knowledge' philistinism, but his attack on Parliament is even more savage:

> Time hustled him [Thomas Gradgrind, senior] into a little noisy and rather dirty machinery, in a by-corner, and made him Member of Parliament for Coketown: one of the respected members for ounce weights and measures, one of the representatives of the multiplication table, one of the deaf honourable gentlemen, dumb honourable gentlemen, blind honourable gentlemen, lame honourable gentlemen, dead honourable gentlemen, to every other consideration. Else wherefore live we in a Christian land, eighteen hundred and odd years after our Master?[73]

Gradgrind, however, has principles of a sort, in contrast to his protégé, the slightly Tancred-like professional politician Harthouse, who fights the Coketown election and whose brother is a railway lawyer skilled in fooling the House about his clients' criminal incompetence. Harthouse is the complete negation:

> '. . . any set of ideas will do just as much good as any other set, and just as much harm as any other set. There's an English family with a charming Italian motto. What will be, will be. It's the only truth going!'[74]

'Che sarà, sarà' was the motto of the great Whig house of Russell which seems to have symbolized for Dickens the irresponsible power of the traditional governing class, the 'national dustmen' who would, at the end of the novel, torture the remoralized Gradgrind.[75] Yet Dickens's personal relationships with Whigs *and* Radicals were friendly; while *Hard Times* was appearing, in June 1854, he wrote to Henry Cole, the organizer of the 1851 Great Exhibition, and a 'steam intellect' *par excellence*, about Gradgrind in almost affectionate terms: 'Perhaps by dint of his going his way and I going mine, we should meet at last at some halfway house where there are flowers on the carpets and a little standing room for Queen Mab's chariot among the Steam Engines.'[76] This ambiguity probably contributed to Dickens's complaint of being driven 'three parts mad' by the novel.[77] In March 1854, Britain declared war on

Russia, to enormous public enthusiasm and Dickens's own disgust. By the end of the year his friend the archaeologist and radical MP Henry Layard, a fellow-enthusiast for Carlyle, helped bring down the Aberdeen ministry, and involved Dickens in the Association for Administrative Reform, a middle-class bid to destroy Whig government. Dickens had, in fact, switched to Gradgrind's side, and the 'message' of *Hard Times* vanished in war fever.[78] The counterpoint to Gradgrind's materialism provided by the co-operative Bohemia of Sleary's Circus – man and nature as partners in horse-riding – was also present in the Crimea, which promoted non-economic qualities like bravery and endurance, and was also a circus of a sort.[79] Tennyson's 'patriotic' assault on John Bright in *Maud* (1855) –

> This broad-brimmed hawker of holy things
> Whose ear is crammed with cotton, and rings
> Even in dreams to the clink of his pence

– employed the Gradgrind persona *against* the politician who came closest to expressing Dickens's view on the war.

An 'old radical' assaulting 'old corruption', Dickens lapsed into confusion when confronted with actual complex political divisions. He shared many values and symbols with Disraeli: distaste for economism, a secularized religion, and a fascination with symbolism and entertainment (compare Sleary's Circus with the humanity of the troupes of actors in *Coningsby* and *Tancred*). But Dickens, Orwell's 'free intelligence', created his morality from individual decisions – Stephen Blackpool doesn't blackleg in *Hard Times* because he is anti-union, but because he has given his word to his Rachel.[80] To Dickens the circus represents true morality, against the falsity of political life. In Disraeli the two are entangled: morality is only possible or intelligible in a political context.

Despite his 'Englishness', Dickens remained a 'man of 1848' who believed that discontent was explosive and that government could not check it. He wrote to Layard in 1855:

> . . . I believe the discontent to be so much the worse for smouldering, instead of blazing openly, that it is extremely like the general mind of France before the breaking out of the first Revolution, and in danger of being turned by any one of a thousand accidents . . . into such a devil of a conflagration as never has been beheld since.[81]

The very qualities which Bagehot saw as contributing to British political stability seemed to destroy real reform: '. . . representative government is become altogether a failure with us . . . the English gentilities and subserviences render the people unfit for it.'[82] Yet Dickens took Peel's side in 1846, regarding Disraeli's desertion as 'dunghill politics', and saw little hope on the left. He reported the Preston strike sympathetically for *Household Words*, but in *Hard Times* libelled organized labour in the repellent Slackbridge.[83] His alienation from politics became as pronounced as Carlyle's, until he joined him, along with Kingsley and Ruskin, in commending Governor Eyre's ruthless suppression of disorder in Jamaica in 1865.[84]

Was a Manichaean view of government being frozen out by the *literati* of the establishment? C. P. Snow asserted that Cambridge dismissed Dickens even in the 1920s 'as . . . not suitable for serious literary discussion', and attributed this to his clash with Fitzjames Stephen, Leslie's brother, over his denunciation of the civil service in *Little Dorrit* (1856–7).[85] But that highly literate man Albert Venn Dicey, Victorian Britain's leading constitutionalist, Fitzjames's cousin and the friend of George Eliot and Mrs Gaskell, gave Dickens credit for inspiring the intervention by government in social and economic life which had stabilized constitutionalism in Britain – a position broadly similar to Cazamian's.[86] Dicey opposed a separate system of administrative law as incompatible with parliamentary sovereignty, an assimilation of public and private law crystallized in his *Law of the Constitution*, published in 1885. Shortly after, Parliament rejected Gladstone's attempt to give home rule to Ireland. This did two things: it confirmed Disraeli's 'Westminster Ethos'; Parliament lost its last vestiges of a 'thing', a 'sinister interest', and became a 'great individual', responsive to the complaints of the citizenry and able to take rapid action thereon. Dickens the sentimental social reformer could be incorporated as a prop to the system, at the cost of a sourer and greater critic.

IX

Disraeli pillaged the social critics and previous writers of political fiction, but made the issue the legitimacy of the State. His performance as a social reformer was mediocre.[87] He borrowed Carlyle's sense of crisis, and much of his 'métèque' diction, but his grasp of history was sketchy.[88] He adopted the Cobbettite–Tractarian vision of an 'organic' Church plundered by the nobility, but never developed it.[89] He reinterpreted the Venetian constitution – once a 'country party' ideal – as a Whig oligarchy which had to be combated, and reinvented Bolingbroke as a Tory prophet.[90] However eccentric his notion of Venice, Blake sees it as apt for the 1840s and 1850s, when 'the power of the "Venetian" aristocracy was immense . . . [and] whole counties took their political colour from their leading "magnifico"'.[91] But what would happen when this power receded, and new social classes developed? Both Disraeli and Marx believed that British parties could coalesce into a defensive alliance of the propertied, on terms dictated by the new wealth; then would come the moment of the organized proletariat.[92] But Disraeli saw that the political system – not only Parliament but also its whole cultural penumbra (elections, press, monarchy) – could be mobilized to obviate class conflict. The message of the trilogy is the same as he delivered in his assault on Peel for abolishing the Corn Laws: 'Maintain the line of demarcation between the parties, for it is only by maintaining the independence of parties that you can maintain the integrity of public men, and the power and influence of parliament itself.'[93] Disraeli was never *parti pris* about Parliament. Throughout his career he dallied with ideas his opponents could regard as Caesarist. But, ironically, *because* of the hated Peelites, Peel himself and Gladstone in particular, Parliament grew into the rôle of competent supervisory mechanism as well as theatre that he had advertised for it.[94] In 1847 the Commons entered Pugin's chamber, redolent of the mansions from which Disraeli's neo-feudalists doled out their alms. By the time he wrote *Lothair* in 1870 the parliamentary system had reached a position of unquestioned authority, where challenges to it could be dismissed as the machinations of international ne'er-do-wells. Dickens's objection, however, remained. Parliament might *work*, but was it *moral*? Did it cope with the issues the Chartist writers, the radical ideologues, even the Christian Socialists, had raised? The mid-Victorians viewed Parliament as an educational institution and review body, not as a legislative machine, and to such a view Disraeli, fashioning cabinets from unpromising material, and sustaining wobbly majorities, contributed little. A moral commitment to representative government was still needed. The next – and greatest – generation of political novelists supplied it.

NOTES

1   Michael Foot, 'The good Tory', in *Debts of Honour* [1980] (London: Picador, 1981), p. 46.

2   James Ogden, *Isaac Disraeli* (London: Oxford University Press, 1969), pp. 188, 63.

3   For the contribution of Defoe, Richardson and Fielding, see Watt, *The Rise of the Novel* (Harmondsworth: Penguin, 1963); and see J. F. Stephens, *The Censorship of Drama in England* (Cambridge: Cambridge University Press, 1979), p. 1.

4   Watt, *Rise of the Novel*, p. 55.

5   Jeremy Bentham, *A Fragment on Government* (1776), in *Works* (1844), Vol. 1, p. 235.

6   Gary Kelly, *The English Jacobin Novelists, 1780–1805* (London: Oxford University Press, 1976), pp. 5–6; John David Moore, 'Coleridge and the

modern Jacobinical drama', *Bulletin of Research in the Humanities* (Winter 1982), pp. 443 ff.

7 Kelly, *English Jacobin Novelists*, p. 6.
8 Thomas Holcroft, *Hugh Trevor* (Oxford: Oxford University Press, 1973), p. 280.
9 Kettle, 'The Early Victorian social problem novel', in Boris Ford (ed.), *The Pelican Guide to English Literature* vol. 6 (Harmondsworth: Pelican, 1958), p. 172.
10 Kelly, *English Jacobin Novelists*, p. 182.
11 ibid., p. 222, 240 ff.; Robert Blake, *Disraeli* (London: Eyre & Spottiswoode, 1966), pp. 90, 128.
12 Maurice Colgan, 'Ascendancy nationalism in Maria Edgeworth's later Irish novels', in Heinz Kosok (ed.), *Studies in Anglo-Irish Literature* (Bonn: Bouvier, 1982), pp. 37–42.
13 Marilyn Butler, *Maria Edgeworth* (London: Oxford University Press, 1972), pp. 181–4.
14 See David Hewitt, 'Scott's art and politics', in Alan Bold (ed.), *Sir Walter Scott: The Long Forgotten Melody* (London: Barnes & Noble, 1983), pp. 43–63.
15 Christopher Harvie, 'Scott and the image of Scotland', in ibid., pp. 17–42.
16 See John H. Cahalan, *A Fanatic Heart: The Irish Historical Novel* (Dublin: Gill & Macmillan, 1988), ch. 1.
17 There is a Colonel Hauton in Maria Edgeworth's *Patronage* (1815), and this may be an early instance of the borrowing of fictional names. This can mean conscious acknowledgement – or that the author is playing safe with the libel laws.
18 See Carl Van Doren, *The Life of Thomas Love Peacock* (London: Dent, 1911), pp. 78–104; and Marilyn Butler, *Peacock Displayed* (Oxford: Oxford University Press, 1979), p. 163; for political Arthurianism, see Gwyn A. Williams, *When Was Wales?* (Harmondsworth: Penguin, 1985), pp. 123 ff.
19 Peacock, *The misfortunes of Elphin* [1829], in *Novels of Thomas Love Peacock* (London: Pan, 1967), p. 183
20 Ogden, *Isaac Disraeli*, pp. 143, 61; see Richard Dorson, *The British Folklorists* (London: Routledge, 1968), p. 38; Blake, *Disraeli*, p. 191.
21 See Eric Hobsbawm, *The Age of Revolution* (New York: Mentor, 1962), pp. 164 ff.
22 See F. B. Artz, *Reaction and Revolution* (New York: Harper Torchbooks, 1963), pp. 64–9; A. J. P. Taylor, *The Hapsburg Monarchy* (Harmondsworth: Penguin, 1976), p. 33; and Christopher Harvie, 'Legalism, myth and national identity in Scotland in the imperial epoch', *Cencrastus*, Summer 1987. (On the strength of his 'dramatic spectacle' *Rumpel-Stiltskin* (1823), Disraeli certainly knew of the Grimms' work, first published 1812–18.)
23 John Galt, *The Member* [1832] (Edinburgh: Scottish Academic Press, 1985), p. 62.
24 ibid., p. 119.
25 P. H. Scott, *John Galt* (Edinburgh: Scottish Academic Press, 1985), p. 76.
26 John Galt, *The Provost* (Edinburgh: T & N Foulis, 1913), p. 23.
27 Scott, *Galt*, p. 56.
28 ibid., p. 23.
29 Galt, *The Member*, p. 36.
30 Benjamin Disraeli, *Coningsby* (London: Longmans Green, 1900), p. 103; Galt, *The Member*, p. 7.

31 H. A. L. Fisher, 'The Political Novel', *Cornhill Magazine*, vol. 64 (1928), p. 69.
32 See Alison Adburgham, *The Silver Fork: Society, Fashionable Life and Literature, 1814–40* (London: Constable, 1983).
33 Francis Russell Hart, 'The Regency novel of fashion', in S. Mintz, A. Chandler and C. Mulvey (eds), *From Smollett to James* (Charlottesville: University Press of Virginia, 1981), p. 93.
34 G. M. Young, *Victorian England: The Portrait of an Age* (London: Oxford University Press, 1953), p. 157; Q. D. Leavis, *Fiction and the Reading Public* (London: Chatto & Windus, 1932), pp. 159 ff.
35 See T. H. S. Escott, *Edward Bulwer* (London: Routledge, 1910), pp. 164, 252.
36 Hart, 'Regency novel', p. 123.
37 Escott, *Bulwer*, p. 238; and see John Mullen, 'The language of sentiment', in Andrew Hook (ed.), *The History of Scottish Literature*, vol. 2, 1660–1 (Aberdeen: Aberdeen University Press, 1987).
38 Phipps, *Robert Plumer Ward* (London: John Murray, 1850), Vol. 2, p. 137; Canning cited in *DNB* entry on Ward (by William Carr).
39 Escott, *Bulwer*, p. 238.
40 Phipps, *Robert Plumer Ward*, Vol. 2, p. 159.
41 'Cherry and Fair Star', *A Year at Hartlebury; or, The Election* [1834] (London: John Murray, 1983); see app. 1 for its publishing history.
42 *Hartlebury*, p. 173.
43 Cited in John Gross, *The Rise and Fall of the Man of Letters* (Harmondsworth: Penguin, 1973), p. 314; *Coningsby*, p. 368.
44 *The Provost* [1822] (Edinburgh: T & N Foulis, 1913), pp. 328–9; *Sybil* (Harmondsworth: Penguin, 1954), pp. 138–9.
45 T. B. Macaulay, 'Southey's colloquies' [1830], in *Critical and Historical Essays* (London: Longman, 1903), p. 368.
46 Victor Kiernan, 'Class and ideology: the bourgeoisie and its historians', *History of European Ideas*, vol. 6, no. 3 (1985), p. 270.
47 Bernard Shaw, *The Perfect Wagnerite* (London: Constable, 1923), pp. 30–4.
48 Karl Marx and Friedrich Engels, *The Communist Manifesto* (Harmondsworth: Penguin, 1973), p. 77.
49 E.P. Thompson and Eileen Yeo (eds), *The Unknown Mayhew* (Harmondsworth: Peguin, 1974), pp. 15–16.
50 Walter Besant, 'The first Society of British Authors' [1843] in *Essays and Historiettes* (London: Chatto & Windus, 1903), pp. 271 ff.
51 See Duncan Forbes, *The Liberal Anglican Idea of History* (Cambridge: Cambridge University Press, 1952), p. 109.
52 Blake, *Disraeli*, p. 193.
53 Mark Girouard, *The Return to Camelot* (New Haven, Conn.: Yale University Press, 1981), pp. 18, 57; a Lord Egremont actually existed, who entertained 6,000 tenantry and labourers with a giant ox-roast in 1834. See Langer, *Political and Social Upheaval* (New York: Harper, 1969), p. 19.
54 For Anglo-Saxonism, see L. P. Curtis, jnr, *Anglo-Saxons and Celts*, Conference on British Studies, 1968, pp. 11 ff.
55 See H. W. C. Davis, *Balliol College* (Oxford: Blackwell, 1899), p. 187; M. E. Speare, *The Political Novel: Its Development in England and America* (New York: Oxford University Press, 1924), p. 159, on Disraeli's relations to the Oxford Movement; Fred Kaplan, *Thomas Carlyle: A Biography* (Cambridge: Cambridge University Press, 1983), pp. 154–5.

56 Disraeli, *Coningsby*, p. 65.
57 Stephen, 'Mr Disraeli's novels', in *Hours in a Library* (London: Smith Elder, 1892), Vol. 2, pp. 206–7.
58 Foot, *Debts of Honour*, pp. 52–3.
59 This attained its fullest development in *Lothair*, see Blake, *Disraeli*, p. 517.
60 Disraeli, *Sybil*, p. 280.
61 ibid., p. 96.
62 Speare, *Political Novel*, p. 74; Sheila M. Smith, *The Other Nation: The Poor in English Novels of the 1840s and 1850s* (London: Oxford University Press, 1980), p. 98.
63 Walter Bagehot, *The English Constitution* (London: Oxford University Press, 1928), p. 9; and see Ferdinand Mount, *The Theatre of Politics* (London: Weidenfeld & Nicolson, 1972), pp. 245–7.
64 Karl Marx, 'Morning Post gegen Preussen', p. 220, preface to *Grundrisse der Kritik der politischen Ökonomie*, written 1857–8 (Vienna: Europa Verlag, n.d.), p. 31; and see S. S. Prawer, *Karl Marx and World Literature*, (London: Oxford University Press, 1976), pp. 86 ff.
65 See Donald Southgate, 'From Disraeli to Law' in R. A. Butler (ed.), *The Conservatives* (London: Allen & Unwin, 1977), pp. 123–32.
66 Anthony Trollope, *Autobiography* [1883] (London: Oxford University Press, 1946), p. 230.
67 Blake, *Disraeli*, pp. 68–9.
68 *Tancred* (London: Longmans Green, 1900), p. 222.
69 Disraeli, *Coningsby*, pp. 117–18.
70 James Bryce, 'Lord Beaconsfield', in *Studies in Contemporary Biography* (London: Macmillan, 1903), p. 51.
71 Una Pope-Hennessy, *Charles Dickens* (Harmondsworth: Penguin, 1970), p. 171.
72 Charles Dickens, *Hard Times* (Harmondsworth: Penguin, 1988), p. 65.
73 ibid., p. 129.
74 ibid., p. 162.
75 ibid., p. 312.
76 Dickens to Henry Cole, 17 June 1854, cited in Edgar Johnson, *Charles Dickens: His Tragedy and Triumph* (London: Gollancz, 1953), p. 797.
77 Pope-Hennessy, *Dickens*, p. 432.
78 ibid., p. 426; and see Karl Marx, 'On the Reform movement', *Neue Oder Zeitung*, 20 May 1855, reprinted in D. Fernbach (ed.), *Surveys from Exile* (Harmondsworth: Penguin, 1973), p. 287.
79 F. R. and Q. D. Leavis, *Dickens the Novelist* (London: Chatto & Windus, 1970), pp. 187 ff.
80 George Orwell, 'Charles Dickens', in *Critical Essays* (London: Secker & Warburg, 1946), p. 60; Jack Lindsay, *Charles Dickens* (London: Allen & Unwin, 1950), p. 310.
81 Dickens to Layard, 10 April 1855, quoted in David Paroissen (ed.), *Selected Letters of Charles Dickens* (London: Macmillan, 1985), p. 265.
82 Dickens to John Forster, 30 September 1855, in ibid., p. 266.
83 See Geoffrey Carnall, 'Dickens, Mrs Gaskell, and the Preston strike', *Victorian Studies*, vol. 8 (September 1964), p. 34.
84 C. P. Snow, 'Dickens and the public service', in Michael Slater (ed.), *Dickens 1970* (London: Chapman & Hall, 1970), p. 148.
85 ibid., p. 137.

86 A. V. Dicey, *Law and Opinion* (London: Macmillan, 1904), pp. 418–22, and *Law of the Constitution* (London: Macmillan, 1885), p. 188.

87 Asa Briggs, *The Age of Improvement* (London: Longman, 1959), p. 332.

88 Blake, *Disraeli*, p. 273.

89 Horst Rössler, *Literatur und Arbeiterbewegung: Studien Zur Literaturkritik und Frühen Prosa des Chartismus* (Frankfurt: Peter Lang, 1985), p. 221.

90 Kelly, *English Jacobin Novelists*, pp. 222 ff.

91 Blake, *Disraeli*, p. 273.

92 'The Chartists', *New York Daily Tribune*, August 1852, reprinted in D. Fernbach (ed.), *Surveys from Exile* (Harmondsworth: Penguin, 1973), p. 264.

93 Quoted in Briggs, *Age of Improvements*, p. 342.

94 ibid., pp. 328–35; and, for Gladstone's reforms which placed the Treasury under firm parliamentary control, see H. C. G. Matthew, 'Disraeli, Gladstone and the politics of mid-Victorian budgets', *Historical Journal*, vol. 22, no. 3 (1979), pp. 615–43.

4

Landscape with Candidates

NOT A MAN disposed to this sort of thing, Anthony Trollope allowed himself to be moved to awe at the sight of the two lamps which guard the entry to the Members' Lobby of the House of Commons:

> I have told myself, in anger and in grief, that to die and not to have won that right of way, though but for a session, – not to have passed through those lamps, – is to die and not to have done that which it most becomes an Englishman to have achieved.[1]

That a powerful *genius loci* could inhere in a new building shows the strength of the parliamentary ethos in the 'age of equipoise', that period which gives political fiction two essential qualities: actuality and – no less important – profitability.[2] The mid-Victorian output was limited – perhaps seventy titles published between 1848 and 1886 – but enough now stayed in print and were treated seriously by critics to consolidate the genre. Some paid very well: Trollope's Palliser novels earned him around £3,000 each (over £100,000 in our money), George Eliot made £5,000 on *Felix Holt* in 1866, and Disraeli broke all records with the £10,000 Longman gave him for *Endymion* in 1880.[3]

In the 1850s Whitehall and Westminster established themselves as part of the landscape of British domestic fiction. H. G. Nicholas wrote in 1956 that the election scene, for example, 'became for fifty or sixty years . . . a regular part of the English novelists' stock-in trade'.[4] By the 1870s writers were aiming political propaganda at the enlarged electorate, and in the 1890s the 'political thriller' arrived. As the mid-Victorians established the landscape of British political fiction, this seems the point to chart it: the ways in which it was written and published, how it reached and was received by the public.

The genre is, inevitably, broader and less coherent than the tradition of social criticism explored by Raymond Williams in *Culture and*

Society – varying from complex cultural and psychological analysis to the near-pulp of most 'political thrillers'. Writers can have influential positions in the political élite or churn out potboilers or, these days, 'books of the TV series'; but if, as Doris Lessing argues, Britain has failed to achieve the European metropolitan novel there has been no slide into the assembly-line production of, say, hospital and war novels. As entertainers, writers of political fiction have to be sensitive to a wide social constituency, and even the worst are forced by their subject-matter to write with some individuality and practical authority.

The concerns of political fiction parallel the political structure: *legislature* (elections, party activity, Parliament); *executive* (legislation, authority, intrigue); and *judiciary* (moral qualms about the foregoing). 'Party' politics also parallels the business of writing, publishing or staging the 'product' – reabsorbing it into the political culture – since much of British print-capitalism is embedded in a politically created *milieu*. In Peacock's *Melincourt* (1817), Desmond the moralist-turned-peasant found in the London of the 1810s:

> . . . everywhere the same indifference or aversion to general principles, the same partial or perverted views: every one was the organ of some division or subdivision of a faction; and had entrenched himself in a narrow circle, within the pale of which all was honour, consistency, integrity, generosity and justice; while all without it was villainy, hypocrisy, selfishness, corruption, and lies.[5]

Mature print-capitalism diminished this partisanship, but not totally. Even when the novel displaced poetry as 'serious' imaginative communication, it was subject to strong 'small-p political' constraints: not just because some publishers had party links but through agreements on distributing and pricing books. As binding as Disraeli's conventions, these created a distinctive literary world, with a largish number of authors living on the copyright of three-volume novels. In the United States the rock-bottom prices of the free market meant many books but few native authors; German publishers, decentralized in the various states, found more authors but little profit. British publishing, like other élite activities – the Bar or the universities – had a 'political' structure which, intentionally or otherwise, mimicked the conventions of Westminster.[6]

If the British constitution was representative without being democratic, British publishing was commercial without being truly competitive. It 'restricted its franchise' by agreeing with the circulating libraries a high price – equivalent to the weekly wages of a skilled man – for new novels. Published authors got around £300 the three-decker, and indeed grew in number: 31 three-deckers were published in 1837, 184 in 1887.

But this meant that few novels got beyond the 'library edition'. Authors were like parliamentary candidates, most of them Tories in Welsh mining valleys: a few weeks of prominence, and then obscurity. For the winners, who could partly control their market, negotiations about publication became almost as complex as forming a Cabinet.[7] The parallels can be extended, not utterly fancifully: Mudie's subscribers as the electorate, Paternoster Row as Parliament, publishers' readers as whips, copyrights as foreign policy, agents as agents . . .

The literary industry, largely centralized in London, had self-government (not a foregone conclusion elsewhere in Europe) and a readership (or at least a male readership) similar to the parliamentary electorate. Its freedom was remarkable (obscenity, only, being constrained by Lord Campbell's Act of 1856), and power was devolved to 'creative' rather than 'money-making' groups, like editors and literary advisers, in a set-up which endured until the 1960s.[8] During this time the stage – potentially much more effective than the novel: a run of three weeks in an average theatre would reach more people than most three-deckers ever managed to – remained under strict control by the Lord Chamberlain. A stage version of *Coningsby* by Shirley Brooks was suppressed in 1847 because it was 'a kind of *quasi*-political piece, exhibiting a sort of contrast between the manufacturing people and the lower classes'. When film censorship was set up - not by the State but by the film exhibitors – in 1912, nothing changed.[9]

II

These relationships are 'political' in an institutional sense. But the political novel evolved just when, as Benedict Anderson has argued, liberal nationalism and print-capitalism made it a means of imposing a 'national' history. Writers 'imagined' a community, using realism to render in concrete terms the subjective conviction of an élite.[10]

Take the 'Introduction' to George Eliot's 'political novel' *Felix Holt the Radical* (1866) where the Midlands are surveyed from a stagecoach rolling through them in 1830, on the eve of Reform:

> But everywhere the bushy hedgerows wasted the land with their straggling beauty, shrouded the grassy borders of the pastures with catkined hazels, and tossed their long blackberry branches on the corn-fields. Perhaps they were white with May, or starred with pale-pink dogroses; perhaps the urchins were already nutting amongst them, or gathering the plenteous crabs. It was worth the journey only to see those hedgerows, the liberal homes of unmarketable beauty . . . Such hedgerows were often as tall as the labourers' cottages dotted

along the lanes, or clustered into a small hamlet, their little dingy
windows telling, like thick-filmed eyes, of nothing but the darkness
within.[11]

At first glance, this looks like straightforward natural history; on second
reading, more powerful images emerge. Hedges are man-made. Yet the
'straggling beauty' of these 'wastes' and 'shrouds' potentially efficient
agricultural land. 'The liberal homes of unmarketable beauty': is this the
coming fight between 'liberal' political economy and the 'unmarketable'
relationship of the landlord society the hedges belong to? But does
'liberal' also mean that, if the hedges are left alone to grow, they will
be ecologically generous? At any rate, George Eliot's hedges are old. If,
by historians' rule of thumb, every century adds a new species, these
ones are very old indeed. In fact, by the time we come to the stunted
cottages, we don't just have a description, but a pretty good idea what
the chapter, even the book itself, is going to be about.
    Contrast this with Balzac's sketch, in *The Member for Arcis*, of the
country round Arcis:

> Champagne looks, and is, a poor country . . . As you pass through
> the villages or even the towns, you see none but shabby buildings of
> timber or concrete. Stone is scarcely used, even for public buildings.
> At Arcis the chateau, the Palais de Justice and the church are the only
> edifices constructed of stone.[12]

The reader is certainly primed to expect the descent on Arcis of characters
he already knows from *The Human Comedy*, but Balzac, the metropolitan
conservative, simply sees Arcis as 'not-Paris', lacking a political culture
of its own. Eliot's evaluation is far more complex, and becomes more so
as the coach traverses different types of community: the isolated hamlet
'away from everything but its own patch of earth and sky, away from the
parish church by long fields and green lanes, away from all intercourse
except that of tramps';[13] the 'trim, cheerful, village' 'with a neat or
handsome parsonage and grey church set in the midst; the pleasant
tinkle of the blacksmith's anvil, the patient cart-horses waiting at his
door; the basket-maker peeling his willow wands in the sunshine; the
wheelwright putting the last touch to a blue cart with red wheels'; and
then the incursions of the industrial revolution:

> . . . as the day wore on, the scene would change: the land would begin
> to be blackened with coal-pits, the rattle of handlooms to be heard in
> hamlets and villages . . . The gables of dissenting chapels now made
> a visible sign of religion, and of a meeting place to counterbalance the
> ale house . . . Here was a population not convinced that old England

was as good as possible; here were multitudinous men and women aware that their religion was not exactly the religion of their rulers, who might therefore be better than they were, and who, if better, might alter many things which now made the world perhaps more painful than it need be, and certainly more sinful.

These descriptions not only underline the argument of the hedgerow passage; they also emphasize Eliot's choice of epigraph to the chapter – out of Michael Drayton's *Polyolbion*:

> Upon the midlands now the industrious muse doth fall,
> The shires which we the heart of England well may call.

This landscape is symbolic of England as a whole. Eliot's Midlands were anything but remote, as a glance at any map will show that the nodes of every English transport system – road, canal, railway, motorway – fall within a dozen miles of Nuneaton, *Felix Holt*'s Treby Magna.

Anderson argues that fiction is central to the 'imagining of community. 'The representative mechanism', he writes, 'is a rare and moveable feast. The generation of the impersonal will is . . . better sought in the diurnal regularities of the imagining life.' In the liberal epoch

> The search was on for a new way of linking fraternity, power and time meaningfully together. Nothing perhaps more precipitated this search, nor made it more fruitful, than print-capitalism, which made it possible for rapidly-growing numbers of people to think about themselves, and to relate themselves to others, in profoundly new ways.[14]

Combine the 'representative mechanism' with the novel, as Eliot did, and you have a near-perfect example: the peculiarities of the English, carefully established in time and place, set against the main political change of the nineteenth century.

Eliot stressed the impact of society on landscape. Loamshire is 'landlord's country', in the phrase of a later literary politician, Charles Masterman: '. . . the open woods, the large grass fields and wide hedges, the ample demesnes . . . signify a country given up less to industry than to dignified opulence.'[15] Eliot knew the Continent well and deliberately sets Loamshire against the undifferentiated landscape of peasant Europe.[16] *Felix Holt* reflects (as did most other mid-Victorian political novels) the centrality of land to the politics of the British élite. Even in the 1860s over half the *Commons* were related to, or in some way dependent on, the territorial nobility.[17] Primogeniture led ambitious younger sons into politics and the civil service; heiresses meant much more than 'romantic interest'. Trollope, always keen on his love-stories, can be cursory about the physique of his girls; he is always precise about their expectations.[18]

Loamshire is not eternal. 'Grey steeples . . . and churchyards . . . sleeping in the sunlight' reads uneasily; so does 'multitudinous'. Change had accelerated since 1832; stagecoaches had vanished, and this complex countryside could follow them, dissolved by the railway and the 'multi-tudinous' history-less city. Where participatory community didn't exist, and the old landed order yielded to the mechanism of the new, where can space for an honourable political society be found? Eliot tries to reassure through a type of dialectic – between land and commerce, church and dissent, stagecoach and train, Tory and Liberal – to give the political adversary system at least a temporary appropriateness. Felix Holt – both the hero of the novel and the 'author' of 'An Address to Working Men' in 1867 – pleads for the workers to adopt the old political framework until they educate themselves into conceiving a better.

This was close to the position of younger political writers, many of them members of the Eliot–Lewes circle, who resembled liberal nationalists on the Continental model. Opposed, in the *Reform Essays* of 1867, to 'mechanistic' utilitarians such as John Stuart Mill on the left and Robert Lowe on the right, they insisted that the institutions of a British *commonwealth* should gradually adapt towards a democracy (unspecified, but their examples were mainly Swiss or American), a process requiring as much political art as political science. Like Eliot, they believed that this process could only function within the traditional framework.[19]

III

Felix Holt imagined 'Britain' at a decisive transition from land, locality and deference to Parliament, nationality and print-capitalism. It also *embodied* the new order, being 'managed' as a major publishing event – the country's most serious novelist *on* politics *in* the year of franchise reform. Yet Eliot also exploited a tradition of politics-as-entertainment, *and* the expertise of the *Reform Essays* élite.[20]

The Loamshire election is *Felix Holt*'s main political element. 'That mysterious distant system of things called "Gover'ment"' remains mysterious, and it's quite easy to forget who actually got elected, but the election is the catalyst which changes the fates of all the main characters. In this Eliot reflected – not for the last time: *Middlemarch* (1871–2) was still to come – the fascination which elections exerted on British novelists, even the most apolitical. To take only two examples: in Mrs Gaskell's *Ruth* (1854) the heroine re-encounters her seducer when he stands for Parliament; and Mrs Henry Wood in *East Lynne* (1861), the most popular novel of the century, with 500,000 copies sold by the mid-1890s, uses an election to bring her villain to book.[21]

Why did elections have this fictional popularity? For a start, they were technically useful in constructing a novel. According to Nicholas, the election scene became 'one of the stock incidents that a novelist uses to diversify his narrative and intermingle his classes and characters, like a church scene in opera – which it also resembles in the incitement it provides to bravura and virtuoso treatment'.[22] Elections were when the community could penalize wrong-doing or – as with Mr Brooke in *Middlemarch* – impractical pretensions. Such rituals were in Europe the province of town or Church; these had continuity while representative government was episodic. Obviously all novels which include elections are not political yet they can't be neglected, as elections are where the British public encountered the routines of politics. The more such scenes tended to appear, the greater the chance for the political novel proper to establish itself.

Trollope, to Frederic Harrison the 'photographer' of mid-Victorian Britain,[23] makes his elections almost a documentary of British political geography. These range from the country town of Barchester in *Dr Thorne* (1858) and the rural pocket borough of Silverbridge in *Can You Forgive Her?* and *The Prime Minister*, to the Scottish 'grouped burgh' of Strathbogy in *The Three Clerks* (1858) and the London seats of Chelsea in *Can You Forgive Her?* and Westminster in *The Way We Live Now* (1876). He moves Phineas Finn from the Irish borough of Loughshane to Loughton in Essex, and then to the northern mining seat of Tankerville in *Phineas Redux* (1873). Trollope's own contest at Beverley, transmuted into Percycross in *Ralph the Heir* (1871), was plainly grim, but he put it to good use, while George Meredith could make the Bevisham election in *Beauchamp's Career* (1875) as emblematic of the 'condition of England' before the Second Reform Bill as *Felix Holt* had been of politics at the time of the First.[24]

British elections were frequent – at every accession, otherwise at least every seven years. They were a political weapon, as the Prime Minister could choose the most favourable date, and ideologically important, as the 'first past the post' system meant that what a candidate stood for was significant (in a proportional-representation system party programmes are essentially something to be haggled about by coalition partners *after* the contest). Britain also had more by-elections than anywhere else – when MPs died, or inherited peerages, or when, before 1918, ministers had to recontest on taking office. Before opinion polls (which date from 1945) public opinion could only be tested at such contests; thereafter, as the stability of the system dwindled, anonymous London suburbs or remote counties would briefly be granted the status of oracle to the nation.

Elections also emphasized the link between the representative and his seat, and the way in which, even after 1832, party bargains shaped political geography. The big towns, the Scots and the Irish remained badly represented. The Whigs kept their small boroughs (Calne in 1851 returned as many MPs as Leeds), the Tories their tame county freeholders. Open voting, with 'influence', bribery and coercion, lasted until 1872; unrestricted expenses until 1883. Only in 1884 was the grant of the suffrage to male householders accompanied by even roughly equal electoral districts.[25]

The election was a substitute for a participating local community, which allowed Parliament to domesticate party conflict. Most European assemblies symbolized confrontation. Ministers faced a horseshoe of representatives, with a speaker's podium in the middle, and some lonely MP speaking *at* his colleagues, conscious of Bismarck, or someone like him, glowering at his back. Westminster, on the other hand, both dignified and 'froze' the securities of the two-party system. When not barracking one another from the parallel green benches, members sprawled or chatted or read among their 'friends' – the old name for party; friendships extended beyond party boundaries; a Labour MP might be closer to his Tory 'pair' than to his party colleagues. 'Make friends with the other side', says Jim Hacker in 'Yes, Minister', 'at least they're not after your job.' This was not unique: the sociologist Robert Michels noted of the pre-1914 German Reichstag that there was more difference between party activists and MPs than between MPs of different parties.[26] But in Britain, with a far more stable constitution, this gap was even wider.

In Continental and American political fiction party struggles or regional-central conflicts tend to matter more than elections. Balzac's *Member for Arcis* is about the *selection* of the candidate not his election, and many American novels and films about politics tend to climax at the Nomination Convention. British elections persuaded electors that, in a very remote and predictable system, their opinion still mattered. If they were too boisterous or too boring, something was wrong. Nicholas thought that after 1880 the quality of fictional elections declined, as party machines grew more dominant, but this was in 1956 when the two-party system was unquestioned.[27] Greater uncertainties since then have brought elections back into prominence; exalting and destroying 'third force' contenders, yet somehow maintaining the *status quo*. To the Labour MP Joe Ashton, in *Grassroots* (1983) they are still 'the blood transfusion of politics, necessary to keep up the old aggro and the old fear'.[28] Whether they are an adequate substitute for a participative community is another matter.

Elections were where politics intervened in 'ordinary life' – with candidates, canvassing, slogans and 'favours', the tension of the hustings and the count – testing the will of the voter as well as the nerve of the candidate. Minds could actually be changed, small majorities snatched. Disraeli laid this on. After Bohun's one-vote win in *Hartlebury: The Election*, a by-election in *Coningsby* floors the pretentious party hack, Nicholas Rigby. Although, as Trollope would point out, such successes defied the facts of landlord influence and the labours of the registration court, they passed effortlessly into mythology, even that of the Labour Party. In the novels of Howard Spring or James Welsh, elections are where the young movement puts to flight the old men and their fly-blown slogans.

The epic element is obvious enough – the joust or contest trans-muted into politics – but there were also those who saw elections demeaning 'true' self-government. Hogarth ridiculed their corruption in his engravings based on the Oxford election of 1754, and in that great mid-Victorian icon, Ford Madox Brown's painting *Work* (1852), there appears in the distance, between Carlyle and F. D. Maurice and the noble navvies, a file of shabby men carrying sandwich-boards with 'Vote for Bobus' on them – an allusion to the 'Houndsditch politics' of 'beer and balderdash' in Carlyle's *Past and Present*. Nicholas regards the satiric presentation of elections as a pre-1832 phenomenon, but it was probably the stronger reaction.[29]

Dickens's Eatanswill was written in 1837: in a market-town awash with booze and slogans, the guileless Pickwickians stroll from Blue to Buff to Blue; crack reserves of electors are too drunk to get to the poll. Dickens had it in for the manipulators more than for the mob, but so, too, did Tories like Samuel Warren, whose enormously popular *Ten Thousand a Year* appeared in 1841, and W. E. Aytoun's sprightly 'How I stood for the Dreepdailly Burghs' in which 'reformed Scotland' has fallen into the hands of the clique which 'in almost every town throughout Scotland, . . . leads the electors as quietly, but as surely, as the blind man is conducted by his dog. These are modelled on the true Venetian principles of secrecy and terrorism.'[30]

Radicals were similarly sceptical. At elections the true citizen had to stand out against 'corruption' in every sense of the term. Mark Ruther-ford's *The Revolution in Tanner's Lane* (1887) shows how the reawakening of the spirit of 1789 in the 1841 election calls the Congregationalists of Cowfold to judgement, and finds their minister wanting. In Lewis Grassic Gibbon's *Cloud Howe* (1934) another minister's abandonment of the radical cause leaves his wife, Chris Colquohoun – and the handful of Liberals left in the little town of Segget – to champion 'Liberty Mere' against 'the Tory cars piled black with folk, getting off to vote for the gentry childes that had promised them reischles and reischles of tariffs'.[31] In this, Chris expresses solidarity not with Gibbon's own schema of Marxist 'development' but with the thrawn integrity of her peasant forebears, who would forfeit a tenancy rather than betray their politics.

This scepticism seems to have a strong Scots or Irish flavour. Scotland was until 1832 'the largest rotten borough in Britain' where elections were total formalities. In Ireland, after a relatively open period after Catholics gained the vote in 1793, elections were manipulated in favour of the Ascendancy.[32] Maria Edgeworth in *Castle Rackrent* begins a treatment of the election as farce, which is carried on by Samuel Lover in *Handy Andy* (1827) and in such early novels of Charles Lever as *Charles O'Malley*, in which the antics of the 'genial Paddies' mask a Tory–nationalist protest against mechanism and manipulation in politics:

> In the goodly days I speak of, a county contest was a very different thing from the tame and insipid farce that now passes under that name, where a briefless barrister, bullied by both sides, sits as assessor – a few drunken votes – a radical O'Connellite grocer – a demagogue priest – a deputy grand purple something from the Trinity College lodge, with some half-dozen followers, shouting 'To the devil with Peel!' or 'Down with Dues!' form the whole corps de ballet.[33]

The notion of elections as 'Vanity Fair' revived in the twentieth century, from Robert Tressell's *The Ragged Trousered Philanthropists* (written in 1911) and the ingenious election comedies in John Buchan's *John MacNab* (1925) and *Castle Gay* (1928), to, almost in our own day, David Walder's *The Short List* (1964) and Dennis Potter's television film *Vote, Vote, Vote for Nigel Barton* (1966). In this acidulous piece, judged sufficiently malign to be postponed until after the general election of that year, the demonic rôle is taken by the Labour agent, a figure who could have been in charge at Eatanswill or Percycross:

> Believe me, there have been better mornings. Sometimes you can get a door-step conversation, Billy Graham style. But usually they tell you what they think you *want* to hear. I could see that all this raw politics upset poor old Nigel like nobody's business. He's over behind that hedge, being sick. He had this old-fashioned idea that . . . well . . . I don't like to say it really . . . that (*sniggers, and stops*) . . . 'conviction' and passion – I do beg your pardon, folks, really I do – should come into it somewhere.[34]

Perhaps the British election is a successor of the 'ridings' or 'rough music' of the seventeenth century, whereby public figures were chastised by the people – in Europe the Fastnet or Carnival still contains such elements – but its ethos has always been that of 'letting off steam', not of free citizens making rational decisions.[35]

IV

Moral self-realization and 'representation' gave the election scene a place in the English domestic novel; to pursue matters into legislation and executive action required knowledge of Parliament and administration, even if the intention was satirical.[36] Writing which vividly re-creates local class or family conflict can falter when presented with Whitehall politics. In a novel by a Scottish miner who eventually became a Labour MP, James Welsh's *The Underworld* (1922), his hero Robert Sinclair, a miner, is called to an industrial conference in London. Its chairman, the Prime Minister, Asquith, is brilliantly sketched by an old trade unionist:

> Look at that auld fermer-collier lookin' chiel, wi' his white heid an' his snipe-nose an' a smile on his face that wad mak' ye believe he was gaun tae dae you some big service. That's the smile that has made him Prime Minister. You'd think frae his face that he was just a solid easy-gaun kindly auld fermer, who took a constant joy in givin' jeelie-pieces to weans. But when he speaks, and gets a grip o' you, he's yin o' the souplest lawyers that ever danced roun the rim o' hell withoot fallin in. He'd do his faither, that yin. He wad that.[37]

When 'thae chaps get round about ye', the miners will be played like trout. This didn't just apply to Welsh's characters; his own Scots vocabulary evaporated, leaving only a limp English, when he described metropolitan and parliamentary life, something with an *arcana* of language, conventions and relationships only vaguely to be perceived from outside. John Buchan, in *John MacNab*, has the Foreign Secretary, on a day off from poaching game, deliver a speech to a Highland audience. Oratorically perfect, it fails to engage with a single actual issue, and wins wild applause. This reflected, perhaps, Buchan's own doubts, as a presbyterian Scot, about Westminster. Others, more reverent, were not thought by insiders to have made the grade. James Bryce had his doubts on Trollope:

> He was a direct and forcible speaker, who would have made his way had he entered Parliament. But as he had no practical experience of politics either in the House of Commons or as a working member of a party organisation in a city where contests are keen, the pictures of political life which are so frequent in his later tales have not much flavour of reality. They are sketches obviously taken from the outside.[38]

Could the outsider ever be accepted? Mrs Humphry Ward wrote her political novels *Marcella* (1894) and *Sir George Tressady* (1896) only after painstakingly absorbing the atmosphere of Westminster (on to whose benches she was intent that no woman should penetrate); less respectably, Marie Corelli teamed up with the Radical MP Henry Labouchere for her satire on the press and politics, *The Silver Domino* (1892).[39] Even in the 1960s another civil servant, C. P. Snow, had to seek out a novel-writing MP, Maurice Edelman, to guide him round Westminster; the result, *Corridors of Power* (1964), is much less atmospheric than his later novel *In Their Wisdom* (1974), written from actual experience of the House of Lords.[40]

These examples stress one unliterary quality: the demand for an 'authentic record' of something hermetic and specialized, Galt's 'community made up of peculiar people'. Edgar Wallace and William Le Queux, both old journalistic hands, managed this sort of thing effortlessly.[41] Jeffrey Archer supposedly wrote *First among Equals* (1984) 'from the inside', and many 1970s bestsellers implied that they offered their readers not only entertainment but also useful facts.[42] 'Insiders' seem to have counted from the start. Of the first generation of political fiction writers, from 1848 to 1886, forty-three authors wrote between them sixty-four works. About a third had occupations – politician, civil servant, journalist – which would make them familiar with Whitehall and Westminster, while only seven (16 per cent) were women, compared with about 25 per cent among authors as a whole. Granted that statistics are distorted by Trollope's remarkable output - fourteen works during this period – insiders produced half the political novels written in this period.

This literary deference before public men persisted. Arnold Bennett captured it when he made Sam Raingo, northern industrialist summoned into wartime Whitehall, consider the deviousness of his political chief: '. . .he might have put me through an intensive inside course of politics, but he's more important things to think about. And I couldn't learn politics in three months more or less - nobody could. I've got to do the best I can and avoid moral indignation, and go through with it.'[43] Bennett wrote out of his own experience at the Ministry of Information in 1918. But a claw of irony is perceptible. Raingo was an innocent, whose fate was to be destroyed by politics; Bennett was a deeply read and shrewd professional author, who realized two things: one, that writers – and industrialists – operate in a linear fashion, in which the goal – the book or the firm – demands and defines a certain organization of life, while politicians have to cope with a constantly changing mix of factors, in which the stress is often simply on survival; two, despite this existential predicament, irony is to politicians what garlic is to vampires.

Irony is not sarcasm – in which politicians excel – but the ability of the author to manipulate his readers' feelings: to induce first belief in, then scepticism about, his characters. This creative autonomy is what writers seek but politicians must at all costs avoid. Disraeli possessed it, but he was a rare example. Well-placed writers can fictionalize politics, and there have been some original writers who were politicians – Harold Nicolson, Maurice Edelman, David Walder – yet no politician since Disraeli has managed to express his own individuality and succeed.

V

Such literary approaches had a twofold effect. First, they publicized the themes and language of politics. Think of the formulas – 'Two Nations', 'Tadpoles and Tapers', 'All Power Corrupts', 'Corridors of Power', 'Wets' – which have been broadcast by political fiction, or of the incisive treatment of the semantics of Whitehall in 'Yes, Minister'. Second, they suggested that political society's conventions had only a blurred line separating them from fiction. Richard Crossman noted, on taking office in 1964, a

> . . . curious sense of fiction, the feeling that I am living in a Maurice Edelman novel. All this business of being a Cabinet Minister is still unreal to me . . . every time we left Downing Street or moved along Whitehall there was always a crowd of people watching, cheering, clapping as we went in and out – it's as if we are taking part not in real life but in a piece of reportage on the British constitutional system.[44]

Political fiction sometimes achieved the same unity of imagination, description and action as the Elizabethan stage, appealing to groundlings as well as to intellectuals, and retailing the 'shop' as well as the great themes. 'Social history at last . . . attains the reality of fiction, which is the highest reality of all', wrote George Dangerfield at the end of *The Strange Death of Liberal England* (1935), in which he had employed the techniques of the novelist – the debt to Trollope, Meredith and Wells is obvious – to reorder events which had taken place only twenty years earlier.[45] In the 1980s his images still shadow British politics with a vividness few 'scientific' writers could ever match. Are there, then, affinities between politicians and writers? This hinges on the point at which the genre gained acceptance, and on the relations between fiction, criticism and political journalism.

Novels came late into the critical canon. Up to the 1840s 'escapist' themes of love, adventure, travel and fashionable society dominated.[46] In 1855 Fitzjames Stephen deplored Thackeray's levity towards 'the serious business in life', and in 1859, W. R. Greg stressed their social importance while deprecating their moral effects. Novels preyed on the unsuspecting: busy men relaxing 'when the fatigued mind requires rest and recreation, when the brain, therefore, is comparatively passive', the young 'at the exact crisis of life when the spirit is at once most susceptible and most tenacious', and women 'who are always impressionable, in whom at all times the emotional element is more awake and more powerful than the critical . . .'.[47] Carlyle's 'long ear' again! But in the same year another of the Sage's disciples, David Masson, Professor of English Literature at University College, London, claimed that the novel had become 'a Natural History of British Life', far from escapist in its choice of agenda: contemporary history had moved in, with

> . . . a determination . . . to deal with incidents and situations of the order of those historically recent – political conspiracies, club-meetings, strikes in the manufacturing districts, mill riots, &c.; while, as addition to the novelist's traditionary stock of ideal characters, we have had the Socialist, the Red Republican, the Foreign Refugee, the Government Spy, the young Chartist Orator, the Emancipated Women, and the like.[48]

This was marginal to a literary criticism still dominated by poetry and the classics, whose assessment of the novel moved only creakily towards endorsement. Masson, like E. S. Dallas, another early and prescient novel-critic, was out of the Scottish common-sense tradition, which accepted the 'theoretical history' claims of the novel – ironically just at the point where it was defeated by the assault of J. S. Mill on Sir William Hamilton. But by the 1870s a definitive *critique* had evolved, with an appreciation of formal qualities, style and characterization.

The key document is Leslie Stephen on Disraeli in 1874. Stephen, the father of Virginia Woolf, was as editor and critic the great legislator of late-Victorian Eng. Lit. and, equally typically, had shifted from 'committed' political journalism to a more detached 'academic' analysis. As a Liberal, Stephen had to account for Disraeli's political success, but he found himself facing no pamphleteer but a complex and well-read writer whose 'ambiguous hovering between two meanings . . . [and] oscillation between the ironical and the serious' stretched his own capabilities as a critic. Disraeli could be both a purveyor of fairy-tales and illusions, and a shrewd realist about politics: his worship of intellect was 'a double-edged weapon: it is at once the faculty which reads the dark riddle of the universe, and the faculty which makes use of Tapers and Tadpoles'.[49]

Stephen rated *Coningsby* close to *Vanity Fair* as a study of politics and society: 'Nobody has described more vigorously all the meaner forms of selfishness, stupidity, and sycophancy engendered under "that fatal drollery", as *Tancred* describes it, "called a parliamentary government".'

Disraeli, however, could not match negative satire with positive ideas. Young England was never more than a 'flimsy collection of sham beliefs'. For Stephen the trilogy only really made sense and had weight when viewed from the vantage-point of Sidonia. Here there was 'a touch . . . of tragedy, and real mystery': 'The lights and shadows fluctuate, and solid forms melt provokingly into mist; but we must learn to enjoy the uncertain twilight which prevails on the borderland between romance and reality, if we would enjoy the ambiguities and the ironies and the mysteries of *Coningsby*, Stephen remained perplexed. Did Disraeli care at all for Parliament? Was he serious about race and his mystic attachment to intuitive intellect? He concluded, rather startlingly: 'We can only solve the problem by accepting the theory of a double consciousness . . .' It is a pity that, on the edge of this profundity, he declined to speculate about the parallels between Disraeli's Semitism and the attitude of the Scots or Irish to their British identity. Although a strong historicist, he recognized that Disraeli had somehow imposed himself on a politics whose rules were not altogether written by Tadpole and Taper. Indeed, as later on he commented on Trollope's Barchester novels, the rules might be made on the margin of acceptable behaviour: '. . . by the excision of all that is energetic, or eccentric, or impulsive, or romantic, you don't really become more lifelike; you only limit yourself to the common and uninteresting.'[50] This gained Stephen a purchase on the experimentalism of his daughter's generation, while the much younger Henry James was more orthodox and rebuked Trollope for his coyly intrusive authorial personality: 'It is only as an historian that [the novelist] has the smallest *locus standi*. As a narrator of fictitious events he is nowhere.' Despite such lapses, James commended Trollope for doing this: 'He never wearied of the pre-established round of English customs – never needed a respite or a change – was content to go on indefinitely watching the life that surrounded him, and holding up his mirror to it.'[51] James wrote that he found the political novels 'distinctly dull' and hadn't read them (although he knew their plots and characters quite thoroughly) but as one of the first theorists of novel criticism, he accepted the realistic novel of English establishment life. Serious radicals might still cavil – John Morley calculated fiction as 70 per cent of public-library issues in 1886, 30 per cent more than it ought to be – but it was now as much a part of society as the railway timetable or the daily newspaper.[52]

There was some retrospective self-justification. Frederic Harrison did much to establish George Eliot, Disraeli and Trollope as central to the mid-Victorian canon, and his advice to Eliot over the legal issue at the centre of *Felix Holt* was crucial, yet his purposes for the novel were totally didactic, and he tried to pressure Eliot into writing a propaganda tract for Comteian Positivism. Eliot resisted: 'I think aesthetic training is the highest of all teaching because it deals with life in its highest complexity. But if it ceases to be purely aesthetic – if it lapses anywhere from the picture to the diagram – it becomes the most offensive of all teaching.'[53] Her terms assigned qualities to the novel which were as monumental as the non-fiction contributions of, say, Mill, Arnold or Bagehot. They ensured that the Victorian classics would not, in future, lack imitators. But how, precisely, was this triumph achieved?

VI

Published literary criticism is less important here than the values of the mid-Victorian intellectual élite and the organization of print-capitalism. Criticism was perhaps more significant *before* publication, as the heads of family-owned firms, concerned with mastering and exploiting new technology, delegated the discovery and promotion of all but the most important authors to subordinates like publisher's readers. The word-of-mouth evaluations of small literary groupings could often be more important than anonymous reviews, particularly when, between 1860 and 1885, these were related to other innovating groups in politics and academic life.

Publishers' readers and periodical critics often knew one another at university, worked for the same periodicals, were personal friends or even relatives.[54] In the 1860s W. R. Greg was the brother-in-law of Walter Bagehot, editor of *National Review*, and *The Economist*, who was in turn a close friend of Richard Holt Hutton, editor of the *Spectator*. Hutton had many friends among the Christian Socialists and contributed to *Essays on Reform* in 1867, along with Stephen, Bryce, Dicey and Harrison. Harrison was the close associate of G. H. Lewes, George Eliot and John Morley, editor after Lewes of the *Fortnightly Review* (Trollope was its chairman), literary adviser to Macmillan and friend, with Harrison, of George Meredith, literary adviser to Chapman & Hall. If such strings of relationships were repeated for other figures, very few in the mid-Victorian literary firmament would be left out. Even fairly outrageous figures like Ouida or Marie Corelli had a foothold in this *milieu*. The important thing was to live in or near the metropolis. 'It is sheer madness', wrote Charles Lever in 1856, 'for any man who has to live by his brains to be removed from this great market. I can now see how recklessly I have played my cards this life – and that if I had settled down here I should have been a rich man today.'[55]

Most publishing had been based in Paternoster Row, near St Paul's and Fleet Street, since the last challenge from Edinburgh – Scott and Constable's vision of a truly mass readership – had ended in the disaster of 1825. Here, the mid-Victorian classics were produced 'as the outcome of collaboration, compromise or commission'.[56] Yet those involved were more than businessmen, and the novels they handled something more than entertainment. Their values – according to Tom Nairn – still informed the intelligentsia of the 1970s: '. . . literature is their bible. It has become the element which resumes that moralised romanticism which is the nerve of the English middle class . . . its job is the creation of a myth-world that bolsters the ailing body.'[57]

'Great' literature took over, in the 1860s and 1870s, some of the functions of religion, appealing to those who were losing their orthodox faith, or who wanted to modernize the central cultural tradition and the universities.[58] Morley, Stephen and Harrison were in retreat from Evangelicalism; Greg, Hutton and Bagehot were, or in Hutton's case had been, Unitarians. Without much civic confidence – London lacked any reputable tradition of autonomy - and disturbed by the scientific method, exemplified by Darwin's *Origin of Species* in 1859, they could still incline towards a 'humanized' religion like Comteian Positivism.

Besides Harrison, Positivism was to involve George Eliot, Lewes and Gissing and, on its fringes, Meredith and Leslie Stephen.[59] The Positivists were radicals; advocates of the trade unions and particularly close to Marx.[60] Yet they were also explicit and confident élitists who had no fear that mass politics would destroy deference and impose (at best) an Americanized materialist egalitarianism. They fitted into an enduring type of radicalism: mixing authoritarianism with the 'sectarian' small group, viewing representative government with only theoretical favour. In the largely plebiscitary system they envisioned, political fiction was an exemplary unity of morality and action. Biography might also serve, or the infant political science - Bagehot's *English Constitution*, or Morley's 'English Men of Letters' series – but fiction stressed both the manners of politics and their language.

In both of these, the essential conventions were inferred from accepted morality, as with Dicey's thesis about the sovereignty of Parliament and the unity of law, and presented lucidly, with wide literary reference. This gave a vocabulary in which irony and inference could transmit an unparalleled range of meanings, with the word 'politics' standing at the centre of a dozen or so formulations, each quite distinct. 'The politics of education', 'education policy', 'a politic educational programme', 'educational politicking' can still convey a subtlety of approach far beyond the single available German term, *Bildungspolitik*.[61] To this would be added such 'scientific' terms from other languages as *hegemony* or *Gemeinschaft*, which were then used by the English in an essentially literary way.

VII

Such critics and 'higher journalists' made fiction part of a political culture which has, even in textbooks, been lyrical rather than analytic. H. G. Wells dramatized the political psychology of his friend Graham Wallas's *Human Nature in Politics* (1908) in his novel *The New Machiavelli* (1910–11), and the argument of a contemporary Conservative, Sir Ian Gilmour, in *Inside Right: A Study of Conservatism* (1977) is substantially couched in literary terms. This has never implied an unqualified endorsement of Parliament, about which both Disraeli and Trollope were ambiguous. Disraeli's novels always stressed the superiority to it of ideas – whether the Church, the monarchy, the press or public opinion. Even in *Can You Forgive Her?* Trollope's devotions were shortly followed by a vignette of a dull, earnest, reforming MP being choked by the indifference of the House. Yet neither could think of an alternative.

The loyalties of the literary intellectuals had in the 1860s lain abroad, with radical movements in France (for the Positivists), in Italy (for most young Liberals), or in the North in the American Civil War (for practically all of them). Alienated from Palmerston's Britain, they wanted to infuse some foreign radicalism (up to and including, in some cases, republicanism) into an ossified politics.[62] Bagehot, who demontrated the utility of convention, they all but ignored, until the age of Grant and Crispi showed democracy as nurturing its own vices. But growing conservatism and academic specialization in the 1880s meant a recognition that the British political structure had comparative advantages, The defeat of home rule, coupled with Dicey's *Law of the Constitution* cleared the way for the Bagehotian constitution, which even its inventor had despaired of, to attain the status of a governing myth.[63]

VIII

By 1900 many European intellectuals, far from becoming revolutionaries, had been incorporated into their establishments: usually as academic 'experts' on social conflict and its avoidance – like the Katheder-Sozialisten in Germany or the sociologists around Emil Durkheim in France. Others were still in Bohemia: in the equivalent of the Sezession movement in the visual arts, which drew to it groups like socialists and Jews who were excluded from government patronage. The rôle of both groups was clearly defined, and the 'official' intellectuals were firmly restricted in their political activities, particularly in Germany. The politicization induced by the Dreyfus affair made this less marked in France, but both societies lacked a 'political class' – an élite composed of elements from aristocracy, bureaucracy and bourgeois – which combined, in Schumpeter's words, 'adherence to formal tradition with extreme adaptability to new principles, situations and persons . . . [and] is quite ready to rule on behalf of changing interests'.[64]

On two levels, however, the British élite was ill-fitted for its function. It was recruited via a secondary and tertiary education system backward by European standards; it existed within a notably centralized and secretive governmental system. It compensated for this by continuing to recruit from a 'non-England' grown wider through imperial expansion, and from exiles – voluntary and otherwise – attracted by the relative openness of British society.[65] This attraction increased when publishing cashed in on the linguistic community of the North Atlantic, after copyright was extended to the United States in 1891. The 'Britain' of print-capitalism bore little relationship to any orthodox national community.

In this existential situation, intuition and inference took over. If Bagehot stressed the element of illusion in politics, then by the 1890s a seamless web existed between literary politicians, journalists and commentators, reinforced by conventions like the privileged access of lobby correspondents to ministers (recognized in 1886). To the peculiarity of a 'satirical' magazine – *Punch* – fustier by far than the actual establishment, was added the overlapping of what passed for political and literary criticism, from Bagehot and St Loe Strachey to Bernard Levin and Auberon Waugh. Eng. Lit. 'presented' Parliament, warts and all. A wart, however, is a blemish, not a crippling malfunction; such writers colluded in sanctioning eccentricities, while ignoring more intractable problems.

NOTES

1 Anthony Trollope, *Can You Forgive Her?* (London: Oxford University Press, 1953), Vol. 2, p. 53.
2 For the power of the *genius loci* in the 1850s, see Sheldon Rothblatt, 'Newman and the idea of Oxford' – draft for *History of Oxford University*, Vol. IV (Oxford: Oxford University Press, forthcoming).
3 Anthony Trollope, *Autobiography* (London: Oxford University Press, 1946), pp. 302–3; Gordon S. Haight, *George Eliot* (London: Oxford University Press, 1968), p. 384; Thom Braun, *Disraeli the Novelist* (London: Allen & Unwin, 1981), p. 7.
4 H. G. Nicholas, introduction to *To the Hustings: Election Scenes from English Fiction* (London: Cassell, 1956), p. vii.
5 T. L. Peacock, *Melincourt* (London: Constable, 1924), pp. 137–8.
6 John Sutherland, *Victorian Novelists and Publishers* (London: Athlone Press, 1976), pp. 17, 69.

7   cf. Sutherland's account of the negotiations surrounding the publication of *Felix Holt* and *Middlemarch* between George Eliot, G. H. Lewes and John Blackwood, in ibid., pp. 190–201.

8   For the break-up of this system, see John Sutherland, *Fiction and the Fiction Industry* (London: Athlone Press, 1978), pp. 3–25.

9   J. F. Stephens, *The Censorship of Drama in England* (Cambridge: Cambridge University Press, 1979), pp. 1–5, 184; and Jeffrey Richards, *The Age of the Dream Palace* (London: Routledge, 1984), p. 91.

10 Benedict Anderson, *Imagined Communities* (London: Verso, 1983), pp. 31–2.

11 Citations are from George Eliot, *Felix Holt*, ed. Fred C. Thomson (Oxford: Oxford University Press, 1980), pp. 6 ff.

12 Honoré de Balzac, 'Le Deputé d'Arcis' in *La Comédie Humaine*, Vol. VIII (Paris: Gallimard, 1977), p. 749.

13 Eliot, *Felix Holt*, pp. 6–8.

14 Anderson, *Imagined Communities*, p. 40.

15 C. F. G. Masterman, *The Condition of England* (London: Methuen, 1960), p. 157.

16 The *Felix Holt* description seems closely connected to her article 'The natural history of German life', *Westminster Review*, vol. 66 (July 1856), reprinted in *Essays of George Eliot*, ed. Thomas Pinney (London: Routledge, 1968), p. 274.

17 Bernard Cracroft, 'The analysis of the House of Commons', in A. O. Rutson (ed.), *Essays on Reform* (London: Macmillan, 1867), p. 177.

18 Trollope, *Autobiography*, p. 186.

19 'Felix Holt', 'An address to working men', *Blackwood's Magazine*, January 1868, reprinted in *Essays of George Eliot*; see Rutson, *Essays on Reform*, and also G. C. Brodrick, review of Mill's *Thoughts on Parliamentary Reform* in *The Times*, 1859, reprinted in his *Political Studies* (London: Kegan Paul, 1879), p. 153.

20 See Haight, *George Eliot*, p. 464.

21 Charles W. Wood, *Memorials of Mrs Henry Wood* (London: Bentley, 1894), pp. 241 ff., and see Mrs Henry Wood, *East Lynne* (London: Dent, 1984), pp. 453–519.

22 Nicholas, *To the Hustings*, p. ix.

23 Frederic Harrison, *Studies in Early Victorian Literature* (London: Arnold, 1895), p. 208.

24 Trollope, *Autobiography*, pp. 242–53; and see Lance O. Tingay, 'Trollope and the Beverley Election', *Nineteenth Century Fiction*, vol. 5 (1950–1), pp. 24–6; George Meredith to Moncure Conway, 18 June 1874, in *Letters of George Meredith*, ed. C. L. Cline (London: Oxford University Press, 1970), p. 523.

25 See H. J. Hanham, *Elections and Party Management in the Age of Disraeli and Gladstone* (London: Longman, 1959), pp. 211 ff.; and Geoffrey Alderman, *British Elections: Myth and Reality* (London: Batsford, 1978), pp. 9–41.

26 Robert Michels, *Zur Soziologie des Parteiwesens* [1911] (Stüttgart: Krämer, 1970), pp. 179 ff.

27 Nicholas, *To the Hustings*, p. xvii.

28 Joe Ashton, *Grassroots* (London: Quartet, 1978), p. 121.

29 See Thomas Carlyle, *Past and Present* (London: Chapman & Hall, 1899), pp. 31, 33, 295; and Nicholas, *To the Hustings*, p. viii.

30   W. E. Aytoun, 'How I stood for the Dreepdailly Burghs', *Blackwood's Magazine* (1847), reprinted in W. L. Renwick (ed.), *Aytoun: Stories and Verse* (Edinburgh: Edinburgh University Press, 1966), pp. 46–7.

31   Lewis Grassic Gibbon, *Cloud Howe* (London: Jarrold, 1934), p. 132.

32   I. C. R. Hutchison, *A Political History of Scotland, 1832–1922* (Edinburgh: John Donald, 1986), pp. 33 ff.; and J. C. Beckett, *The Making of Modern Ireland* (London: Faber, 1966), pp. 250–1, 296 ff.

33   Charles Lever, *Charles O'Malley* (London: Downey, 1897), pp. 78–9 (first published in the *Dublin University Magazine*, March 1840–December 1841); for Lever's disquiet over Irish politics, see W. J. Fitzpatrick, *Charles Lever* (London: Chapman & Hall, 1879), Vol. 1, pp. 290–2, Vol. 2, pp. 56–66.

34   Dennis Potter, *The Nigel Barton Plays* (Harmondsworth: Penguin, 1967), p. 104.

35   Martin Ingram, 'Ridings, rough music and "popular culture" in early modern England', *Past and Present*, no. 105 (1985), p. 81.

36   James F. Davidson, 'Political science and political fiction', *American Political Science Review*, vol. 55 (1961), p. 858.

37   James Welsh, *The Underworld* (London: Herbert Jenkins, 1919), p. 204.

38   James Bryce, 'Anthony Trollope', in *Studies in Contemporary Biography* (London: Macmillan, 1903), p. 121.

39   Mrs Humphry Ward, *A Writer's Recollections*, and see M. E. Speare, *Political Novel: Its Development in England and America*, (New York: Oxford University Press, 1924), p. 268. For Marie Corelli, see Brian Masters, *Now Barabbas Was a Rotter* (London: Hamish Hamilton, 1978), pp. 106, 120.

40   Quoted in Philip Snow, *Stranger and Brother* (London: Macmillan, 1982), p. 157; and see C. P. Snow, *In Their Wisdom* (London: Macmillan, 1974).

41   See Margaret Lane, *Edgar Wallace* (London: Hamish Hamilton, 1964), pp. 130 ff., and St Barbe Sladen, *The Real Le Queux* (London: Nicholson & Watson, 1938), p. 3 (Le Queux started as parliamentary reporter of the *Globe*).

42   John Sutherland, *Best Sellers: Popular Fiction of the 1970s* (London: Routledge, 1981), pp. 137–53.

43   Arnold Bennett, *Lord Raingo* (London: Cassell, 1926), p. 260.

44   Richard Crossman, entry of 22 October 1964 in *The Diaries of a Cabinet Minister*, Vol 1, *Minister of Housing, 1964–66* (London: Hamish Hamilton Jonathan Cape, 1975), p. 29.

45   Dangerfield, *The Strange Death of Liberal England* (London: Macgibbon & Kee, 1966), p. 365.

46   Based on a random sample of c.500 titles taken from A Block, *The English Novel, 1740–1850: A Bibliography* (London: Dawson, Pall Mall, 1961). Of these, only about 5 per cent fall into the socio-political category.

47   Fitzjames Stephen, 'The relation of novels to life', in *Cambridge Essays* (Cambridge: Parker, 1855), p. 161; W. R. Greg, 'False morality of lady novelists', *National Review*, vol. 8 (January 1859), reprinted in *Literary and Social Judgements* (London: Trübner, 1877), p. 104; and see Richard Stang, *The Theory of the Novel in England, 1850–1870* (New York: Columbia University Press, 1959), p. 46.

48   David Masson, 'Naturalism in art', in *British Novelists and Their Styles: Being a Critical Sketch of the History of British Prose Fiction* (London: Macmillan, 1859), pp. 257–64.

49   All citations from Leslie Stephen, 'Mr Disraeli's novels', *Fortnightly Review*, October 1874, reprinted in *Hours in a Library* (London: Smith Elder, 1892), Vol. 2, pp. 108 ff.

50   Leslie Stephen, 'Trollope's Barsetshire novels', *National Review*, no. 38 (1901), p. 84.

51   Henry James, 'Partial portraits', reprinted in *The Art of Fiction and Other Essays by Henry James*, ed. Morris Roberts (New York: Oxford University Press, 1948), pp. 59–60.

52   John Morley, 'On the study of literature', address to London Society for the Extension of University Teaching, 26 February 1887, reprinted in *Studies in Literature* (London: Macmillan, 1891), pp. 202–3.

53   George Eliot to Frederic Harrison, 16 August 1866, *The Letters of George Eliot*, ed. Gordon S. Haight (New Haven, Conn.: Yale University Press), Vol. 4, pp. 300–1.

54   For a general study, see John Gross, *The Rise and Fall of the Man of Letters* (Harmondsworth: Penguin, 1973), pp. 75–147.

55   Quoted in Sutherland, *Victorian Novelists and Publishers*, p. 65.

56   ibid, pp. 6, 17.

57   Tom Nairn, 'The English literary intelligentsia', in *Bananas*, ed. Emma Tennant (London: Quartet, 1977), p. 59.

58   For an example of this, see D. A. Hamer, *John Morley: Liberal Intellectual in Politics* (London: Oxford University Press, 1968), pp. 1–15.

59   See ibid., p. 50, for their influence; T. R. Wright *The Religion of Humanity: The Impact of Comtean Positivism on Victorian Britain* (Cambridge: Cambridge University Press, 1986), pp. 38–9.

60   See Royden Harrison, 'The Positivists: a study of Labour's intellectuals', in *Before the Socialists* (London: Routledge, 1965).

61   Arnold J. Heidenheimer, 'The language of politics', paper delivered at Nuffield College, Oxford, October 1983.

62   See J. R. Green on *Essays on Reform* in *Saturday Review*, vol. 23, 6 April 1867, p. 438.

63   cf. Bryce MSS, Bodleian Library, Oxford: Bryce to Dicey, 27 April 1916; and see C. T. Harvie, *The Lights of Liberalism* (London: Allen Lane, 1976), ch. 8; and 'Ideology and home rule: James Bryce, A. V. Dicey and Ireland, 1880–87', *English Historical Review*, no. 91 (April 1976), pp. 298–314.

64   Joseph Schumpeter, *Capitalism, Socialism and Democracy* (London: Allen & Unwin, 1942), p. 110.

65   Perry Anderson, in 'Components of the national culture', *New Left Review* (1968), reprinted in *Student Power* (Harmondsworth: Penguin, 1969). Of the sixty-six writers active 1900–10 cited in the bibliographical appendixes to the *Pelican Guide to English Literature*, Vols 6 and 7 (1969 edn) thirty-two, or just under half, had nonconformist/provincial, Scots, Irish or foreign backgrounds.

5

The Golden Age: The Mid-Victorian Political Novel

I

'IT'S ALL IN TROLLOPE', said Harold Macmillan in the 1950s, when asked about the principles of parliamentary government.[1] The themes and characters of mid-Victorian political fiction seemed peculiarly alive, even after total war. Angela Thirkell revived Barsetshire, and the Palliser novels loomed over Snow, Powell and Raven's *romans fleuves* in the 1960s. The enthusiasm was, like Macmillan's own ancestry, transatlantic: American academics outperformed their British counterparts, through a formidable fusion of Eng. Lit. and Germanic research – and perhaps a mental flight from a less than tranquil *academe*.[2] Did their predecessors of the 1870s and 1880s likewise retreat to Barsetshire from Tammany Hall and Washington lobbyists? Or did the Victorian political novel go transatlantic because it interpreted two political systems, closely linked in their ideological debates, to a market which absorbed almost anything which came off the British presses?[3] Two polities were evolving in circumstances which invited comparison: America coping with the aftermath of civil war, immigration and a widening frontier; Britain detaching itself from aristocratic control, trying to contain national divergences, population change and accelerating industrialization.[4]

Trollope became 'the most perfect exponent' of the British experience by studying Fitzjames Stephen's 'serious business in life', and that succession of political novels to which he contributed – from *Can You Forgive Her?* in 1863 to *The Duke's Children*, and Disraeli's *Endymion*, in 1880 – were, as George Watson writes, 'conscious of being something momentous'.[5] After 1865, with Thackeray and Mrs Gaskell dead, and Dickens forsaking writing for his dramatic readings, it imposed its categories even on fiction written on a different, domestic or parochial, scale.

The tide ebbed after 1875 – Trollope felt it, and *Endymion* was a slow seller – and recovery was asymmetrical. Speare in 1924 lauded

Disraeli and deprecated Trollope, but the latter's stock rose with Michael Sadleir's *Commentary* in 1931, and G. M. Young's *Portrait of an Age* which forced a serious reconsideration of the Victorians.[6] Fire-watching and the boredom of troopships completed the restoration, in the shape of the tiny Oxford World's Classics volumes, so that after the war Britain's archaic but reliable élite could balance its collectivist experiments with deference to the past. When, in 1953, Asa Briggs, writing on Trollope and Bagehot, quoted Gladstone in 1860: 'We live in anti-reforming times. All improvements have to be urged in apologetic, almost supplicating term .'[7] He stressed this resilience and a success in constitutional politics which enabled Britain to instruct its less fortunate European neighbours, through 'traditions that embody experience, with a professional code and with a common fund of views'.[8] By 1983 commentators were less indulgent. In the eyes of one influential interpretation this 'composure' was toxic to any successful industrial society. Trollope and his contemporaries had connived at a complacency grown pathological.[9]

Yet the image of tranquillity common to both groups was false. Between 1851 and 1880 politics and culture were constantly in movement. The Crimean War knocked Britain as well as Russia out of European politics, leaving it to the French and the Prussians. Science and organized religion collided noisily over natural selection in 1859–60; radicals fêted Garibaldi in 1864, and Irish Catholics rioted bloodily against him; other radicals staged menacing demonstrations for franchise reform. In 1865 there was a sharp panic about Britain's apparently dwindling coal reserves, and a year later a real slump. In 1873 imports pitched agriculture into permanent decline, and provoked unrest in Ireland which was by 1886 threatening to dismember the United Kingdom itself. If Trollope is synoptic in his views, he is in no way the wise-owlish literary gent of his own highly misleading autobiography and the deeply conservative Trollope exegetical industry. His views are fractured and contradictory, always withstanding the same pressures which threatened to tear 'the age of equipoise' apart.

II

Trollope acclaimed *Felix Holt* on its publication in 1866: 'I think it has more elaborated thought in it, and that it is in that way a greater work . . . than anything that you have done before.'[10] This was not flattery. *Felix Holt* is fundamental to our whole enterprise both as 'imagined community' and as exemplification of the dense strategies and structures of the Victorian novel, in its plot, rich in mystery and coincidence, its uplifting theme, its tragedy and ultimate 'happy ending'. The standard commentaries assume that Eliot intended to centre a domestic tragedy on the fate of the adulterous Mrs Transome, and was side-tracked into rather incompetent politics.[11] Yet politics was omnipresent in 1865. Palmerston was at last looking mortal. A Reform League was forming to agitate for universal manhood suffrage, after the Northern victory in America had settled a fierce, highly articulate debate on democracy. In her radical intellectual circle, any pronouncement would be awaited with respect.[12]

Eliot had, with her growing success, moved from the provincial *milieu* of the Brontës and Mrs Gaskell to ideological issues. *Romola* (1863) was, in J. G. A. Pocock's sense, a discussion of the actual 'Machiavellian moment' in fifteenth-century Florence, where individual moral judgement was counterpoised with the imperatives of civic humanism: its lessons equally apt for a newly united Italy or for Britain.[13] Although *Felix Holt* deals with the reform crisis thirty years before, its agenda was contemporary. The 1830s were to mid-Victorian intellectuals what 1945 has been in our day to David Hare or Trevor Griffiths: the incomplete revolution. The forces represented in the novel – gentry, church, lawyers, nonconformists, workers – were still to hand, their relations still unsettled.[14]

I believe Eliot intended to invoke the theme of civic virtue in her own epoch; to show how the corrupt relationship of land and political power brought tragedy to guilty and innocent alike. This both made a case for reform and insisted that tragedy - 'irreparable collision between the individual and the general' - could be, in its ennobling elements, a possession of ordinary people.[15] Forebodings of collision are latent in the 'introduction'. In her essays on the European peasantry Eliot had contrasted the collective power which stemmed from their relative undifferentiation, forcing land reform from the liberals in 1848 – and then deserting them – with the complex and 'cultured' nature of English society: '. . . the cultured man acts more as an individual; the peasant, more as one of a group.'[16] The English paid for this by the political powerlessness of the workers, the weakness of the State, the isolation of the intellectuals. The journey into 'the heart of England', with what Henry James called its 'retarding persuasiveness which allows her conjured images to sink slowly into your very brain', is also *politically* retarding, showing a landscape inured against civic virtue.[17]

Felix Holt's plot has drawn criticism for complexity and overmuch coincidence. But E. S. Dallas – one of the Eliot circle – found that its logic was the conflict of a virtuous with a vicious triangle: virtue being the Independent minister Rufus Lyon, his step-daughter Esther and her suitor Felix Holt, and vice Mrs Transome, her former lover Lawyer Jermyn and their illegitimate son Harold Transome. Although Harold's return to contest the county as a radical at the first election after the Reform Act sets in train a sequence of events which expose his parentage and bring his family down, no one in either triangle seems endowed with tragic potential. Esther, who turns out to be the heiress to Transome Court, seems a tiresome shallow girl, while Leslie Stephen found Felix 'much too cold-blooded for the time when revolution and confiscation were really in the air'.[18] It is Rufus Lyon who essentially embodies the qualities of a collective tragedy. He catechizes Harold in terms which sound pedantic:

> 'You will not deny that you glory in the name of Radical, or Root-and-branch man, as they said in the great times when Nonconformity was in its giant youth.'
> 'A Radical – yes; but I want to go to some roots a good deal lower down than the franchise.'
> 'Truly there is a work within which cannot be dispensed with; but it is our preliminary work to free men from the stifled life of political nullity, and bring them into what Milton calls "the liberal air", wherein alone can be wrought the final triumphs of the Spirit.'[19]

Lyon's faith had, two centuries earlier, brought Charles I to the scaffold; now he is marginalized while opportunist members of the 'old enemy' – such as Harold Transome – annex the radical cause.

Eliot's problem was similar to that of Dickens in *Hard Times*: to unite an urgent social metaphor with a realistic plot. With one volume finished, and flagging, Eliot invoked Frederic Harrison to provide an opinion in which the Transomes' right to their property would collapse when the last representative of the old line died.[20] So, when bribery and treating inflame an election riot, Felix, trying to stop it, is imprisoned for injuring a policeman (who dies), and the town drunk, Tommy Trounsem, is killed. As the last of the old Transomes, his death brings the Durfey-Transome lien on the estate to an end, although the real heir remains a mystery.

This the novel-reading public appreciated. 'I am uneasy as to what Mrs Transome has done', John Blackwood, her publisher, wrote to Eliot. 'Poor Felix is in a terrible fix . . .'[21] Eliot had followed Disraeli in throwing in menace and mystery, and met critics of the Fitzjames Stephen sort by grounding the novel in actuality. From this point, Norman Vance has argued, she uses law as the central metaphor for English society. The opposition of 'customary' law and true equity is the basis both of the 'civil' case – the ownership of Transome Court – and of Felix's own trial, in which he claims he knocked down the policeman to prevent a far worse riot.[22] The fact that this claim of 'moral right' is ultimately accepted is the closest Felix comes to the heroic. The mismatch between this moralism and the 'general' – Loamshire society at election-time – gives him, in Eliot's definition, a tragic potential. Not enough, alas, to convince. But, for someone excluded from parliamentary life, Eliot's imaginative dissection of the constituency – its inns, vestries, chapels and mansions – was unprecedented. Whatever they are, the Treby people are not an anonymous mob. Moreover, her Owenite education with the Brays made her as sceptical about Parliament as Harrison and his Comtist friends. In her own contribution to the reform debate, was it surprising that pedagogy came before party?[23]

Eliot acutely linked the 1832 election with her main theme. A new social confrontation, which the landed order will lose, draws the net tight over the Durfey-Transomes, now as degenerate as Tommy Trounsem. The legitimate heir has died of dissipation; Harold Transome is doubly disbarred, by the end of the Durfey lien on the estate in favour of Esther Lyon, and by his own illegitimacy. Esther, with the puritan integrity of Rufus Lyon, renounces her inheritance in Harold's favour and marries Felix. The Transomes, as a legitimate line, die out. As do their Tory rivals, the Debarrys. Philip Debarry wins the election; we know he will die a Catholic priest. Felix Holt may be conservative in preferring education to the vote, but the old governing order is choking in its internal decay – misappropriated inheritances mirroring its 'beer and balderdash' corruption of the lower orders. Harold's uncle, the squarson John Lingon, rationalizes his family's position: 'If the mob can't be turned back, a man of family must try and head the mob, and keep the country up on its last legs as long as he can. And you're a man of family, my lad – dash it! You're a Lingon, whatever else you may be . . .'[24] This gets Harold nowhere. The mob is literally headed off by Felix, the man of no family, implying that civic virtue can only inhere in the common people. The middle class – the Jermyns and Johnsons – are too implicated in the old order to offer stable government on their own. Eliot doesn't argue, like the writers of *Essays on Reform* (1867), for deference as a check on democratic excess. On the other hand, she was increasingly apprehensive about any violent challenge to the system. So *Felix Holt* – the novel-hero and the pamphlet – could only end circumspect.[25]

Felix dead or transported would be a revolutionary statement. Eliot reprieves him through upper-class intervention and turns him into a schoolmaster: on the face of it a surrender to the élite. But the violence in *Felix Holt* is peculiarly emblematic. In 1865 there was a rising in Jamaica, whose governor, Edward Eyre, seized a prominent Negro leader, George Gordon, had him hanged, and six hundred others executed. The pro-reform Hyde Park riots on 23 July 1866 coincided with the formation of the Jamaica Committee to prosecute Eyre, whose leading figures – Herbert Spencer, Frederic Harrison, T. H. Huxley, J. S. Mill – were members of Eliot's circle. Eyre was backed by most MPs and peers and many literary notables – Dickens, Kingsley, Carlyle,

Ruskin – men who had failed to come to terms with the liberal political order.[26] Eliot's position was quite clear. Indeed, the way in which Felix is saved from gaol may have intentionally pointed a contrast with the judicial murder of Gordon.[27]

'There is no private life', Eliot wrote in chapter III, 'that is not determined by a wider public life', yet *Felix Holt* seems least satisfactory as a novel of ideas. There is little political dialogue, no interest in Parliament or 'statesmanship'. Much of this is explained by the tragedy of Rufus Lyon, his life constricted by the Test Acts, his wife killed by this ghetto existence. Even when he has the chance to testify to his faith the curate chosen by the Debarrys to debate with him (they would never have demeaned themselves to answer him personally) turns and runs. There is not even the beginnings of a *polis* here. A woman like Eliot, similarly constrained, was bound to empathize: she and Lyon had both followed Carlyle's injunction and got right with themselves before tackling the ills of the world, but the old order made that world deaf and blind.[28]

Felix Holt is emphatically not 'Mrs Transome's Tragedy'. Mrs Transome is passive, class-bound, and devoid of that moral determination which will provoke conflict: 'She had no ultimate analysis of things which went beyond blood and family . . . She had never seen behind the canvas with which her life was hung.'[29] Mrs Transome is bloodstock, but she can neither save the Durfey-Transomes nor fend off the predatory Jermyn. She is as much a victim as Rufus Lyon's sad French wife. That 'evil usage that women receive at the hands of men', which John Morley, among others, observed as a constant theme, was appropriate on the eve of John Stuart Mill's introduction of the first parliamentary motion for female suffrage.[30] With the frustration and belittlement of Rufus Lyon, and of Felix himself, her fate contains elements of George Eliot's definition of tragedy, but also cries out for reform.

'Felix is a fragment', wrote Henry James in the New York *Nation*. 'We find him a Radical and we leave him what?'[31] But as medical man, watchmaker and schoolmaster Felix was almost an anthology of Enlightenment virtue. Was his propaganda for improved education a logical extension of the Positivist programme, with its demand that 'the brute element of mere numbers should be made respectable by being combined with intelligence and love of order'?[32] Or was it an escape from a Loamshire throttled, in 1866 as much as in 1832, by gentry politics? At any rate it was close to the opinions which, in 1862, Trollope had brought from the United States: 'They have educated their people, as we have not educated ours. They have given to their millions a personal respect, and a standing above the abjectness of poverty, which with us are much less general than with them.'[33]

III

'It is not like a novel', Blackwood wrote to Lewes of *Felix Holt*, 'but . . .
a series of panoramas where human beings speak and act before us.'[34] The
novel's descriptive solidity – an entire volume dealing with the effect of
the election on all social levels in Loamshire – gave it the documentary
presence of Mayhew or Scott, and an 'extraordinarily well-defined social
and historical context' for other writers.[35] Notably Trollope. Asa Briggs,
among many others, has seen him as the embodiment of the age of
Palmerston. But only the first of the Palliser novels was written in
Palmerston's lifetime, and when Briggs cites the Tory leader in *The
Prime Minister* 'to confirm that the main work of Parliament is not to
legislate but to raise supplies', and that 'positive legislation' ought to
be confined to building battleships, he fails to stress that a Trollope
Tory is speaking, not the author himself. Not surprisingly, the largely
American Trollope industry, turning out ninety volumes between 1977
and 1982, seems to have 'appropriated the novelist to the conservative
cause'. There are, according to the inimitable Professor Halperin, 'no
Marxist studies of Trollope'.[36] But there ought to be, because Trollope's
was a political intellect, concerned to project many of the voices and
concerns of his age, through a surprisingly wide range of techniques.

Structure, in Trollope, is progressive. Conservatives, as élitists, make
their literary–political pattern a sort of dance - the characters perform a
sequence of movements and end up where they started – while Trollope's
sense of linear development is strong.[37] *The Warden* coincides with the
Whig–Peelite reform of the old endowed institutions, notably Oxford
and Cambridge, the Palliser novels with the debate on democracy in the
mid-1860s. By the 1870s all these institutions had changed completely,
and Trollope's political aristocrats had given way to professionals from
middle- and even lower-class backgrounds. Franchise extension disrupted
all Bagehot's generalizations about the 'Palmerstonian constitution'.[38] To
Trollope it was a fact of life.

Frederic Harrison praised Trollope's realism, but regarded his plots
as worn and his incidents as commonplace; his characters are 'seldom
very powerful, or original, or complex'.[39] There are certainly *lacunae*.
Out of Ireland, Trollope's social range is narrow; few working people,
manufacturers, nonconformists. Nor does he seem to use, like Meredith,
any philosophical or symbolic means of involving such groups, replicating
instead the defensiveness of the 'in-groups' – the clergy or civil service
- which fascinated him.[40] His chronology is hit-or-miss. Glencora Palliser,
for example, is betrothed and under twenty-one in 1862. In 1876 she is
dead, her family grown-up.[41]

But the Glencora example contradicts the 'sordid realist' (Henry James)
classification of Trollope. Consider the first sighting of her, in *The Small*

House at Allington, with half of Scotland as dowry: 'the property in Fife, Aberdeen, Perth, and Kincardineshire, comprising the greater part of those counties, and the coal-mines in Lanark, as well as the enormous estate within the city of Glasgow'; and compare this with the passage from *The Prime Minister* describing Tenway Junction, just before 'the morning express down from Euston to Inverness . . . coming round the curve at a thousand miles an hour' knocks Ferdinand Lopez 'into bloody atoms':

> Not a minute passes without a train going here or there, some rushing by without noticing Tenway in the least, crashing through like flashes of substantial lightning, and others stopping, disgorging and taking up passengers by the hundreds. Men and women, – especially the men, for the women knowing their ignorance are generally willing to trust to the pundits of the place, – look doubtful, uneasy, and bewildered. But they all do get properly placed and unplaced, so that the spectator at last acknowledges that over all this apparent chaos there is presiding a great genius of order.[42]

Glencora is not simply a skittish heiress; she is a fabulous figure, a Queen of Sheba, who will make her presence felt. Similarly Tenway Junction doesn't just have a lot of trains running through it; it is a metaphor both for Parliament and for the complicated nation it controls. Lopez has tried to master it, and it is now taking its revenge.

Such passages suggest Dickensian symbolism (fog in *Bleak House*, rubbish in *Our Mutual Friend*) and hyperbole out of Disraeli, who offers some parallels with the younger Trollope. In the 1840s both were attracted by the Oxford Movement; both were sympathetic to Ireland and Catholicism; both devoured Scott, revered Carlyle and detested Peel.[43] Although there is one sarcastic reference to a Jewish money-lender called Sidonia, the hatred evinced in the *Autobiography* seems to have come later, provoked by Disraeli's foreign policy in the 1870s.[44] Similarities emerge even in Trollope's first novel. *The MacDermots of Ballycloran* is emphatically about the 'Condition of Ireland'. If its realism and pessimism are far from Disraeli's ultimately reassuring pantomimes, the tragic Feemy MacDermot is still, like Sybil, an allegory of her people.

To Owen Dudley Edwards, Trollope remained 'possessed, obsessed, and in some way mauled by Ireland'.[45] The *Autobiography* marginalizes his Irish concerns, even claiming that it was a mistake to make Phineas Finn an Irishman, but is no more reliable here than elsewhere. For Edwards, Trollope's dialogues and speeches, his plots, the names of his characters, above all his feeling for 'marginal' people, in from the frontier, are conspicuously Irish traits: 'Much of the workmanship after his return to England was still based on the rough designs he had initially executed on Irish soil, with Irish stories, about Irish characters, and with Irish insights.'[46] There is a lot in this case. The deafening ceaseless argumentation of the London 'megatherium' was, after all, anything but an English upper-class characteristic. Trollope went to Ireland at twenty-six in 1841, from misery in England. Although his period there coincided with the Famine (emotionally equivalent to being in Berlin in the latter days of the Third Reich?), he loved the Irish and matured through writing about them.[47]

The *Autobiography* wilfully exaggerates the failure of his Irish novels – they sold quite respectably throughout his life – and the anglocentric Sadleir extends this depreciation.[48] *The MacDermots* is 'naïve and over-detailed' in its descriptions, and when its author 'strays beyond the actual thoughts and doings of his men and women, he is bleakly unpoetical, and lapses readily into either sociology or politics'.[49] To turn from this to the book itself is a revelation. The story is simple and the sense of impending tragedy palpable, as Thady MacDermot, the proud bewildered squireen in his crumbling mansion at Drumsna, falls to the gombeen men and the police and their informers. Trying to save his estate, he joins a group of Ribbonmen or agrarian terrorists; trying to protect his sister Feemy, he kills her police-inspector seducer. As land unrest has broken out, the authorities decide to make an example of him and hang him.

The understated didactics of the novel are impressive. The people make their own case, in their own language, Trollope trying like Scottish contemporaries to render local speech-patterns honestly.[50] Far from Ireland choking 'the very genius that she had vitalised by her insane absorption in her own wrongs and thwarted hopes',[51] Trollope vividly portrayed individuals being destroyed when a community falls apart. Thady isn't just the first of many culturally dislocated characters – Josiah Crawley, Robert Kennedy, Phineas Finn – his predicament is a 'theoretical history' out of Galt, and has much of the desperate pessimism of Scott's last stories.

'He saw Ireland with the mind of a jury', wrote a later Irish novelist and politician, Stephen Gwynn, while Professor John Cronin has praised Trollope's 'ability to probe beyond the trite official explanations . . . and search out the fundamental causes of Irish misery'.[52] But, though Ireland gave Trollope a *polis*, it was one in collapse; it could have resulted in complete pessimism, instead of that deft grasp of the organizations which integrated the multi-national kingdom. Frederic Harrison talked of Trollope's 'unity of texture and perfect harmony of tone', something which concurred with the assumed unity of private and public ethics. So he was able both to parallel the intelligentsia's shift from an ordained clerisy in the 1850s to a secular meritocracy in the 1870s, and to expand his *polis* from Ireland to Barsetshire and London.

Trollope was a curious amalgam of the progressive and the traditionalist. Trains, which produced paroxysms in Dickens, were just somewhere he wrote his books; he expected his characters to travel on them without being symbolic about it. Yet he was uninterested in the application of the 'scientific method' to the novel, by Flaubert or Zola. His closest parallel was with Scott, another administrator who wrote in his spare time and at great speed. Scott had intended his Waverley novels to cover all the main regions of Scotland; he travelled through them and tried to adapt to them his minute knowledge of the Borderland. Trollope, faced with a much larger, industrialized country, used not the law but the Post Office as a unifying mechanism, at the juncture when railways and telegraphs were making communications industrialized and international. Sidonia may have travelled everywhere, but Disraeli hadn't got past the Mediterranean and knew little of Britain beyond London and Buckinghamshire. Trollope travelled all over Britain and most of the world – and wrote cogently about what he had seen.

This did not lead him to the metropolitan novel, because there was no centralized administrative state, no *culture* of national unity such as existed in Imperial Germany, France, Russia and German Austria. Yet his knowledge and approachability – and perhaps his Irish sympathies – gave him a peculiar empathy with this set-up: an ability to create an eloquent dialectic between bourgeois and aristocrat, centre and province, man and woman. Take the evolution of Barchester. Trollope had probably read the passage in *Coningsby* in which Mr G. O. A. Head denounces Manchester as 'dead and buried': 'We all of us have a very great respect for Manchester, of course; look upon her as a sort of mother, and all that sort of thing. But she is behind the times, sir, and that won't do in this age . . . If you want to see life . . . go to Staleybridge or Bolton. There's high pressure.'[53] This is very Carlyleian, and Trollope, contemplating a Carlyleian comedy about the clash between the 'mechanical' mentality and its opposite – and always symbolic when it came to christening his characters – surely devised Barchester as the antithesis of Manchester.[54] The *Autobiography* tells us he got the idea while visiting the close of Salisbury Cathedral in 1851, plainly intrigued by the survival of the quiet opulent world of close and chapter, usually High Tory in its politics, into the age of the Crystal Palace and Peelite reform.

His curiosity wasn't theological or antiquarian. Barchester theology is simply a brisk allocation of High, Low or High-and-Dry affiliations – and its architectural 'atmosphere' is sketchy. But its politics, as a form of upper-middle-class self-government, was in some ways more complex and fascinating than that of Westminster. There are few novels about life, love and intrigue in European cathedral cities because European clerics – even when married – were state servants: their affairs directly part of national politics. Moreover, in 1851 the disestablishment of the Church was a real possibility; the management of much of its property remained, according to Geoffrey Best, 'virtually untouched by the spirit of reform, and horribly inviting to the anticlerical muckraker', while close and chapter defensively interacted with Westminster, the universities, the borough authorities and the great landowners.[55]

The universities were being forcibly reformed, and two particularly lurid cases of endowment abuse, at Winchester and Rochester, which irrupted in 1852, provoked the intervention of Charles Dickens in *Household Words*. Even the Christian Socialists, who wanted to open the Establishment to all believers, could find little good to say of the cathedrals, Kingsley thoughtfully offering them as 'winter gardens' for the working classes.[56] *The Warden* directly tackles this conflict of polities, by basing an ironic comedy on Carlyle's text in *Heroes and Hero-Worship*: 'The writers of Newspapers, Pamphlets, Poems, Books, these *are* the real working, effective Church of a modern country.'[57]

Mr Harding, the Warden of Hiram's Hospital, is technically an abuse but personally a benevolent and scholarly man. The 'working, effective church', of such as Tom Towers, Dr Pessimist Anticant (Carlyle) and Mr Popular Sentiment (Dickens), transform him into a white-collared Squeers. But, when a tragedy akin to the fate of Thady MacDermot seems to impend, Harding's son-in-law Archdeacon Grantly, a worldly ambitious Tory, successfully counterattacks the 'working, effective church's' over-extended lines of communication. While both churches collide like armies, the Warden makes the Christian gesture of renunciation This could ruin him, but he ends up sustained by his other daughter and her husband, Harding's former antagonist John Bold. The losers – by the game of high politics and, ironically, by the Warden's high *principle* – are the pathetic bedesmen, whose ingenuous greed leaves them worse off than before.

The fate of Hiram's Hospital could be out of Pugin's *Contrasts*: '. . . the whole place has become disordered and ugly. The warden's garden is a wretched wilderness, the drive and paths are covered with weeds, the flower-beds are bare, and the unshorn lawn is now a mass of unwholesome moss. The beauty of the place is gone; its attractions have withered.'[58] The Hospital has gone the way of the MacDermots' Ballycloran: a real loss has been registered to the intimacy and generosity Trollope saw accompanying secure adequate property. Barchester, an asylum from the world, in part created by Trollope himself, 'of telegrams and anger', has been breached. On the other hand Harding's own salvation is due to politics as well as to his daughter's love-affair. When he goes to London to meet the Attorney-General about his case, he observes the Commons debating the 'Convent Custody Bill' and sees how party discipline can defuse a particularly nasty religious witch-hunt. Party pig-headedness – trooping into lobbies to vote that two and two make five – is bad, but ideological fanaticism is much, much worse.[59]

In the 1850s the pressure was taken off Barchester. Matthew Arnold, John Henry Newman, even Thomas Hughes followed Coleridge in successfully counterposing the *genius loci* of provincial tradition to the 'march of mind' of the Crystal Palace, and the fiasco of the Crimea discredited centralization.[60] In 1854 the General Board of Health was dissolved and its Benthamite secretary, Edwin Chadwick, fired. It was in this atmosphere of mingled reform and inertia that Trollope began, in April 1855, *Barchester Towers*, his best-organized, most Disraelian and also most conservative-minded novel.

Barchester remains what it was, despite the challenge of a new bishop representing, as one of the commissioners reforming Oxford, the new order. Mrs Proudie, his Scottish gorgon of a wife, and their chaplain Obadiah Slope are evangelical Tartuffes. They are frustrated, not by Dr Grantly, his Tractarian friends, and absurd reactionaries like the Thornes of Ullathorne, but through the confusion caused by the amoral and alluring Madeleine Stanhope Neroni and her dilettante brother Bertie, a couple with all the mischief of Vivian Grey. The concluding appointment of Arabin as Dean endorses a Tractarian victory which both Trollope and Disraeli would – at that stage in their careers – have approved.

Barchester Towers appeared in 1857. Two years later the equipoise it celebrated was shattered by *Essays and Reviews* and *The Origin of Species*, which polarized religious opinion and drove liberal Anglicans to appeal to Parliament and the law-courts. The battle is muted in Barsetshire, but the later novels are increasingly secular and political – the election for Barchester of Sir Roger Scatcherd in *Dr Thorne* (1858), Nathaniel Sowerby's ruinous parliamentary career in *Framley Parsonage* (1861) and the first, unprepossessing, appearance of Plantagenet Palliser, the Duke of Omnium's nephew, in *The Small House at Allington* (1864). Barsetshire's parliamentarians are unimpressive. Bishop Proudie, archetypal member of the Great and Good, is always running up to London, and is morally as well as materially elusive in Barchester Close. The Earls de Courcy are indolent, mean and snobbish, Plantagenet Palliser is callow and dull, and Harold Smith, MP, Lord Petty Bag, is inflated by his dignity into crazy self-conceit. Sir Roger Scatcherd may be a drunkard who has killed his man, but he is also an entrepreneur of genius. Being elected and then trapped by unworkable electoral laws finishes him. Parliament's embassy in Barsetshire is the glacial, uninhabitable Gatherum Castle, where the Duke of Omnium entertains his Whig colleagues. Invited there to lunch, Dr Thorne sees the Duke enter among the local notables, eat rapidly and silently, and then leave. He senses himself in the presence of a political Bonze caste, immeasurably remote from local life.

Up to *Can You Forgive Her?*, in fact, we have yet to meet a single sympathetic politician. Yet then comes that heartfelt passage about the lamps in the Members' Lobby. What dissipated this robust provincial scepticism? Trollope's other writings of the 1850s wander far from 'that western county'. The Barchester election in *Dr Thorne* recycled material from an abortive and highly Carlyleian social critique *The New Zealander* (1854), which also contributed much to the fiction, experimental in theme, which he wrote in his last Irish years: *The Bertrams* (1859), on religious unbelief, *Castle Richmond* (1859), on the Irish famine; and *The Three Clerks* (1857), on the civil service. The last is not very successful, but subject, style and his own high valuation suggest that Trollope wanted a new departure, and also to get in another jab at Dickens and his abuse of Whitehall in *Little Dorrit*.[61] *The Three Clerks* is a critique of the panacea of competitive examination and Treasury supervision. Surveying the careers of the high-flying Alaric Tudor, the undemonstrative reliable Henry Norman and the wayward Charley Tudor, Trollope proves to his own satisfaction that brilliance does not guarantee probity. The ambitious Alaric starts by cutting corners to achieve promotion, commits fraud and ends up, after imprisonment, in exile in Australia.

The political theme of *The Three Clerks* was important throughout Europe, where centralized bureaucracies, with or without elected parliaments, were contrasted with the 'corruption' of American democracy, as interpreted by Tocqueville or, indeed, by Frances Trollope. Trying to suggest the 'character' bureaucrats should cultivate in a free society, Trollope adopts symbol and allegory. Tony Bareham has argued that the Thames is the connection between the heart, the villa at Surbiton where they meet their girls, and the head, their London offices. The examinations Alaric Tudor institutes and the mines he inspects are the ladders and pits of his career. His Weights and Measures Department finds him wanting.[62] This combination certainly seems to be present but doesn't really work. The courtship and domestic comedy element is too trite. But the portrait of Alaric Tudor implies that enlightened officialdom was, for Trollope, no alternative to responsible participation. *The Three Clerks* suggests that Trollope, by now senior in the Post Office and contemplating a return to Britain, was clearing the ground for a more ambitious project.

By 1860, Whitehall was drawing politics away from Barchester. The recoil against centralization had proved temporary, and interest in institutional and electoral reform picked up again. Trollope wanted to be on hand: 'I thought that a man who could write books ought not to live in Ireland, – ought to live within reach of the publishers, the clubs, and the dinner parties of the metropolis.'[63] By 1865 he was wallowing in politics, publicity and journalism. His reputation and his enthusiastic publisher, George Smith, gained him entry to the society of Lewes and George Eliot, Thackeray, Fitzjames Stephen and Henry Reeve, and little dining clubs where coming men such as W. E. Forster and William Harcourt 'used to whisper the secrets of parliament with free tongues'. Although without any Bohemian apprenticeship, he dominated it – megatherium-like – within five years.[64]

IV

The outcome was the Palliser sequence of novels. Trollope's own estimate of these was high, and has received recent endorsement from academic critics, both *literati* and historians.[65] Where Speare had depreciated Trollope's political grasp – 'Trollope never took his politics more seriously than as a means of creating another background for the portrayal of human beings, for the telling of a good story, for the chance of reflecting more "heart interest"'[66] – to James Kincaid the novels' 'comprehensiveness and subtlety make them Trollope's finest achievement', while Roy Foster, the biographer of Parnell and Lord Randolph Churchill, has praised Trollope's 'remarkable verisimilitude': 'the artifices and collusions of the mid-Victorian political world, as well as the unspoken assumptions of the age' are therein contained.[67]

The main interpretation, however, has been conservative. Trollope begins in 1863 reverent towards politics, but the 'democratization' of 1867 and his humiliation at Beverley in 1868 disillusion him, and he ends with bitter forebodings about a legislature divided between unscrupulous plutocrats and democratic fantasists – between the Augustus Melmottes of *The Way We Live Now* (1874–5) and the Ontario Moggses of *Ralph the Heir* (1870–1). This unease he conveys both by set-pieces like corrupt elections, and by a running theme about the rise into Parliament of ambitious but impecunious young men. Phineas Finn may have been a better-class example, but he left Speare, for example, aghast: '. . . it would be a sad day for England if men of his weak moral fibre and mental flabbiness become samples of "an ambitious younger generation" struggling with public affairs.'[68] Ambition provokes venality, while the decline of the old aristocratic obligation to serve weakens continuity and responsibility. As Halperin writes:

> Is it possible to succeed in politics without compromising one's integrity? Can one please others and still retain one's soul? Trollope's answer is that the preservation of moral integrity in such circumstances is both possible and impossible – possible for the exceptional man, impossible for the ordinary man. Thus it is important that exceptional men should interest themselves in politics.[69]

This echoes Walter Bagehot and Robert Lowe, but was it Trollope's own line? Two points suggest otherwise: the rejection of 'enlightened bureaucracy' in *The Three Clerks* and the fact that Trollope took six months unpaid leave in 1861–2 to study American politics.

The *Autobiography* dismissed his *North America* as 'tedious and confused',[70] but Trollope took seriously this huge project, which implied a commitment to the unpopular cause of the federal government. Henry Adams found Thackeray's hostility to the North typical of the 'sacred eccentrics' of the British establishment.[71] Trollope both defended American democracy and watched it operate close up. When Britain and the United States came to the brink of war in 1861, over the seizure of Confederate envoys from a British steamer, Trollope was at the State Department: 'I dined with Mr Seward on the day of decision, meeting Mr Sumner at his house, and was told as I left the dining room what the decision had been.'[72] The militarization of Washington – 'the rough-shod generals were the men of the day'[73] – at a time of Southern successes worried him, but he endorsed the achievement of Congress: 'For sixty years Congress has fully answered the purpose for which it was established. With no antecedents of grandeur, the nation, with its Congress, has made itself one of the five great nations of the world.'[74] Two main conclusions stemmed from *North America*. Trollope believed the South would eventually be allowed to secede, as a smallish non-slave Confederacy, on the North's terms.[75] The United States would remain one of the five great nations, but not overtake Britain as the greatest. He also believed, contrary to Tocqueville, that 'Leading men in public life have been much less trammelled by popular will than among us. Indeed with us the most conspicuous of our statesmen and legislators do not lead, but are led.' So he claimed for England 'a broader freedom in political matters than the States have, as yet, achieved'.[76]

On this 'broader freedom' depended Britain's future supremacy. Being socially not constitutionally derived, it had to be investigated empirically, so Trollope combined in the Palliser novels a sociological investigation with the popularity of fiction, taking an almost programmatic approach to 'displaying' the political machine. Disraeli's picture of government was vague, loosely endorsing claims about the arrogance of Parliament and appeals to the monarchy or public opinion. But, where Eliot had examined a single constituency, Trollope omitted no important element – cabinet and party meetings, Whitehall offices, select committees, newspapers, patronage – of the central government structure.

Bradford Booth characterized Trollope's political position as 'republican', and this seems a reasonable definition with which to start.[77] In the *Autobiography* Trollope considers the relationship of friendship and equality in somewhat delphic terms: 'It seems to me that intimate friendship admits of no standing but that of equality. I cannot be the

Sovereign's friend, nor probably the friend of many much beneath the Sovereign, because such equality is impossible.'[78] The implication seems to be that the sovereign simply doesn't enter Trollope's field of reference. Trollope's *was* a Venetian constitution, dominated – but not monopolized – by a patrician land-owning class. But how did this class renew its power, and how did it cope with a multi-national country? On what terms did it admit new wealth? Or ingest talent unaccompanied by wealth? What limits were set to parliamentary convention? These questions made the Palliser novels, first, into a sort of *Bildungsroman* in which various individuals were inducted (or not inducted) into the political world; second, into an experiment in which one central convention was distorted and the reaction of the various principals observed. Both phases were focused, successively, on two characters: the first on Phineas Finn, the second on Plantagenet Palliser, Duke of Omnium.

Attempts have been made to identify Trollope's politicians with originals. It is more important to equate them with themes and types – and to follow Trollope's injunction to read the Palliser novels as a whole. If we do this, the following 'history' emerges. Before 1863 government was usually in the hands of the Whig Lord Brock, but he was out of office and a Tory minority ministry under Lord de Terrier and Mr Daubeny was in. This was brought down by a vote of no confidence and a Whig–Liberal Mildmay administration took over, holding a further election in 1865 which strengthened its grip, but becoming divided on the ballot and on tenant right. In 1868 the Liberals again won the election, but Mr Gresham's ministry lasted only one year before it split on the ballot and allowed the creation of a minority Daubeny ministry. Mr Daubeny tried to dish his opponents by adopting Church disestablishment but failed, and another Gresham ministry came to power. But this, too, could not gain overall support, so the Duke of Omnium undertook to lead a grand coalition. This lasted until 1876, when it split and Gresham took over again for two years. There was then a short Tory ministry under Sir Timothy Beeswax, which gave way after a general election to a Liberal government under Joshua Monk. This gives ten premierships in fifteen years. In reality, Palmerston's government had been taken over in 1865 by Lord John Russell, who resigned in 1866 over reform, and left the resolution of this to a minority Derby–Disraeli ministry, 1866–8. Gladstone then won the election and remained in until 1874, and Disraeli from 1874 to 1880. A total of six premierships. Trollope's serene mid-Victorian scene was, in his 'history', tumultuous and experimental: a 'critical' rather than an 'organic' period.

This was what confronted the 'young man making his way in politics'. Halperin believes this *Bildungsroman* element shows the necessity of wealth and solid political tradition. The alternative is instability and venality. But are Trollope's young men thus imperilled? Although nearly all are MPs, candidates or peers (so much for Speare's notion of the marginality of politics), most are unspectacular in terms of birth or talent. George Vavasor, Phineas Finn, Lord Fawn, Frank Greystock, Ferdinand Lopez and Frank Tregear are all short of money, but only Vavasor and Lopez behave really badly. John Grey, Plantagenet Palliser, Arthur Fletcher and Lord Silverbridge have means, but Grey's career in Parliament is short, and Silverbridge is innocent of a single political idea. Lord Fawn comes of a family of hereditary legislators but, timid and dim, seems simply an indictment of the breed.

The ambitious young man is a stock figure for two reasons. First, he develops 'heart interest' in a less sublime direction. Young men in politics need money, and are after heiresses, even if they are still attached to devoted but impecunious girls. This both stitched together Trollope's statutory double plots and opened out a fascinating moral ambiguity: love 'from the full heart' versus the economically secure marriage.[79] Second, the young man is socialized into the 'in-group': the rituals of elections, the House and government. He either has to practise such ethical freedom as circumstances allow him or, like Vavasor and Lopez, carry arrogance and defiance to the point of self-destruction.

Most of Trollope's young men don't last beyond one novel, but both Phineas Finn and Plantagenet Palliser develop until they dominate their parts of the sequence. Phineas has obvious picaresque elements, out of *Tom Jones*, Charles Lever's cheery Irish mercenaries and Byron's *Don Juan*. At first glance he would not be out of place in a Disraeli story. But, after a rapid education in politics and social life, he takes on the moral seriousness which underlay *Don Juan* – in Trollope's view, something Disraeli was incapable of. Phineas's debating-society ideas melt under the critique of a parliamentary manipulator like the Whig Barrington Erle, but he then gingerly attaches himself to the philosophical radical Joshua Monk. Against this, his conformism is strengthened by the patronage of Lady Laura Kennedy and her father, the Earl of Brentford, and the favour shown him by his former rival, her husband Robert Kennedy. But then the price of this essentially parasitic behaviour falls due: severe for Phineas, appalling for Lady Laura. It's a revulsion against this, as much as a solidarity with the rebellious Monk, which after five years drives Phineas out of Westminster and back to Ireland.

There is, among the structures that Trollope stuck to, a comedy of love and ambition, at its most perfect in *Barchester Towers*. There is also a darker drama, of ordeal and ambiguous consolation, which he reserves for his more complex characters: Mr Harding, the Reverend Josiah Crawley, Plantagenet Palliser. Phineas, too, must endure this. In *Phineas Redux* his reabsorption into high politics is balanced by the traumas of his personal life. He has lost his wife and child; the patronage of the Brentfords has become the obligation to protect Lady Laura and her senile father from her demented husband. His enemies Slide and Bonteen, aided by the capricious career of Lady Eustace, move forward to engulf him. Accused of the murder of Bonteen, isolated and desperately lonely, he is only rescued by a similarly isolated but morally much more resolute figure, Marie Goesler. Parliamentary society seems revealed at its most callous: 'What does it matter who sits in Parliament? The fight goes on just the same. The same falsehoods are acted. The same mock truths are spoken. The same wrong reasons are given. The same personal motives are at work.'[80] Is this a terminal disillusion with politics? No, Phineas's himself again – now in the Cabinet – in *The Prime Minister*: a rather conservative First Lord of the Admiralty, useful and 'British', but now a man without any real moral investment in politics.

This career has elements of real tragedy and suggests the Marxist interpretation which Professor Halperin dreads. Phineas's passion for Laura is the chief emotional – and indeed sexual – theme of both books but it plays itself out in a changing society. Laura, trapped by the debts of her brother Lord Chiltern and the fact that the Brentfords' wealth no longer matches their ambitions, sells herself to Kennedy. Kennedy, like Phineas, is an outsider: a Scots Presbyterian where Phineas is an Irish Catholic. A quiet, honest, almost touching figure on his Scottish estate, the tensions in his marriage – and his wife's intimacy with Phineas, which he permits because Phineas saved his life – drive him towards religious mania, madness and death.

The struggle against Kennedy brings Phineas and Laura into a relationship which would – in any country other than Victorian England – have been sexual. This is, indeed, what the press surmise and what finally drives Kennedy out of his mind. Defending himself against these charges, Phineas confronts Bonteen, and thus becomes prime suspect when Bonteen is murdered. Phineas's rescue by Marie, who uses her money and her international business connections to produce evidence which exonerates him, means that he must marry her, and part for ever with Laura.

Laura ends as lonely as *Felix Holt*'s Mrs Transome: imprisoned in the Whig cage of politics rather than in the Tory cage of family, but even more hopeless. The symbolism of both is identical: isolation in a country house with an imbecile for companion. As for Phineas, perhaps his marriage resembles what might have happened had Harold Transome actually married Esther Lyon. In *The Prime Minister* Phineas and his wife seem to spend most of their time apart. Phineas, the man of principle who had 'gone out' on the Irish issue of tenant right, now stays in by opposing his countrymen over home rule. Although he and Marie are both in their thirties, they have no child.

Phineas is an outsider: Catholic, Irish, poor. Plantagenet Palliser is a Whig born to govern. He begins, unpromisingly, in Barsetshire. He narrowly saves his marriage to Lady Glencora in *Can You Forgive Her?* at the (temporary) cost of his political career. In the Phineas novels he climbs to the Cabinet, first as Chancellor of the Exchequer, remaining there as President of the Board of Trade on the death of Bonteen and after his own translation to the Lords as Duke of Omnium. He is one of Disraeli's Venetians. Macmillan, who married a Cavendish, remarked that the political capacity and conscience of the great Whig houses distinguished them from the Tory aristocracy, which stayed on its estates and left running the party to recruits from other social classes or parties.[81] Peel and Gladstone were only one generation away from trade; Bentinck and Derby – Disraeli's colleagues – were former Whigs. Disraeli we have already met.

Palliser is becoming an anachronism. The noblemen that Barchester looked to in the 1850s – Lord Brock and Lord de Terrier – have given way, by the end of *The Duke's Children*, to lawyers like Sir Timothy Beeswax and career politicians like Joshua Monk. Omnium bows out, comparing himself to an old draught-horse, in the dignified but honorific post of Lord President under Monk, a stonemason's son. But Palliser is not a complete Whig, like the Duke of St Bungay. The maker of Cabinets for decades, supposedly modelled on that Marquess of Lansdowne whose son Macmillan described as the last of the race, St Bungay believes in governing, not in reforming. Such Whigs were exclusive. Even when progressive, they spent their time with other Whigs, addressed few meetings, wrote few pamphlets and fewer articles. Lord Amberley, Earl Russell's radical son, still found a wife, Kate Stanley, in another Whig family.[82] Palliser believes in family – which is what the tensions in *The Duke's Children* are all about – but he mixes readily with non-Whigs: the dreadful Mr Bott from Manchester in *Can You Forgive Her?*, Julius Monk, later on Phineas Finn. Moreover, he has ideas – 'crotchets' – which is definitely a radical habit. The most obvious of these is decimal coinage, and a lot of the fun which Trollope derives from this obsession stems from the ordinary Briton's view of decimals as subversive, revolutionary and French. Planty Pal is a mild but still progressive descendant of those Whigs who in the afterglow of 1789 styled themselves the 'Friends of the People'.

If the Phineas story is essentially a biographical *Bildungsroman* – let down in the second part by a very weak subplot – Palliser's moment comes in the very tightly structured *Prime Minister*. The subordinate plot – the rise and fall of Ferdinand Lopez – has been dismissed as an irrelevance to the fortunes of the coalition government that the Duke of Omnium heads, but in fact it intersects with the main plot like the convergent railway-tracks at Tenway Junction. A collision between Lopez' unscrupulous careerism and the Duke's burdensome ministry becomes inevitable, and is provoked when Glencora's wilful promotion of Lopez in the Silverbridge election clashes with the Duke's wish to dismantle his family's patronage. Lopez is destroyed. The Duke, while still on the rails, so to speak, is stricken, his career in eclipse.

Speare recognized the circumstances out of which Palliser's predicament springs: 'The men are so near to each other in all their convictions and theories of life that nothing is left to them but personal competition for the doing of the thing that is left to be done.'[83] The grand coalition seems, at the beginning of the novel, a way out of chronically unstable governments. It satisfies the 'Old Duke', St Bungay, probably now more Conservative than Liberal, and the labours of Omnium keep it together for three years – very good going for any Trollope politician. But to dispense with party conflict was to throw away the rule-book, and to let adventurers like Lopez (the young Disraeli? – playing the stock exchange, writing importunate letters to the premier, that South American mining company . . .), Lizzie Eustace and Quintus Slide get themselves power. For Omnium, this menace is symbolized by the gigantic hall of Gatherum, no longer a Liberal fortress, but an entry for opponents like Drought, parasites like Lopez and Major Pountney. The Duke is thin-skinned because the coalition has removed his usual shell.

The upshot is, however, a new faith in Liberalism – and that great passage with which I began this book. Palliser has seen an undivided British political class in action and feels well rid of it. A grey man for most of his career, only now does he emerge as an individual. In the course of the book he has taken several portentous walks on his estates: at Gatherum fending off Drought and his battleships; at Matching, to Glencora's disgust, talking cork soles with Lady Rosina de Courcy. With the coalition in ruins, he takes Phineas Finn to his favourite view at Matching, and tries to communicate his Liberal vision. He considers the Tory millenium of a benign aristocratic élite, and dismisses it:

'We know that power does corrupt, and that we cannot trust kings to have loving hearts, and clear intellects, and noble instincts. Men as they come to think about it and to look forward, and to look back, will not believe in such a millennium as that.'

'Do they believe in any millennium?'

'I think they do after a fashion, and I think that I do myself. That is my idea of Conservatism. The doctrine of Liberalism is, of course, the reverse. The Liberal, if he have any fixed idea at all, must I think have conceived the idea of lessening distances, – of bringing the coachman and the Duke nearer together, – nearer and nearer, till a millennium shall be reached by —'

'By equality?' asked Phineas, eagerly interrupting the Prime Minister, and showing his dissent by the tone of his voice.[84]

This represents the quintessential moment of the 'liberal' fiction of politics, a fallible man conscious of the distance of his own life both from the practice of the parliamentary system and from his own ideals. It ends in embarrassment and confusion as Palliser, who has seen his God, comes back to reality and his sceptical Irish interlocutor.

V

'I look on Catholicism as my religious flag, on Liberalism as my political faith.' Lord Acton (usually credited with one of Trollope's lines in the foregoing) articulated what is apparent throughout the Palliser novels: the secularization of English society. Omnium's millennium is not religious, although presented with quasi-religious imagery. If we are reminded of another believer, Josiah Crawley in *The Last Chronicle of Barset*, it is only to confirm the drying-up of Crawley's 'sea of faith'.[85] In the Palliser novels religion scarcely features, except to provide a murderer, the Reverend Joseph Emilius, and to figure as the centre of a party manoeuvre when, in *Phineas Redux*, disestablishment threatens to destroy Barsetshire. Roy Foster takes Daubeny's scheme as shorthand for the reform issue in 1867, but Trollope could have adopted other symbols for Disraelian ingenuity – disarmament or home rule.[86] The imperilment of the Church at the hands of its Tory ally is simply another instance of the triumph of the metropolitan political game.

There is such assurance in Trollope's portrait of his ideal statesman – ideal, admittedly, in his faults as well as in his virtues – that we have to remind ourselves that *The Prime Minister*, when published in 1876, was judged a failure. This hurt Trollope deeply, and he cut much political material out of *The Duke's Children* which, as published in 1880, was more about psychology than about politics. Why did Trollope and his readership start to part company? The failure of the *St Paul's Magazine* (1867–70), from which he emerged 'slightly blown upon', lost him his close publishing connection with George Smith.[87] Economic decline hit the landed society on which he had always focused. And among the 'classes', the archetypal Mudie's subscribers of London and its suburbs, there was in 1874 'a considerable middle-class movement against a radical government, a garnering of votes of which the Tories had been deprived by Palmerston'.[88] If Trollope was a Palmerstonian, this did him no good; if he was an intellectual Liberal of a distinctive sort, he would certainly be hit. Moreover, in late 1876, he was particularly outspoken in Gladstone's campaign on the Bulgarian Atrocities, an issue which set the pro-Disraeli South-East against the North and the Celtic Fringe.[89]

'An advanced, but still a Conservative, Liberal' was not just 'a rational and consistent phase of political existence':[90] since an 'advanced Liberal' *tout court* meant a 'faddist', probably a Nonconformist, with a thing about India or peace or drink. Party was Trollope's remedy for a personal *accidie* – although elections had a horror all their own – and he stuck to his side. What he lacked was the deep collaboration which other liberal intellectuals acquired at school and university. For all his gregariousness, Trollope knew loneliness, and conveys its qualities, whether in the chambers of the former Solicitor-General Sir Thomas Underwood, in *Ralph the Heir*, in the misery of Phineas Finn during and after his trial, or in the widowed Duke, not knowing 'how to look out into the world'. Trollope's dilemma was that his moral liberalism grew just as its social foundation – his simple equation of property and security – was becoming a Tory cry.

VI

As a Conservative literary *démarche*, Disraeli's *Lothair*, published on 2 May 1870, was sensational in every sense of the term. Henry James regarded it as a holiday from 'the new realism, the hard, sordid, pretentious accuracy . . . of Trollope'.[91] He couldn't take it seriously as politics. Others did. Trollope and Lord Houghton hoped it would ruin Disraeli – or at least Longman, his publisher.[92] But Frederic Harrison, who could never be accused of flippancy, regarded it as 'a political event', providing an essential entrée to 'the mature thoughts of one who has governed an empire'.[93] Disraeli would have agreed. Longman's £10,000 was always useful in keeping his creditors at bay, but the novel's fanciful plot contained a palette of political initiatives, and styles of propaganda typical of the mass-political epoch, which would evict the republicanism of the intelligentsia.

Disraeli encountered a workable vein of romanticism – 'what gorgeous palaces of Geneva' – among suburban Londoners, and *Lothair* reads like one of their Christmas pantomimes.[94] Set in the period of Disraeli's premiership, between August 1866 and August 1868, it contrives to ignore it. Its naïve, wealthy hero, reared in the Free Church of Scotland, turned loose in London society, woos and loses the daughter of a Tory magnate, and is then courted by glamorous temptresses from the Secret Societies and the Catholic Church. Seduced by one into joining Garibaldi's assault on Rome, he is almost converted by the other. Lothair escapes, wanders to the Holy Land, gets an abridged version of the revelation offered to Tancred, and returns to marry his Corisande.

Can *Lothair* be described as political fiction, since Parliament scarcely figures in it? A clue may be given in one of the few conversations that the hero and Corisande manage to have:

'You are a most ardent politician,' said Lothair.

'Oh! I do not care in the least about common politics, parties and office and all that; I neither regard nor understand them,' replied Lady Corisande, 'But when wicked men try to destroy the country, then I like my family to be in the front.'[95]

Developing the paranoiac-thriller element in *Sybil* – but without any of *Sybil*'s social criticism – *Lothair*'s 'popular aristocracy' is threatened by radical nationalism and Catholicism, a serious enough message, although put over with wit, gaiety, luscious scene-painting and a daft plot.[96] Its success brought back into print earlier works which the Tories found it useful to publicize. Although Disraeli had travelled far towards orthodoxy since writing *Sybil*, the next generation were able to construe 'One Nation' as meaning Unionism rather than class reconciliation.[97] *Lothair*'s anti-Catholicism endorsed the help militant Protestants had given to the Conservatives at the election of 1868, especially in Lancashire, and, by making Lothair's guardian Lord Culloden the defender of the faith (Lothair's original, the young Marquis of Bute, who had 'gone over' in 1868, was a substantial Scots landowner), adapted this to Scottish ends. Irish discontent was played down – 'Their treason is a fairy-tale, and their sedition a child talking in its sleep' – but Disraeli could exploit the expected Vatican decrees on papal infallibility.[98] Although Michael Foot sees Disraeli as radical and feminist, he doesn't notice how skilfully the party man plays off the Garibaldians against the Irish, and how the revolutionary Bruges, wanting to do 'something for the freedom of mankind on the banks of the Danube', endorses a pro-Turkish foreign policy.[99]

Vernon Bogdanor argues that Disraeli valued the 'national' Church but he disbelieved in all nationalisms.[100] The Catholic Church intrigued him because it actually *functioned* in the sort of international arena that, *pace Tancred*, he envisaged for himself, as did the Secret Societies: Disraeli's King Charles's Head. This obsession showed an odd respect for movements which were often internally chaotic, like Marx's First International – the 'Holy Alliance of Peoples'? – founded in 1864 and already on its last legs. The Conservatives even troubled themselves to infiltrate it in 1871.[101] When the Balkan Crisis broke out in 1876, Disraeli denounced it as 'the conspiracy of the Secret Societies of Europe against the Turkish Empire'.[102] The irony was that in the subsequent conflict the Catholics and Marx both took Disraeli's side.

Lothair 'relaunched' the literary Disraeli. It constructed a 'Britishness' which integrated Scotland and posited Ireland as a specific 'Catholic' problem. It could become an embarrassment only if a Tory settlement of home rule were possible. In the suburbs, among militant Protestants and future members of the Primrose League, it filled the bill, and appealed to the new bestseller market provided by mass literacy. *Lothair* has all Q. D. Leavis's bestseller *desiderata*, but rarely has 'the magnificent vitality of the author' been more in evidence.

VII

Lothair, moreover, accords with a type of fiction which irrupted during this period with particular force, directed at readers as voters, using new developments in publishing, and reflecting the political instability of a time which saw reform in Britain, war and insurrection in France, and a brief efflorescence of republicanism. Such Carlyleian *frissons* of internal corruption and external menace were revived by the Edinburgh Tory John Blackwood, George Eliot's publisher. In 1865 he was approached by a young diplomat with a social satire; in 1870 by an engineer colonel with a grudge. In both cases he aimed to disrupt his more orthodox competitors.

Blackwood got Laurence Oliphant, Orientalist, journalist and radical, to put together a satirical series in *Maga*, 'loosely about unaccountable, generally bubble-spawned, fellows who keep an establishment in London, and entertain every one of note for a season or two, and then burst with some disclosure of bankruptcy or fraud'.[103] *Piccadilly*, which printed ten editions before 1891, combined the bite of *Vanity Fair* and the conviction of Bunyan, with the witness of a gifted man living under severe mental and religious stress: Oliphant's father had been an Irvingite, and Oliphant himself was involved in various projects of a millennial socialist sort.

Piccadilly assaulted a society suffering from:

> Morbid activity of the national brain, utterly deranged action of the national heart . . . Due to the noxious influence of tall chimneys upon broad acres, whereby the commercial effluvium of the Plutocracy has impregnated the upper atmosphere, and overpowered the enfeebled and enervated faculties of the aristocracy; lust of gain has supervened upon love of ease.[104]

Where the clergy 'are only a paid branch of the civil service, exercising police functions of a very lofty and important character', the real morality is money: aristocracy and fashion prostitute themselves and their children before the wealthy, and prey on the already disadvantaged, the Irish or the aborigines in the colonies.[105] Over this the parliamentarians are simply lords of misrule:

> 'Have you ever been in an asylum for idiots, Broadhem?' I asked abruptly.

'No' he said, timidly.

'Then you are in one now. Look at them; there is the group to which you belong playing at politics. Look at the imbecile smile of gratified vanity with which they receive the applause that follows a successful hit. That poor little boy has just knocked a political tobacco pipe out of Aunt Sally's mouth, and he imagines himself covered with lasting glory.[106]

Oliphant's critique was informed but, ultimately, unstable. He was elected a radical MP in 1865, and in 1867 helped push Disraeli and Gladstone much further towards universal suffrage than they wanted to go. Then he vanished into semi-imprisonment in a Utopian community in the United States with his mysterious 'instructor' Joseph Lake Harris, remaining there for nearly twenty years.[107]

Other publishers joined in. In 1870, Alexander Strachan, who had just ejected Trollope from *St Paul's*, launched Edward Jenkins's *Ginx's Baby*, a mocking tale about an abandoned child's fate at the hands of brawling and disorganized religious bodies, local authorities and political parties. This ran into thirty-seven editions by 1877, and had by then – along with another two satires – made Jenkins, as a 'socialistic liberal', an MP.[108] In 1872, Eliza Lynn Linton published *The True History of Joshua Davidson, Communist*, really a revival of her ex-husband W. J. Linton's *Records of the World's Justice*, in which her Christ-like hero, returning from the Paris Commune, gets stoned to death by a mob incited by the local rector. Frederic Harrison and John Bright applauded; Bradlaugh bought a thousand copies. It ran into three editions in 1872, and ten by the end of the century.[109]

Jenkins and Mrs Linton claimed to be radicals, though soon shifted rightwards. Much more emphatically right-wing was the engineer officer George Chesney's *The Battle of Dorking*, the most successful of invasion-scare stories, engagingly summarized by the author:

We have the quarrel with America and Russia, dispersion of all our forces, followed by rising in India, sudden appearance of Germany on the scene. Sentimental platitudes of Messrs. Gladstone and Co., trimming leaders in the *Times*. Destruction of our 'Field Line' by new torpedoes. Arrival of 100,000 Sanskrit-speaking Junkers brimming over with 'Geist' and strategy. Hurried defence of the chalk-range by volunteers and militia, no commissariat, line turned, total defeat, retreat on London, occupation of that place, and general smash up.[110]

Carried by *Maga* in May 1871, Chesney's philippic caused a political furore. A pamphlet version sold 110,000 copies, and translations, counter-pamphlets and speeches by politicians, notably Bulwer-Lytton and Gladstone, made the 'imaginary war' an almost unbudgeable element of right-wing propaganda, visible in Sir Orlando Drought's battleships and the crisis-packed beginning of George Meredith's *Beauchamp's Career* (1875).[111]

This volatility extended to 'the most imbecile and depressed portion of our literature', the London theatre.[112] Charles Reade staged *Free Labour*, an adaptation of his *Put Yourself in His Place*, in 1870, worrying the Lord Chamberlain, even though it was strongly anti-trade union.[113] But politics, already figuring in Tom Robertson's *Society* (1866) and *MP* (1870), irrupted in earnest in May 1873 when W. S. Gilbert's burlesque *The Happy Land* at the Court Theatre so mauled Gladstone's ministry that the Lord Chamberlain closed it down until direct portrayals of cabinet ministers were dropped. It ran for seven months and was succeeded by similar efforts which persisted until the election of 1874.[114] Gilbert's Tory satire sends the Liberal Cabinet to fairyland, which it rules through competitive examination and 'Liberal principles' – party discipline, discarding British interests, and ignorance. A Gladstone-figure tells a representative fairy that she is 'eminently qualified for First Lord of the Admiralty, *because* you don't know anything about ships. You take office – you learn all about ships – and when you know all about ships, the opposition comes in and out you go.'[115] The reforming energies of the Government were certainly flagging, but the success of Gilbert's burlesque showed the pronounced – and continuing – rightward shift of the metropolis.[116]

By contrast, in the provinces, a 'conscious regionalism' intensified after 1870.[117] In the Palliser novels Scotland appears as a vast bleak sporting estate, and Ireland raises only a fist-sized cloud. When Phineas Finn is accused of murder no one links him with the Fenians, and Omnium's coalition leaves '[the] Irish party . . . without an inch of standing ground'.[118] Phineas, as Chief Secretary, is eager to head off nationalism by creating a prosperous farming class and local authorities, and worries that, although 'the power of the Church is going to the wall' in Ireland, ultramontane Catholicism 'is infinitely stronger now than it was fifty, or even twenty years ago'.[119] But, when he goes to the Admiralty, Ireland disappears from the agenda.[120]

Other writers were more responsive. Lynn Linton set much of *Joshua Davidson* in Cornwall, and Edward Jenkins appealed to anti-landlord sentiment in Scotland in *Lord Bantam*, but these were totally overshadowed by William Alexander's classic of vernacular radicalism in Aberdeenshire, *Johnny Gibb o' Gusheteuk* (1871), which reached fifteen editions by 1908, while Charles Kickham's *Knocknagow* was scarcely less popular in Ireland. There, Ascendancy writers shifted to a pessimistic nationalism. Trollope's old friend Charles Lever, in *Lord Kilgobbin* (1870–2), saw

Ireland trapped between insensitive governors and dispirited or rebellious natives. His heroine escapes from the rain-sodden fields of Kilgobbin Castle to America with her Fenian lover; the parliamentary nationalist, with his hopes of modernization, is left irresolute. Mary Laffan Hartley's very Trollopian *Hogan MP* (1876) is no more sanguine. Hogan, a young Dublin Catholic lawyer, is a straw man, created and destroyed by speculative finance and a complacent 'Castle Catholic' bourgeoisie waxing rich as importers, not as entrepreneurs. Her images are vivid: Hogan's journey to his constituency, the train steaming from the elegance of Kingsbridge into the darkness and desolation of the post-Famine West; the welcome at a great house blazing with light, and the morning sight of its damp collapsing outbuildings, the wretched cabins of his constituents scattered over a hillside reverting to bog.

Intensely unreassuring, *Hogan MP* looks back to the 'Irish Trollope' and forward to George Moore's *A Drama in Muslin* (1886), the claustrophobic decay of Somerville and Ross's *The Real Charlotte* (1894) and George Bernard Shaw's *John Bull's Other Island* (1904). Ironically, while these advanced into the realism of Flaubert and the Russians, Catholic nationalists reverted to the earlier methods of English domestic fiction. *Knocknagow*, the 'great Fenian novel' written by Kickham in 1869 after his release from an English prison, drew on Dickens and George Eliot's *Adam Bede* to create a 'national epic' for an increasingly militant Irish rural society, lauding virtues not all the efforts of J. M. Synge and James Joyce's 'Ivy Day in the Committee Room' could dislodge.[121]

Knocknagow was one of countless serials in the Irish and Scottish local press. Twenty-five Scottish towns had a paper in 1845, and a typical circulation was the *Aberdeen Free Press*'s 600 a week.[122] By 1900, 125 towns had papers (many had more than one) with dailies in the bigger towns and a weekly like the radical *People's Journal* selling at least 250,000.[123] In serial form there may be around 5,000 full-length novels by Scottish writers in newspaper files - and some of this fiction was political, usually radical. David Pae, their acknowledged master between the mid-1850s and his death in 1884, interleaved social protest in his melodramas: 'Between the two − between the selfishness and cruelty of Mammon and the heaven-directed desires of the heart − there is a bitter contest, in which the heart generally comes off the worst . . . crushed between the wheels of iron which now whirl ceaselessly in our factories.'[124] Pae was a millennialist, raised in an Owenite household. In *The Coming Struggle among the Nations of the Earth* (1853) he expected the Kingdom of God to be inaugurated by a world war in 1866, something which sets another context for Chesney and the 'invasion scare': the appeal of Armageddon rather than of political propaganda.

While 'in practice, the writing, production and reading of books was a middle class monopoly',[125] such serials - often written in local dialect, which varied considerably from region to region – were the staple of Scottish working-class readers, particularly in the north-east where strong educational and folklore traditions contended with a rapidly developing agriculture-and-fishery capitalism. It was this society that produced William Alexander, editor of the *Aberdeen Free Press*, whose *Johnny Gibb* is the most important Scottish novel between Hogg and Stevenson. Set during the 'Ten Years' Conflict', 1834–43, which split the Church of Scotland, this centres on the struggle between Johnny, the crofter, and the 'muckle farmer' Peter Birse for dominance in their village. Despite Birse's wealth and influence with the absentee laird and his tame minister, Johnny defeats the attempt to deprive him of his tenancy, and becomes a founder of the new Free Church.

Should a Scottish village dispute figure at all as a Victorian political novel? But think of Galt, and of Rufus Lyon in *Felix Holt*. Gibb, like Lyon, is still impregnated with the radical tradition, the experience of the Civil War, and its republican expectations, and his struggle is part of a sequence of serial novels by Alexander, which take the North-East from the small-farmer epoch to that of industrial and urban growth in the last, *My Uncle the Bailie* (1876), registering the decline of religion before a new secular and materialistic politics. Alexander's achievement, William Donaldson argues, is not a marginal one; he is a realist of the age of Zola: '. . . his interest in social causality; his eagerness to find a rationale for human behaviour in external forces like heredity and environment; his broadly deterministic view of society; his underlying pessimism – all contribute to make him a conspicuous figure in Realistic aesthetics.'[126] Alexander was also, as newspaper editor, the leading Liberal of Liberalism's heartland. Why, then, is his work practically unknown outside Scotland? A short extract from his last novel should suggest the main reason:

> We're jist settin' on to hatch a new brodmill o' toon cooncillors. They're the raw material o' baillies and siclike, ye ken – the baillies bein' seleckit wi' due regaird to the size o' a man's painch, an' a' that; though we've aiven seen them win to the bench on the principle o' the scum comin' to the tap. An' fat better stuff hae ye to mak a Provost o' than a weel trackit Baillie? Wudna ye like to be a toon cooncillor than; as something within the limits o' your modesty.[127]

For a non-Scot – or for anyone outwith the north-east – Alexander's accurate dialect made him as difficult to read as for a Dane to read Norwegian 'Nynorsk'. Political fiction in such areas could remain a combination of the popular and the universal, but its closeness to the people excluded it from the metropolitan market, just as *The MacDermots* had been excluded in the 1840s.

Regionalism, sensationalism, violence, Utopia and Dystopia – Bulwer-Lytton's *The Coming Race* appeared in 1870, Samuel Butler's *Erewhon* in 1872, while Ouida's strange mixture of radicalism and *haut ton* brought her £5,000 per annum – provide an unsettling accompaniment to Trollope's liberal republicanism.[128] The connecting factor is 'corruption' in the eighteenth-century sense: the overwhelming of the civic virtues by the wealth and prescriptive power of what John Stuart Mill called a 'kakistocracy'. Trollope in 1870 saw the system as essentially held in balance between 'accumulating wealth . . . and popular energy'. This security seemed to have deteriorated by 1874. He started *The Way We Live Now*, with its savage denunciation of upper-class greed, just as Disraeli won his first commanding majority.

Trollope and the metropolitan Liberal élite were depressed by this frenetic dialectic, but it found both mid-Victorian political leaders oddly well prepared. A Tenniel cartoon shows Gladstone and Disraeli critically examining their productions of 1870. 'Hm . . . Flippant', says Gladstone of *Lothair*; 'Hm . . . prosy', says Disraeli of *Juventus Mundi*. Both were in the business of myth, Gladstone attempting to reconcile Homer with Christian revelation and folk-epics, and Disraeli pursuing the divine mission of the Semites: something which made them open to the unexpected.[129] John Stuart Blackie, a Carlyleian figure at Edinburgh University, as Classicist and Celtic scholar was frequently consulted by Gladstone and also flattered *Lothair* by comparing it with Goethe's *Wilhelm Meister* as 'what the Germans call a *Tendenzroman*'.[130] Like Lothair's original, the Marquis of Bute, Blackie was a romantic Scottish nationalist. Katherine, the youngest daughter of Trollope's close friends the Page Woods, was to become the mistress and co-conspirator of a far more compelling Irish politician than Phineas Finn, one whose martyrdom would create its own myths: Charles Stewart Parnell.[131] The charisma of the two remarkable mid-Victorian leaders kept in check political tendencies which were increasingly centrifugal.

VIII

In 1874, Liberalism seemed in partial abeyance; national rivalries were getting the better of free trade and constitutionalism, and an organized socialist movement was beginning to attack from the left. This atmosphere penetrates Meredith's *Beauchamp's Career* (1875), the Victorian genre's most subtle and symmetrical achievement, also perhaps its epitaph. Meredith, reader to Chapman & Hall, was at the centre of British publishing. One of the Century Club set, with Morley and Bryce, he was also the most European of English novelists, unafraid to include Mazzini and Lassalle among his characters, and warily respectful of the 'intellectual agility' of Disraeli. His impulse to write came from his own experience. In the same 1868 election which had humiliated Trollope, he had helped his friend Admiral Maxse, a Crimean War hero, as a Radical candidate: 'We were badly beaten in Southampton. I had measured, but poor Maxse had not, the far-striking deep root of Toryism in the soil of the country. So it has amazed him and merely distressed me for his sake. But I have the machinery for a very good story.'[132] Many of those involved became the characters of his novel: Maxse, his wife, his family, even Meredith himself. The result isn't a conversation with the great on Disraelian lines or an exploration of the penumbra of Whitehall. Rather, as Arnold Kettle has commented, it is an ironic and intimate comedy whose ingenious construction gives it remarkable symbolic power.[133]

I have tried to avoid plot-summaries, but accounting for the force of *Beauchamp's Career* demands one. Commander Nevil Beauchamp, a hero of the Crimea, is heir to his Whig uncle Everard Romfrey and suitor to the Tory heiress Cecilia Halkett. He jeopardizes both prospects by courting a former love, the French noblewoman Renée, and contesting the borough of Bevisham as a radical. His rival, Cecil Baskelett, provokes Beauchamp's political mentor, Dr Shrapnel, to impute that Romfrey's housekeeper (and Beauchamp's substitute mother) Rosamund Culling is Romfrey's mistress, which causes a total breach between Beauchamp and Romfrey, after the latter horsewhips Shrapnel. Beauchamp demands a full apology, through Rosamund, a situation which brings about the marriage of Romfrey and Rosamund, and the expectation of a new heir. Rosamund forces an apology out of Romfrey, when Beauchamp is near-fatally ill. Beauchamp marries Shrapnel's ward Jenny and, poor and disinherited, stands by his radicalism. Romfrey's child dies, then Beauchamp loses his life saving a workman's child from drowning. But he has already sired a son. Romfrey ends the book, as he began it, with an heir.

Carlyle had told Meredith to write history. Meredith retorted that his novels were truer than history, and *Beauchamp's Career* is a novel about the incompatibility of the Carlyleian hero and mid-Victorian public life. Beauchamp is a hero in the popular sense, in the decade of the Victoria Cross: brave, generous, and a conscious disciple of Carlyle's *Heroes and Hero-Worship* – 'There was a great deal more in the book than there was in himself'.[134] Believing that the hero can still alter the modern world, Beauchamp wins some credibility among the Hampshire gentry, and more among the ladies – dashing off in the middle of his election to aid Renée, mixing wooing with didactics in his siege of Cecilia. Beauchamp treats the class system as casually as the great warships his yacht skirts as he flits about the Solent and across to France. But the sea itself is a brilliant and ominous multiple image: waterway, temperament, 'moat defensive', a free people in politics. It is also the element which *literally* supports, then engulfs him.

Beauchamp is balanced between the 'sea', an untried, potentially limitless, democratic order, and the forts and warships: a powerful establishment, which is regrouping itself. Romfrey and his Whig friend Culbrett have now allied with the Tories, who are changing from the decencies and prejudice of Colonel Halkett and the Baskelett 'best brute vote' type to the tough élitist individualism represented by the coalowner Blackburn Tuckham and Seymour Austin, Bevisham's senior MP. Austin uses a rapier against Beauchamp's cutlass. He outfights Beauchamp over the issue of women's political equality and persuades Cecilia to reject Beauchamp for Tuckham.

Class matters more than love, and equality is more important than either. Beauchamp loses Cecilia because he fails to recognize her as a *political* individual. Trollope didn't settle a love-affair on ideological grounds, or kill his hero off in the last chapter (he had fewer scruples about killing off his heroines). But Trollope obviously likes Finn and Palliser, while Meredith keeps Beauchamp at a distance: immature and bewildered, like the young heroes of Stendhal, Meredith's great discovery. At the end of the novel the 'advanced radical' is reading Plato:

> A translation of Plato had become Beauchamp's intellectual world. This philosopher singularly anticipated his ideals. Concerning himself, he was beginning to think he had many years ahead of him for work. He was with Dr. Shrapnel, as to the battle, and with Jenny as to the delay in recommencing it.[135]

Beauchamp is changing from democrat to élitist: a Liberal of the school of Jowett (whose translation of Plato had just appeared) rather than a follower of Mill. But if Shrapnel is Ruskin (as Meredith's correspondence indicates), then we must be even more pessimistic, as Ruskin's failure to influence politics, and his seeming retreat into madness, emphasize how forlorn the alternative was.

Meredith's construction of *Beauchamp's Career* stands out in a period which saw the decay of plot, and its power as allegory is concentrated by his deft non-realistic handling of time. Historically, the novel spans the years 1852 to 1859, yet Meredith makes it sound contemporary. Beauchamp has to be a young hero, not like Maxse, a middle-aged half-pay officer. Yet the Tories must be the victors of 1874, not the demoralized protectionists of the 1850s. In this he follows Stendhal's strategy in *The Scarlet and the Black* (1830), compressing the politics of several years into as many months.

At the end Shrapnel holds up the little mudlark whom Beauchamp rescued: 'For this we have exchanged Nevil Beauchamp.' Is the boy symbolic of youth and a democratic future, or does Beauchamp's bewilderment show the hopelessness of heroism in a class society? *Beauchamp's Career* is pervaded by ideology, but Meredith's ironic structure, a mock epic in which the hero returns to the tribe, which then defeats him, obscures any dogmatic outcome. Beauchamp ends up not wiser but dead. Would he have continued progressive? Meredith had already noted tendencies which would make Fred Maxse a leading Unionist in 1886, while his son Leo became, as editor of the *National Review*, an almost unbalanced reactionary.

Meredith remained a Liberal, but like the Positivists he ceased to be active. In 1886 he favoured home rule, but his failure to complete *Celt and Saxon*, started around 1881 as his exploration of British multi-nationality, seems a surrender comparable to Harrison's withdrawal into 'religious positivism'. Two intellectual influences, visible in *Beauchamp's Career*, also lead to stasis. Ruskin was to become almost as influential as Carlyle had been in the 1840s, subverting classical economics, pioneering ecological propaganda, and advocating small-scale political organization. Meredith endorsed this but, unlike William Morris, he ingested Ruskin's quasi-sacerdotal élitism rather than his sense of social crisis. Meredith was also influenced by the evolutionary educational ideas of Herbert Spencer, who believed that a modern readership could decode authorial complexities, 'who, as it were, from some slight hint of the straws, will feel the winds of March when they do not blow'.[136] Spencer saw this élitism as part of a process of dismantling civil society in the interests of an order of 'free exchange' as triumphant as the ordained rule of the British over the Irish. To William Morris and Edward Carpenter, even to George Gissing, the conflicts of the 1870s, in particular over foreign policy, provoked commitment *against* such a future, and an absorption in new working-class institutions. Meredith still aimed at a middle-class élite similar to that which worshipped at the feet of the various Comteian deities.

G. M. Trevelyan, one of the radical enthusiasts for Meredith (who in his old age had the same sage-like reputation as George Eliot), regarded *Beauchamp's Career* as a prose-poem, to be read as such, yet Meredith's baroque style went with an admiration of Disraeli, and 'big fleet' patriotism. If *Beauchamp's Career* surveys the choices before British democracy – the 'presidential' system of the Comtists or decentralization – Meredith offers no clear decision. But the inference conveyed by the novel's cyclic structure, the Romfrey estate as alpha and omega, is that democracy might not actually develop at all.

IX

The Victorian political novels seem to have a collective presence, akin to that of the two-party system. Disraeli supplies propaganda and glamour; Trollope counters with an understanding of institutions and human sympathy: together providing an image of metropolitan life – the great club, the rules of the game - against which the constituency, the local arena of individual moral agency, defines itself at election times. Eliot and Meredith elevated the election scene to the level of allegory, Trollope supplied the linkages which bound it to the metropolis. This subjective map of the political world, like a medieval *mappa mundi*, was centred in an immensely detailed West London, the rest of the city rendered adequately; outside it, suburban mansions - the Horns, Belmont, Loughton; beyond them the hunting counties, south-coast resorts; in the far distance the industrial regions, Scotland, Wales and Ireland. Between the known world and these distant regions lie the constituencies – East Barset, West Barset, Barchester: a market-town, two inns which become party headquarters, two newspaper offices, church (or cathedral), chapel, railway station and perhaps one substantial employer, a brewery or a dockyard. Not far away, the Palladian mansion of some Whig magnate, and in the villages the smaller country houses of the Tory JPs.

This solidity is deceptive. Trollope has a distinctive 'Atlantic' political philosophy: a civic humanism precise in a moral sense but uncertain as to community. His emotional Irishness foundered on the country's plight and his own socialization as a civil servant. Once released from this civil society, he became mistrustful again: in the 1870s corruption seemed omnipresent. Eliot and Meredith represented a provincial *polis*. From their viewpoint London appears distant and unfocused. Their local élites are grounded in land, local government, religious communities, but their autonomy is professional rather than regional: the services, the law, the church. Before the rise of the collectivist state, government interferes little in their affairs.

Trollope skilfully 'composed' these two worlds: the caricature politicians of *The Warden* become the sympathetically handled middle-rankers like Barrington Erle, the eternal 'spare man' at dinner-parties, or Sir Thomas Underwood, the lonely former Solicitor-General. Loneliness is the result of the absence of any real community, hence the importance of property and bureaucracy – but such was his humanizing of Parliament that his characters *could* be frozen into ideal types. Allure is not Trollope's strong suit. His sense of change is brisk and empirical: the Church matters less; politics matters more; property matters always. His young ladies have 'so much a year' in land or government securities. Industry is *terra incognita*, while the stock exchange is simply an extension of the gambling habits of worthless young aristocrats and 'limited liability' a device to diminish personal responsibility.

The centrality of property is patent in his last, unfinished novel, *The Land Leaguers* (1882), in which he reverted to Ireland, the didactic style and even the cast of *The MacDermots* (imperilled landlord, more resolute son, policeman in love with daughter, all under threat from agrarian terrorists). The novel is not a propaganda tract for Unionism, though it sometimes seems like it. There is a silly but well-meaning Irish-American home rule MP, whose opera-singer daughter is going to marry the son and balance the plot out in the usual Trollope way. But in a lengthy chapter which is straight documentary, and which the ordinary novel-reader is 'advised to skip', Trollope shows himself absolutely unyielding on property rights – 'the laws for governing the world, which have forced themselves on the world's acceptance'[137] – and bitterly hostile both to the 'dual ownership' of the Liberal government's 1881 Land Act and to the peasant proprietary which was the Tory alternative. This is not just dissent from the New Liberalism, which the Irish Land Act is generally seen as heralding; it is a rejection of a society in which property can no longer be grounded in absolute title to land. This obsession with landed property left its mark. Although the inheritance-plot and the courting of heiresses rapidly recedes after 1886, when land came to have more cash-liabilities than 'rights and duties', the country house persisted – and to some extent still persists – as a setting for political activity: 'Bladesovery' as H. G. Wells called it, after the country house where, 'below stairs', George Ponderevo is brought up in *Tono-Bungay*.

Trollope's prosaic empiricism did not impede the psychological complexity of his characters. Their peculiarities mirror the misfit between community and individual. Eliot, Disraeli and Meredith used a more symbolic vocabulary, derived from German romanticism, directly and through Carlyle. The political life becomes part of a historical process tending, however vaguely, towards an absolute – a residue of their religious upbringing. To all three Goethe – himself of course the statesman-poet – stood at the point where metaphysics gave way to the possibility of perfectible society, something embodied in musical imagery.[138] Rufus Lyon's vision is like Eliot's own 'Choir Invisible':

> . . . in music . . . all obey and concur in one end so that each has the joy of contributing to a whole whereby he is ravished and lifted up into the courts of heaven. So will it be in that crowning time of the millennial reign, when our daily prayer will be fulfilled, and one law shall be written on our hearts . . .[139]

Meredith's Dr Shrapnel launches into an impassioned tirade about music;

organs are despotisms, 'your piano is the Constitutional bourgeois'; a brass band is true democracy:

> But free mouths blowing into brass and wood, ma'am, beat your bellows and your whifflers; your artificial choruses - crash, crash! your unanimous plebiscitums! Beat them? There's no contest: we're in another world; we're in the sun's world, - yonder![140]

This is too much for Rosamund Culling, and her garbled version brings Squire Romfrey round with his horsewhip. The musical image in Disraeli, powerful in *Sybil*, was still present, 'when, with Garibaldi's army in Italy' Lothair hears Theodora 'in a voice which might have maddened nations [sing] the hymn of Roman Liberty, the whole army ranged in ranks along the valley joining in the solemn and triumphant chorus'.[141]

In the 1870s Eliot's notion of harmony changed. In *Daniel Deronda* (1876) her Jewish pianist Klesmer turns on an obtuse Liberal MP, Mr Bult: 'We help to rule the nations and make the age as much as any other public men. We count ourselves on level benches with legislators. And a man who speaks effectively through music is compelled to something more difficult than parliamentary eloquence.'[142] What is speaking here is not the voice of harmony but that of an élite, and a racial one at that. Disraeli's contention that 'God works by races' received little credence in Britain until *Daniel Deronda* which, Dicey later wrote, made him aware for the first time of the power of race and nationality.[143] The eviction of religion coincided with the impact of Wagner: music as the vehicle for social confrontation, not for its resolution. Shaw regarded Wagner as the poet of the class struggle, and the last novels of the period seem to indicate that such supra-national themes were evicting realism and the 'condition of England'.[144]

Just when Disraeli returned to the 1830s with *Endymion* (1880), George Eliot deserted this period and British politics for contemporary life and Zionism, which had gained relevance from the options created by his foreign policy in the 1870s and from the efforts of Laurence Oliphant and Lady Strangford, widow of 'Coningsby,' to publicize the work of Emanuel Deutsch, the original of *Deronda*'s Mordecai.[145] Was this a sort of flight? Eliot seemed in *Middlemarch* to have balanced social intimacy and ideological change, but in *Deronda* political engagement, history and ideals moved away from England – just when British politics seemed, thanks to the Irish and the Nonconformists, increasingly pluralistic.[146] Eliot, like her Positivist friends, retreated from democracy, in her case into the Zionist strategy of converting the élite – something which offered peculiar scope for foreign exiles, upper-class reformers, and intelligent women within the *cosmopolis* of late-Victorian London.

This high-minded *milieu*, which Mrs Humphry Ward was shortly to annex, was closer to Disraeli's *illuminati* than to the puritan radicalism of Rufus Lyon.

About the intentions of his novels, Disraeli always remained a secret society of one. Impressionistic about Parliament, often more interested in *outré* alternatives to it, he was adept at suggesting menaces to the State. *Endymion* is an exception to this, being safe and rather dull. With the Rothschilds converted into Swiss bankers, the Semitic vision vanishes, and even the Secret Societies give up, but there are some odd parallels to *Daniel Deronda*. In both a proud discontented girl is faced with poverty, marries an English aristocrat for money, and then finds her soul through a platonic relationship and a great ideal. What Gwendolen Harleth finds through her patronage of Deronda, Myra Ferrars achieves by promoting her brother Endymion. The parallel can be pushed too far. Myra becomes Queen of France and Endymion Whig premier of England: *The Babes in the Wood* with a happy end, and an act of *pietas* to the memory of Disraeli's talented unhappy sister Sarah, with whom he had written such pantomimes, and his first political novel, half a century before.

Endymion starts well. The downfall of William Ferrars – his exile from politics to the old mansion of Hurstley, attempt at a comeback, frustration and suicide – has the psychological insight of Thackeray's *Henry Esmond*, while Endymion's start in a 'second-class government office' echoes Trollope's *Three Clerks*. But, after an attempt to sketch such new types of politician as the free-trader Thornberry (Cobden) and the railway magnate Vigo (Hudson), the story becomes a frame for a tedious picture-gallery of contemporaries – Metternich, Palmerston, Bismarck, Louis Napoleon – contributing *bon mots*, their own, alas, not Disraeli's.

Disraeli began *Endymion* shortly after writing *Lothair*. He continued it after his wife's death to recuperate from the troubles of his last years in office. The deficiencies of this over-long slack work can't, however, be put down to old age. His last work of fiction, posthumously published in 1905, shows him back to the tightness and pungency of the 1840s. This novel, of which only ten short chapters were written, is usually assumed to be about an unlovable hypocrite of a middle-class MP and is referred to by his name, *Falconet*. As Falconet resembles Gladstone, was this to be the last word in the battle of the century? Instead Disraeli produced something more intriguing, although not (for him) new. A mysterious unknown stranger whose goal seems to be international revolution makes an early entrance. Moving in the highest circles, he probes the weaknesses of civil society:

> Society is resolving itself into its original elements. Its superficial order is the result of habit, not of conviction. Everything is changing,

and changing rapidly. Creeds disappear in a night. As for political institutions, they are all challenged, and statesmen, conscious of what is at hand, are changing nations into armies.[147]

A darker note, after the pantomime of *Lothair* and *Endymion*, and although reminiscent of the 'thriller' element in *Sybil*, it prefigures the obsessions of a later generation of Conservative writers. It's almost as if John Buchan's Andrew Lumley, the Carlton Club's prince of darkness, were presenting his card.

NOTES

1 Quoted by A. O. J. Cockshut in 'Trollope's liberalism', in Tony Bareham (ed.), *Anthony Trollope* (London: Vision Press, 1980), p. 161.
2 See Bradford A. Booth, *Anthony Trollope: Aspects of His Life and Art* (London: Edward Hulton, 1958), p. 3.
3 John Sutherland, *Victorian Novelists and Publishers* (London: Athlone Press, 1976), p. 69.
4 See, for example, Henry Pelling, *America and the British Left* (London: Black, 1956), ch. 1; and Royden Harrison, *Before the Socialists* (London: Routledge, 1965), p. 75.
5 Booth, *Trollope*, pp. 3, 161; Watson, 'The Parliamentary novel', in *The English Ideology: Studies in the Language of Victorian Politics* (London: Allen Lane, 1973), p. 135.
6 Justin McCarthy and Mrs Campbell Praed, *Our Book of Memories* (London: Chatto & Windus, 1912), p. 2; M. E. Speare, *The Political Novel: Its Development in England and America* (New York: Oxford University Press, 1924), p. 185.
7 Asa Briggs, *Victorian People* (Harmondsworth: Penguin, 1965), p. 99.
8 Joseph Schumpeter, *Capitalism, Socialism and Democracy* (London: Allen & Unwin, 1943), pp. 290–1.
9 See Martin Wiener, *English Culture and the Decline of the Industrial Spirit* (Cambridge: Cambridge University Press, 1981), p. 8.
10 Trollope to George Eliot, 3 August 1866, in *The Letters of Anthony Trollope*, ed. N. John Hall (Stanford, Calif.: Stanford University Press, 1983), p. 346.
11 Fred C. Thomson, 'The genesis of Felix Holt', PMLA, vol. 74 (December 1959), p. 576.
12 C. T. Harvie, *The Lights of Liberalism* (London: Allen Lane, 1976), pp. 111 ff.
13 Gordon S. Haight, *George Eliot* (London: Oxford University Press, 1968), ch. 11.
14 See Sir George Young, 'The House of Commons in 1833', in A. O. Rutson (ed.), *Essays on Reform* (London: Macmillan, 1867), pp. 309 ff.
15 Notebook for *The Spanish Gipsy*, quoted in ibid., p. 577; for tragedy as a 'communal' possession, see Stang, *Theory of the Novel*, p. 34, and T. H. Green, 'An estimate of the value and influence of works of fiction in modern times', in *Works*, Vol. 3 (London: Longman, 1888), p. 25, and Angus Easson, 'Elizabeth Gaskell and the novel of local pride', *Bulletin of John Rylands Library*, vol. 67, no. 2 (1985), p. 700.

16　George Eliot, 'The Natural History of German Life', *Westminster Review*, vol. 66 (July 1856) reprinted in *Essays of George Eliot*, ed. Thomas Pinney (London: Routledge, 1968), p. 274.

17　cf. Arnold Kettle, '*Felix Holt*', in Barbara Hardy (ed.), *Critical Essays on George Eliot* (London: Routledge, 1970), p. 114.

18　R. H. Hutton, in *Spectator*, vol. 39, 23 June 1866, p. 258; Leslie Stephen, *George Eliot* (London: Macmillan, 1902), p. 155.

19　George Eliot, *Felix Holt*, ed. Fred C. Thomson (Oxford: Oxford University Press, 1980), pp. 368–9.

20　George Eliot to Frederic Harrison, 9 January 1866, in *Letters of George Eliot*, ed. Gordon A. Haight, Vol. 4, *1862–8* (New Haven, Conn.: Yale University Press, 1955), pp. 215–17.

21　John Blackwood to George Eliot, 26 April 1866, in ibid., p. 245.

22　Norman Vance, 'Law, religion and the unity of *Felix Holt*', in Anne Smith (ed.), *George Eliot* (London: Vision Press, 1980), p. 114.

23　Haight, *George Eliot*, pp. 45–6.

24　Eliot, *Felix Holt*, p. 31.

25　See Leslie Stephen, 'On the choice of representatives by popular constituencies', in Rutson, *Essays on Reform*, pp. 85–126.

26　Bernard Semmel, *The Governor Eyre Controversy* (London: MacGibbon & Kee, 1962), ch. 3.

27　Mentioned as 'that beastly Baptist Caliban', an epitome of the democracy loathed by the corrupt Henleigh Grandcourt, in George Eliot, *Daniel Deronda* (London: Blackwood, 1876), p. 245.

28　See Speare, *Political Novel*, p. 225.

29　Eliot, *Felix Holt*, p. 320.

30　John Morley (unsigned review) in *Saturday Review*, vol. 21, reprinted in Donald Carroll (ed.), *George Eliot: The Critical Heritage* (London: Routledge, 1971), p. 257.

31　Unsigned review in *Nation*, 16 August 1866, p. 127; reprinted in ibid., p. 273.

32　Unsigned review in *The Times*, 26 June 1866, p. 6; in Carroll, *Eliot*, p. 265.

33　Anthony Trollope, *North America* (New York: Knopf, 1951), p. 517.

34　Blackwood to Lewes, 24 April 1866, in *Letters of George Eliot*, Vol. 4, pp. 242–3.

35　Roy Foster, 'Political novels and nineteenth century history', *Winchester Research Papers in the Humanities* (1981), p. 22.

36　John Halperin, introduction to *Trollope Centenary Essays* (London: Macmillan, 1982); W. J. McCormack, introduction, to *Phineas Finn*, p. viii; John Halperin, *Trollope and Politics* (London: Macmillan, 1977), p. 18.

37　R. E. Polhemus, *The Changing World of Anthony Trollope* (Berkeley: University of California Press, 1968), p. 3.

38　Walter Bagehot, *The English Constitution* (London: Oxford University Press, 1928), p. 269.

39　Frederic Harrison, 'Disraeli' and 'Trollope', in *Studies in Early Victorian Literature* (London: Arnold, 1895), pp. 92, 208.

40　Sadleir, *Anthony Trollope* (London: Constable, 1927), p. 131.

41　F. E. Robbins, 'Chronology and history in Trollope's Barset and parliamentary novels', *Nineteenth Century Fiction*, vol. 5 (1950–1), p. 307.

42　Anthony Trollope, *The Small House at Allington*, Vol. 2, p. 358; *The Prime Minister* (London: Oxford University Press, 1938), Vol. 2, pp. 191–2.

43 Speare, *Political Novel*, p. 159; Booth, *Trollope*, p. 27; James Pope-Hennessy, *Anthony Trollope* (London: Jonathan Cape, 1971), p. 147; Briggs, *Victorian People*, p. 98.
44 The vocabulary of this attack – 'The genteel vulgarisms of a hairdresser's man' – seems to have been taken from an otherwise favourable review of *Lothair* by Frederic Harrison in the *Fortnightly Review*, vol. 13 (June 1870), pp. 654–67.
45 Owen Dudley Edwards, 'Trollope: the Irish writer', *Nineteenth Century Fiction*, vol. 38 (1983–4), p. 3.
46 ibid., p. 41.
47 Sadleir, *Trollope*, p. 136; and see Trollope, *North America*, p. 526.
48 Edwards, 'Trollope', p. 7.
49 Sadleir, *Trollope*, p. 141.
50 See William Donaldson, *Popular Literature in Victorian Scotland: Language, Fiction and the Press* (Aberdeen: Aberdeen University Press, 1986), p. 57.
51 Sadleir, *Trollope*, p. 143; contrast with Polhemus, *Changing World*, pp. 11–18.
52 John Cronin, 'Trollope and the matter of Ireland', in Tony Bareham (ed.), *Anthony Trollope* (London: Vision Press, 1980), p. 33.
53 Benjamin Disraeli, *Coningsby* (London: Longman, 1900), pp. 157–9.
54 Sadleir, *Trollope*, p. 166; and see Asa Briggs, 'Manchester, symbol of a new age', in *Victorian Cities* (Harmondsworth: Penguin, 1971), pp. 93 ff.
55 Geoffrey Best, 'The road to Hiram's Hospital: a by-way of early Victorian history', *Victorian Studies*, vol. 5, no. 1 (September 1961), p. 138.
56 Susan Chitty, *The Beast and the Monk* (London: Hodder & Stoughton, 1974), p. 110.
57 Thomas Carlyle, *Heroes and Hero-Worship* (Leipzig: Tauchnitz, 1916), p. 195.
58 ibid., pp. 263–4.
59 Compare Trollope's denunciation of this in his *New Zealander*, written in 1854, but only published Oxford: Oxford University Press, 1972, pp. 121–2.
60 See Olive Anderson, *A Liberal State at War* (London: Macmillan, 1967), pp. 134–8.
61 Cockshut, 'Trollope's liberalism', p. 171; Trollope, *Autobiography*, p. 93.
62 Tony Bareham, 'Patterns of excellence: theme and structure in *The Three Clerks*', in Bareham, *Trollope*, pp. 66 ff.
63 Trollope, *Autobiography*, p. 112.
64 ibid., p. 134; and see Harrison, *Studies in Early Victorian Literature*, p. 200.
65 Trollope, *Autobiography*, p. 155.
66 Speare, *Political Novel*, p. 219.
67 James Kincaid, *The Novels of Anthony Trollope* (Oxford: Oxford University Press, 1977), p. 174; Foster, 'Political novels', pp. 13–14.
68 Speare, *Political Novel*, p. 200.
69 Halperin, *Trollope and Politics*, p. 280.
70 Trollope, *Autobiography*, p. 138; James Bryce dissented. He found *North America* 'excellent' ('Anthony Trollope', in *Studies in Contemporary Biography* (London: Macmillan, 1903), p. 122).

71   Henry Adams, *The Education of Henry Adams* (New York: Houghton Mifflin, 1931), p. 120.
72   Trollope, *Autobiography*, p. 139.
73   Trollope, *North America*, p. 341.
74   ibid., p. 342.
75   ibid., p. 515.
76   ibid., p. 450–1.
77   Booth, *Trollope*, p. 20.
78   Trollope, *Autobiography*, p. 143.
79   See John J. Hagan, 'The divided mind of Anthony Trollope', *Nineteenth Century Fiction*, vol. 14 (June 1959), p. 23.
80   Anthony Trollope, *Phineas Redux* (London: Oxford University Press, 1937), Vol. 2, p. 306.
81   Harold Macmillan, *The Past Masters* (London: Macmillan, 1975), pp. 183 ff.
82   John Vincent, *The Formation of the British Liberal Party* (Harmondsworth: Penguin, 1972), pp. 57–62, 177–82.
83   Speare, *Political Novel*, p. 218.
84   Anthony Trollope, *The Prime Minister*, Vol. 2, pp. 320–2.
85   See Polhemus, *Changing World*, p. 144.
86   Foster, 'Political novels', p. 11.
87   John Sutherland, 'Trollope and St Paul's, 1866–70', in Bareham, *Trollope*, pp. 116–36; Sadleir, *Trollope*, p. 300.
88   Donald Southgate, 'From Disraeli to Law', in Lord Butler (ed.), *The Conservatives* (London: Allen & Unwin, 1977), p. 183.
89   Halperin, *Trollope and Politics*, p. 118.
90   Trollope, *Autobiography*, p. 243.
91   Unsigned review in *Atlantic Monthly*, vol. 26, pp. 249–51, August 1870.
92   Quoted in Robert Blake, *Disraeli* (London: Eyre & Spottiswoode, 1966), p. 520.
93   *Fortnightly Review*, vol. 13 (1870), p. 654.
94   Quoted in Blake, *Disraeli*, p. 526.
95   Benjamin Disraeli, *Lothair*, ed. Vernon Bogdanor (London: Oxford University Press, 1975), p. 69.
96   cf. Jerry Palmer, *Thrillers* (London: Edward Arnold, 1978), p. 86.
97   Foster, 'Political novels', p. 18.
98   Disraeli, *Lothair*, p. 91.
99   Michael Foot, 'The Good Tory', in *Debts of Honour* (London: Picador, 1980), p. 64.
100 Bogdanor, introduction to *Lothair*, p. xiv.
101 J. T. Ward, 'Michael Maltman Barry', *Scottish Labour History Society Journal*, no. 2 (1970), pp. 25–37.
102 Blake, *Disraeli*, p. 602.
103 Blackwood to Oliphant, 27 January 1865, reprinted in Mrs Gerald Porter, *William Blackwood and His Sons* (Edinburgh: Blackwood, 1898), p. 133.
104 Laurence Oliphant, *Piccadilly: A Fragment of Contemporary Biography* (Edinburgh: Blackwood, 1891), p. 74.
105 ibid., p. 30.
106 ibid., p. 249.
107 Rosemary Anne Taylor, *Laurance Oliphant* (London: Oxford University Press, 1982), pp. 190–1.

108 See B. Maidment, 'Victorian publishing and social criticism: the case of Edward Jenkins', *Publishing History*, vol. 11 (1982), pp. 41–57; and 'What shall we do with the starving baby: Edward Jenkins and *Ginx's Baby*', *Literature and History*, vol. 6, no. 2, (Autumn 1980), pp. 162 ff.
109 See G. S. Layard, *The Life of Mrs Lynn Linton* (London: Methuen, 1901), pp. 179–80.
110 ibid., p. 300.
111 ibid., p. 302; and see I. F. Clarke, *Voices Prophesying War* (London: Panther, 1969), pp. 1–2, 29–41.
112 J. F. Stephens, *The Censorship of Drama in England* (Cambridge: Cambridge University Press, 1979), p. 116.
113 ibid., p. 125.
114 ibid., pp. 121–4.
115 Quoted in Ellwood P. Laurence, '*The Happy Land*: W. S. Gilbert as a political satirist', *Victorian Studies*, vol. 15, no. 2 (December 1971), p. 167.
116 Maidment, 'What shall we do', p. 162.
117 Lucien Leclaire, *Le Roman régionaliste dans les Iles Britanniques, 1850–1950* (Clermont Ferrand: de Bursac, 1952), pp. 91–4.
118 Trollope, *The Prime Minister*, Vol. 1, p. 129.
119 ibid., p. 134.
120 Christopher Harvie, 'Ireland and the intellectuals', *New Edinburgh Review* (1977), pp. 35–44.
121 R. V. Comerford, *Charles J. Kickham* (Dublin: Wolfhound Press, 1979), p. 210.
122 Donaldson, *Popular Literature*, p. 3.
123 ibid., p. 26.
124 ibid, p. 92.
125 Nigel Cross, *The Common Writer: Life in Nineteenth Century Grub Street* (Cambridge: Cambridge University Press, 1985), p. 2.
126 Donaldson, *Popular Literature*, p. 134.
127 *Aberdeen Free Press*, 6 December 1876, p. 2.
128 Yvonne French, *Ouida: A Study in Ostentation* (London: Cobden-Sanderson, 1938), pp. 55, 104.
129 See my 'Gladstonianism, the provinces, and popular political culture', in Richard Bellamy (ed.), *Victorian Liberalism* (London: Methuen, 1989).
130 Moneypenny and Buckle, *Disraeli* (London: John Murray, 1929), Vol. 2, p. 504.
131 See *Letters of Anthony Trollope*, ed. N. John Hall (Stanford: Stanford University Press, 1983), p. 398.
132 Letter of Meredith, n.d. [1868] in *Letters of George Meredith*, ed. C. Cline (Oxford: Oxford University Press, 1970), pp. 356–7.
133 Arnold Kettle, '*Beauchamp's Career*', in Ian Fletcher (ed.), *Meredith Now* (London: Routledge, 1971), p. 200.
134 George Meredith, *Beauchamp's Career* (London: Constable, 1914), pp. 22–3.
135 ibid., p. 626.
136 George Meredith, *The Ordeal of Richard Feverel* (London: Constable, 1914), pp. 233–4.
137 Anthony Trollope, *The Land Leaguers* (London: Chatto & Windus, 1883), p. 153.
138 Jack Lindsay, *George Meredith* (London: Bodley Head, 1956), p. 27.

139   Eliot, *Felix Holt*, p. 131.
140   Meredith, *Beauchamp's Career*, pp. 20–1.
141   Disraeli, *Lothair*, p. 237.
142   Eliot, *Daniel Deronda*, p. 180.
143   Bryce MSS. Dicey to Bryce, 1914.
144   See George Bernard Shaw, *The Perfect Wagnerite*.
145   Haight, *George Eliot*, p. 470.
146   Graham Martin, '*Daniel Deronda*: George Eliot and political change', in Barbara Hardy (ed.), *Critical Essays on George Eliot* (London: Routledge, 1970), p. 150.
147   *Falconet* was published in *The Times* in 1905 and reprinted in Monypenny and Buckle, *Disraeli*, Vol. 2, pp. 1548 ff.

6

Revolutionaries and Elitists, 1886–1914

I

HERBERT HENRY ASQUITH, 'last of the Romans', premier in 1914, entered Parliament as Liberal MP for East Fife in 1886. His Finn-like career – obscure beginnings, Balliol, success at the Bar, marriage with an heiress, rapid promotion – showed an élite continuing to dominate by assimilation and manipulation. Its spectacular end, with his party overwhelmed by war and the Labour movement, belied fundamental insecurities. Prompted by a protracted economic depression, discontent had been growing – among the middle classes as foreign competition in industry increased, among the workers with the growth of trade unionism. Foreign wars and dynamic state intervention, the norm in Europe, took on a new salience and ultimately ended 'splendid isolation'. Ireland provided unnerving heroics throughout. Particularly in retrospect, politics attracted all too easily metaphors of 'thin crusts', and 'panes of glass' separating civil society from something much darker and more atavistic.

Carlyle and Wagner are lurking here. Less rhetorically, the continuing weakness of bourgeois civic humanism made it 'corruptible' by wealth or by the attractions of centralization, with the executive expertise of aristocrats, civil servants and proconsuls celebrated in the sonorous tributes of Rudyard Kipling. Yet, just as Kipling's poetry and Elgar's music are also pervaded by uncertainty and melancholy, this settlement left problems unsolved, crises postponed. When Henry James settled in Britain in the early 1880s he found the upper classes 'rotten and *collapsible*'.[1] He reconciled himself, but his friend H. G. Wells, so close to Trollope in the scope of his fiction, responded to Westminster in terms diametrically opposed to Trollope's veneration:

There in that great pile of Victorian architecture the landlords and the lawyers, the bishops, the railway men and the magnates of commerce go to and fro – in their incurable tradition of commercialised Bladesovery, of meretricious gentry and nobility sold for riches. I have been near enough to know. The Irish and the Labour-men run about among their feet, making a fuss, effecting little; they've got no better plans that I can see. Respect it, indeed! There's a certain paraphernalia of dignity, but whom does it deceive?[2]

If the collapse had been deferred, it would be all the more dramatic when it came.

The novel of high politics persisted, but without the confident tone of the mid-Victorians. Partisanship, pessimism and sensation seeped in. 'Insiders' found it difficult to write: Justin McCarthy, an MP in the 1880s, observed that the novelist 'carries all his materials within his own mind, and if his mind be disturbed by frequent interruptions the materials are apt to get scattered', something aggravated by the legislative 'congestion' of the House, and increasing party discipline.[3] Yet politicians took novelists and playwrights with ponderous seriousness. Marie Corelli's lurid fantasies were read by Gladstone *and* Salisbury, presumably attempting to fathom her readers, the new electorate, whose irruption out of board schools and new suburbs, 'ill-educated and only half-literate', posed, according to Richard Altick, 'a staggering problem of communication'.[4] Men like John Morley and Arthur Balfour grasped at fiction where their European contemporaries patronized sociology. Even that Muse of 'hard fact' Beatrice Potter was, in the 1880s, not only attracting George Eliot's former entourage, but also intending to write political novels.[5] This 'blending' may explain how the heterogeneity of its views never divided the literary world, as happened in Germany and France. There writers sympathized with the court or were *Sezessionists*, were Legitimists or Dreyfusards, but in Britain politico-literary connections had become even more intense by 1914.

II

No such settlement was in prospect in 1886, when economic and political crisis jeopardized the balance struck in the 1840s. Protectionism revived among the Tories. Liberals questioned the legitimacy of rent: provoked by urban poverty which threatened to make the 'East End' rise in a Jacquerie, propaganda for land taxes, and endemic discontent among the Celts. Gilbert and Sullivan's coy celebration of the two-party system in *Iolanthe* (1882) had uneasy references to Ireland. Agrarian violence drove the Chief Secretary, Trollope's friend W. E. Forster (the near-Chartist of 1848) to resign – after carrying his controversial Land Act. His more conciliatory successor, Lord Frederick Cavendish, was promptly murdered by terrorists. When its electorate was expanded by the 1884 Reform Act, Ireland became even more intractable, its peasantry replacing the last anglicized Liberals of the Phineas Finn type by a disciplined cadre of Nationalists under the implacable leadership of Parnell.

For the few who troubled to read it, one portent was the appearance in 1883, the same year as Trollope's *Land Leaguers*, of Bernard Shaw's *The Unsocial Socialist*, which rejoiced in what had appalled Trollope: capitalism on the defensive and economic radicalism popular for the first time since Owenism's day, in the shape of the doctrines of Marx, who had just died. Characteristically, it resembled a play reduced to prose. Its hero, Trefusis, an overbearing Shavian trapped by his own rhetoric, has an ambiguity foreign to Trollope or George Eliot, and a desire to communicate separates him from the word-bound characters of Meredith. If Trefusis is also callous and inhumane, Shaw blamed in determinist fashion the moral corrosion of the contemporary economy.

Shaw exemplified naturalism's cardinal sin against mid-Victorian fiction: presenting problems without solutions, crimes without punishments. He had defended the claims of Zola's novels and Ibsen's plays that fiction could be a type of political experiment, as legitimate as any treatise: something which implied a fundamental scepticism about politics and the compromises it involved. In 1884, Beatrice Potter read Auberon Herbert's 'brilliant' symposium *A Politician in Trouble with His Soul* and approved that Spencerian republican's preference for 'real Socialists' – 'I should feel it a true pleasure to be shot by a genuine Socialist – or to shoot him, as the matter may turn out' – over 'the modern politician, who smirks and bows like the draper's assistant, while he cheats us out of an inch in every yard'.[6] Did another of her circle, Joseph Chamberlain, the Radical leader, fit into this mould, as in 1885 he campaigned on the 'Unauthorized Programme' of disestablishing the Church of England, taxing land values, and creating provincial parliaments? Or did the future shape of politics lie in the East End problem, which shifted the universities and their products from traditional religious and political issues to economics, Oxford Liberals setting up Toynbee Hall where university men could learn about, and mitigate, the social question?[7]

Other middle-class commentators viewed such developments with misgivings: George Gissing, W. H. Mallock and Henry James published 'socialist problem' novels akin in apprehensiveness to those of 1848. 'If a tale of Socialism does not find abundance of readers', *The Times* commented of Gissing's *Demos* in 1886, 'it is not because the times are not ripe for it.'[8] Such ripeness pervaded even the entertainment literature of the time. Robert Louis Stevenson, who had flirted with radicalism as an Edinburgh student, restated the conservative view in possibly the most famous of all adventure-stories, *Treasure Island* (1883), in which a microcosm of English civil society faces a pirate proletariat, and reacted in *The Dynamiter* (1885) to the Irish challenge. He testified to the unease of the wealthy which his friend Henry James observed in 1886 in *The Princess Casamassima*:

> In these hours the poverty and ignorance of the multitude seemed so vast and preponderant, and so much the law of life, that those who had managed to escape from the black gulf were the happy few, people of resource as well as children of luck: they inspired in some degree the interest and sympathy that one should feel for survivors and victors, those who have come safely out of a shipwreck or a battle.[9]

Lionel Trilling placed the novel in the 'backbone' of English fiction, not because of its rather improbable plot, but because of the problem James identified, that 'of our not knowing, of society's not knowing, but only guessing and suspecting and trying to ignore, what "goes on" irreconcileably, subversively, beneath the vast smug surface'.[10] Although aspects of *The Princess Casamassima* remind one of *Sybil* – the aristo-proletarian at the centre, the conspiracy, the seduction of the country house, the symbol of Venice – in the 1840s the 'enemy' was patent, and manageable: the Chartists, the Irish. Now it was vague and vast, with tastes and ambitions obscure to the 'educated' – and only a mile or so from the West End. Poor Hyacinth Robinson is as baffled by it as he is impressed by the values of the upper classes. Felix Holt would have been less malleable, but James surrendered the enveloping social discourse of the mid-Victorians in favour of a cultural and political élitism, a conservative collectivism which commended itself to the Cold War 'liberals' - often ex-communists – who later defended Arnoldian culture against proletarian anarchy.[11]

As neither group had much notion of political community, they failed to see the real dimensions of 1886. The socialist threat never materialized; the bourgeois challenge collapsed. The thrust towards decentralization and land reform was pre-empted by Gladstone's crusade for Irish home rule – and the collapse of the 'radical' leader, Chamberlain, into a Unionist alliance. But did Gladstone will his own defeat – better a 'great moral issue' than 'positive' programmes which could only offend one section or another of the electorate?[12] Or was his an honest vision of an alternative, localized politics, eccentric to the dominant imperialism of the age, but attractive to those areas which had a democratic tradition – in Wales, Scotland and some of the English provinces?[13]

The year 1886 was one of those rather frequent occasions when the solidity of British political convention snatches stasis from the jaws of change. Unionism fused part of the bourgeoisie with the aristocracy élite to provide a stable élite with Dicey's *Law of the Constitution* as its bible.[14] Dicey had argued privately that, if home rule passed, parliamentary sovereignty would have to yield to a 'rigid' or written – and probably federal – constitution. He could now hold his line.[15] Lord Salisbury, the new Tory premier, spoke of the defeat of home rule as 'awakening the slumbering genius of imperialism'. Yet many home rulers were imperialists, such as Cecil Rhodes and the Round Table group, and 1886 postponed for good the transformation of Britain into a federal superstate along American lines.[16] Neal Ascherson, comparing the 1886 debates with the attempts to grant Scotland devolution in the 1970s, has written of Gladstone in 1886 as 'elastic and sovereign . . . what was only a general principle in 1886 has become a fixed taboo today . . .'.[17] The year 1886 was the constitutional equivalent to the 'short breath' that increasingly afflicted the economy. The commitment to constitutional change fossilized; the party machines gripped harder. With the Liberals now backing home rule, Irish nationalists waited patiently for the 'predominant partner' to take action, while assaulted by the Unionists, in part as the weak link in the Liberal alliance, in part out of sheer race prejudice.

The intellectuals tended either to support this or to retreat from politics. Some distrusted Gladstone as a High Churchman and demagogue; more cultivated the 'intellectual liberalism' almost caricatured in Leslie Stephen, once a fierce radical and now a combination of free-thinker and neurasthenic.[18] From their 'commanding heights' – the old universities, the editorial chairs, the front benches – they brooded about the 'new' public – clerks, teachers, shop-assistants. White-collar workers trebled to 7.1 per cent of the labour force between 1851 and 1911, worried, like small tradesmen, about big business and unionized labour, wanting instruction and security. The first could move them left, to adult education and radical politics; Toynbee Hall and the Fabian Society would map out the route of the talented to the leadership of the Labour movement, carrying on the Positivist alliance of 'brains and numbers'. The second was more likely to move them right. Literature would prove critical in both processes.[19]

Literature was anyway changing rapidly. Three-deckers and high prices were on the way out: a novel which cost 31*s* 6*d* (£1.58) in 1880 would be published at 7*s* 6*d* (38p) in 1895. Authors and publishers adapted because they gained American copyright in 1891 – a market of millions was opened up – and in 1894 publishers enforced on booksellers the net book agreement to fix prices. A corporatist capitalism, patrolled by legal and diplomatic convention, was set up which would last for over eighty years. The system was highly professionalized; the publisher's reader – such as Edward Garnett – being joined by the literary columnist and the literary agent.[20] But would the writers thus favoured reach the readers of Harmsworth's *Daily Mail* or Newnes's *Tit-Bits*? Meredith had been a power at Chapman & Hall, but he had turned down *East Lynne* in disgust. Not something any successor would be allowed to get away with.

III

Given that 1886 *was* a counter-revolution, literary reactions were diffuse. Instead of Trollope's republican virtue, there was silver-forkery with more or less of a social conscience. Radical polemic, like Shaw's novels or William Morris's *Dream of John Ball* (1886), was accessible in small and usually ailing periodicals. More painful individual explorations were also provoked into the clash between ideals and actuality, in the world of mature print-capitalism.

Into the first category falls *The Princess Casamassima*, W. H. Mallock's *The Old Order Changes* (1886) and, later on, novels by T. Fraser Rae and Mrs Humphry Ward. It's worth having a closer look at one such, Justin McCarthy and Mrs Campbell Praed's *The Right Honourable: A Romance of Society and Politics*, published in time for the division on home rule in June 1886, because, although long forgotten, it stayed in print until 1904.[21] Its politics was radical – McCarthy was an Irish nationalist MP – but it may have enjoyed its popularity because the romance between a radical leader and the wife of another MP bore a striking parallel to the private life of Parnell. Sandham Morse extricates himself from a blackmail conspiracy and thwarts a Conservative attempt to provoke a war, but not before a socialist friend is duped into leading an anti-war procession into Palace Yard and is accidentally killed in a clash with the police. The riot scene seems *de rigueur* for the period; business in the Palace goes on as usual. There is no allusion to Irish affairs, or to any democratic alternative to Westminster, although the hero is a former Australian state premier. Perhaps McCarthy showed how unrevolutionary the Irish MPs really were – he was to be instrumental in bringing down Parnell in 1890 – but his popularity shows the continuing attraction of the *milieu*.

George Gissing, a much more profound critic, had no illusions about 'those powers of dulness and respectability which seize upon the best men if folly lures them within the precincts of St Stephen'.[22] Nor had he any enthusiasm for the labour movement. 'I shall call it *Demos*', he announced in 1885 of his new novel (handed in to his publishers on the afternoon of Bloody Sunday), 'and it will be rather a savage satire on working-class aims and capacities.'[23] Yet his wilful isolation, his obsession with the means of literary production reflected the 'commodification' of literature, and in other respects – his anti-imperialism, his feminism, his republicanism – Gissing was on a left of sorts.[24] His predicament shows the problems which afflicted someone reared in the tradition of George Eliot in establishing central metaphors for mass society.[25] Gissing had briefly but enthusiastically been a Comtist, thanks to Frederic Harrison; but what had started out, in *Workers in the Dawn* (1880), as a tract against inequality became a deep pessimism about the whole of *Felix Holt*'s programme, which would simply produce 'a class created by the mania of education . . . whom unspeakable cruelty endows with intellectual needs whilst refusing them the sustenance they are taught to crave'. Eliot's signs of hope became for Gissing something 'blighting the whole social state'.[26]

Demos trailed the bequest of the three-decker: the inheritance-plot which gives the journeyman engineer, Richard Mutimer, the chance to set up a socialist community (of a rather antique Owenite sort) and marry an upper-class girl. A by-election fells him, and a conservative relative with the apt name of Eldon inherits, closes the community down and, after Mutimer's death in a riot, marries his widow. But *Demos* is less a polemic against socialism than an examination of political and literary stasis. Gissing characterizes Mutimer as coarse and ultimately dishonest, and personally identifies with the aesthete Eldon, but the socialist community works well enough, and seems to distance his heroine from Eldon's élitist complacency. The novel simultaneously affirms and rejects the *status quo*.[27]

No man who described the royal jubilee of 1887 as 'the most gigantic organised exhibition of fatuity, vulgarity and blatant blackguardism on record'[28] would have accepted Mallock's defence of the 'naturalness' of wealth and luxury, and Gissing's hatred of imperialism and his sympathy for women's rights are maintained (not, admittedly, with much artistic success) in *Denzil Quarrier*, originally *The Radical Candidate* (1892), and *Our Friend the Charlatan* (1901), with Conservative and neo-Darwinian villains much more unscrupulous than Mutimer.[29] *Denzil Quarrier*'s Ibsenite plot ends with his hero, now an MP, realizing that a friend whom he trusted has been instrumental in driving his wife to her death: 'Now I understand the necessity for social law!'[30] Gissing shared with Dickens, and later on with Orwell, the position that without the application of ethical principles politics would degenerate into animal destruction and violence. But to have 'social law' one must first have a society, and in this Gissing – like many others – was vague.

He will recur. In H. G. Wells's *New Machiavelli* he was, as Britten, a contrapuntal 'back-self' to Wells's progressivism. Wells criticized Gissing for allowing mundane pessimism to reduce his 'faithful presentation of life' to 'the genre of nervous exhaustion'.[31] But, although both authors were more ironic than their confessional style suggests, Gissing's reference to 'the crowd . . . At its best a smiling simpleton; at its worst a murderous maniac', was serious: among the intellectuals the menace of the mass age was a commonplace.[32] His isolation also led him to understand the *real* politics of the metropolitan intellectual – writing and publishing – *New Grub Street* (1891) in particular capturing the commercial pressures which destroyed artistic integrity. Gissing, as Frederic Jameson notes, finds it impossible to 'compose' in Lukacs' sense a political compromise. Like Carlyle, he couldn't touch bottom. He saw through the Positivists as well-heeled *rentiers*, academics or civil servants: his own almost wilful failure as a commercial writer dramatized the cash-nexus and class. He anticipates the social precision of Orwell and was surely one of the first to use the term 'lower middle class', in his study of Dickens.[33] But he saw neither solidity nor solidarity in class, neither philanthropy nor order in an élite. The intellectual would either end as a routine counter-revolutionary or be deposited by the division of labour in a corner of a segmented 'world of letters', his stance no longer one of 'engagement' but of 'failure'. Where the choice was between revolutionary Utopia (impossible) or 'commodification', 'renunciation was the intellectual's characteristic response'.[34]

IV

'Renunciation' was willed on William Hale White, 'Mark Rutherford', although his uncompromising radicalism left its mark on Edward Thompson, Edward Upward, Storm Jameson and Joyce Cary. Those who championed him as a consistent thinker and lucid stylist – André Gide, Trilling, Basil Willey, Donald Davie – detached his politics from his thought as either unimportant or transitory. With palpable effect. *The Revolution in Tanner's Lane* (1887), his study of the impact of French revolutionary radicalism on English nonconformity, figures not at all in E. P. Thompson's re-creation of that historical moment, *The Making of the English Working Class* (1965).

White, a senior civil servant in the Admiralty and the son of a parliamentary official, had campaigned for manhood suffrage in 1867, though greatly sceptical about Westminster. 'No dock labourer', he wrote in his autobiographical *Deliverance of Mark Rutherford* (1881): 'could possibly be more entirely empty of all reasons for action than the noble lords, squires, lawyers and railway directors whom I have seen troop to the division bell.'[35] This fierceness had not lessened by 1887. *The Revolution in Tanner's Lane*, a narrative of episodes in English radicalism between 1814 and 1840, was punctuated with expressions of an impudent, contemporary Jacobinism:

> . . . all the atrocities of the democracy heaped together ever since the world began would not equal, if we had any gauge by which to measure them, the atrocities perpetrated in a week upon the poor, simply because they are poor; and the marvel rather is, not that there is every now and then a September massacre at which all the world shrieks, but that such horrors are so infrequent. Again, I say, let no man judge communist or anarchist *till he has asked for leave to work*, and a 'Damn your eyes!' has rung in his ears.[36]

Far from making the usual Victorian equation of radicalism with drink, loose living and infidelity, White seems in total agreement with his revolutionaries, Zachariah Coleman and Jean Caillaud. These resemble his fellow-Bedfordian John Bunyan rather than Felix Holt: descendants of the regicides of 1649, commemorated with a similar mixture of Calvinist determinism and moral courage, when the 'intellectual aristocracy' was scaring itself stiff over a few outbreaks of Irish violence.

Yet the mood of White's *Revolution* is elegiac. In the second part of the book, set between 1820 and 1840, nonconformity becomes established. Comfortable ingratiating Mr Broad, of Tanner's Lane Chapel, Cowfold, abandons the people's cause. In an election over the Corn Law issue, he is only just saved from a drink-inflamed mob by George Allen, the son of one of Coleman's Jacobin friends. Broad dies disgraced, but his opponents, the Allens, oppressed by public opinion as formerly by spies and the gallows, decide to emigrate.

Davie's disillusioned conservative is discernible neither in the novels nor in the correspondence; yet, as Valentine Cunningham has convincingly argued, White skews nonconformist history to make Broad and Tanner's Lane Chapel much more conservative in 1840 than they would actually have been. Why?[37] Partly because the novel of radical politics still suffered the disadvantage that afflicted it in Chartist days: it could not end in optimism without denying the seriousness of the social situation, and thus tended towards stoicism. But White was also checked by contemporary politics. Nonconformity was courting the establishment; John Bright as well as Joseph Chamberlain had gone Unionist in 1886, and even the nonconformist Liberals who controlled the local 'caucuses' tended, under leaders like the Methodist Hugh Price Hughes, towards imperialism.[38]

Nonconformity, wrote the radical Methodist Edward Thompson in 1939, 'stood for an explosive force such as England had not known for more than two hundred years'.[39] But it did not ignite, and Thompson blamed its culture, an 'inexpressibly dull' world which scowled at Victorian literature, made *causes célèbres* of the cases of Dilke, Parnell and Wilde, and rejected theological innovations – like those which cost Hale White his preaching career.[40] It now quite suddenly embraced both metropolitan politics – the key date is 1894, the founding of the Free Church Federal Council – and literary capitalism. Most prominent among its chosen instruments was a tireless Scots minister, William Robertson Nicoll, who came south in 1886 to edit the *British Weekly*, which he followed up in 1891 with the *Bookman* and in 1893 with the *Woman at Home*.[41] Nicoll made himself the arbiter of the literary taste of organized nonconformity, the Liberal rank and file, housewives, and board-school-trained readers and pupil-teachers who sought guidance through the commercial book-market and proliferating cheap editions of the classics.

Such guidance Nicoll (writing in the *British Weekly* as 'Claudius Clear') duly gave: 'He praises a book, and instantly it is popular. He dismisses one, gently – and it dies . . . What Claudius Clear reads on Wednesday, half Scotland and much of England will be reading before the end of the week.'[42] The *Bookman* coincided with the agent–best-seller–author-as-personality mechanism, itself a second Scottish invasion of London publishing. Nicoll stage-managed the success of the Scottish Kailyard, whose leading writer, 'Ian MacLaren' (the Reverend John Watson, President of the Free Church Federal Council), sold over 7 million copies of his Scottish rustic moralities. He started J. M. Barrie on the road to becoming the wealthiest of all British authors.[43] Nicoll commercialized regionalism and made it tributary to the metropolis. Bennett, Hardy, Quiller-Couch, Birmingham and Barrie appear to follow on from Scott, Edgeworth and Galt, but not even Quiller-Couch, the most politically active, could make a functioning community of a Cornwall riven by industrial depression and a bounding tourist trade. Hardy, alert to the changing agricultural economy and to European history, omits any political dimension from his Dorset. In *The Dynasts* there is no level between the statesmen and generals and the rustics, powerless against higher authorities who might as well be Hardy's 'Spirits' as anyone else. To try to read local government into *The Mayor of Casterbridge* is self-evidently absurd.[44]

Nicoll promoted White, but could have been the Reverend Broad: his sectarian *politique* contradicted the revolutionary ideas of the Puritans and later of democrats like Mazzini. Nicoll could not accept *Clara Hopgood* (1895), where a girl from a puritan background yields up her own lover to her sister, who has borne an illegitimate child, goes as Mazzini's agent to Venice and dies there.[45] What Nicoll found immoral was, again, intriguingly manipulated in the 1950s. Irvin Stock, reflecting the

Trilling line, condemned its last lines, in which Baruch Cohen answers his little daughter's query:

> 'I had an Aunt Clara once, hadn't I?'
> 'Yes, my child.'
> 'Didn't she go to Italy and die there?'
> 'Yes.'
> 'Why did she go?'
> 'Because she wanted to free the poor people of Italy who were slaves.'[46]

Stock writes: '. . . the obliteration of the act which most completely expressed her nature, and might well have crowned her life with glory (her renunciation of her lover), is a second death.'[47] But this rings false. Cohen's lines and Clara's action are in the puritan tradition – putting duty before personal satisfaction – as in Mazzini's advice to Clara: 'Whenever real good is done, it is by a crusade; that is to say, the cross must be raised and appeal be made to something above the people. No system based on rights will stand. Never will society be permanent until it is founded on duty.'[48] Davie claims this as a statement of White's conservatism, but it comes from White's memory of his own encounter with Mazzini, in the company of W. J. Linton: no abdication of radicalism, but a presentation of its metaphysical nature in the mid-nineteenth century, now overlaid by the numbing effectiveness of metropolitan politics.

V

The success of Mary Augusta Ward suggests a third response to the crisis. As the grand-daughter of Arnold of Rugby and the niece of Matthew Arnold, she was at the heart of the intellectual aristocracy and almost as representative of her generation as Trollope had been of his.[49] Uncle Forster had passed the 1870 Education Act and been Irish Secretary, 'the man of Quaker training at grips with murder and anarchy';[50] she had assisted the Liberal triumph at Oxford, knew all of its leading figures (Morley and Harrison, inevitably, included); she took Henry James under her wing when he finally settled in England in the early 1880s, even before the publication in 1888 of *Robert Elsmere* transformed her from the translator of Amiel into a bestseller.[51] *Elsmere* prompted Gladstone to agonize publicly over the portrayal of the conflict, in and around Oxford, of faith and doubt in what was really a silver-fork novel cum painless introduction to mid-Victorian intellectual history. The 'civic virtue' preached by T. H. Green (Professor Grey in the novel) sends Elsmere out of the Church to preach a 'social gospel' in the East End, where he dies – rather like Alton Locke, bequeathing a 'Christian Socialism' akin to internal imperialism on Toynbee Hall lines. Thereafter Mary Ward went well ahead of Disraeli, with an income of £20,000 from *David Grieve* in 1892, and showed how a radical impulse – the waning of orthodox religious belief – could become a useful prop for centralized élitist politics.

Of Mary Ward's casts, Gwynn remarked that it was 'characteristic of her . . . to show lovingly how much they have', something manifest in her political novels.[52] The first of these, *Marcella* (1892), concerned the maturing of an impulsive young woman from a decayed and disreputable landed family, who breaks with her aristocratic fiancé, Aldous Raeburn, when he refuses to help reprieve a poacher condemned for murdering a gamekeeper. She then links herself to a radical MP through the Venturist Society, only to find that his gambling debts make him sell out his working-class allies. Working as a nurse in the East End, she is threatened by a drunken husband, only to be rescued by Raeburn, whom she then marries.

Mary Ward never left it to the reader to infer her views. Before (finally) engaging herself to Raeburn, Marcella reviews the state of her radical ideals:

> She had ceased to take a system cut and dried from the Venturists, or anyone else; she had ceased to think of whole classes of civilised society with abhorrence and contempt; and there had dawned in her that temper which is in truth implied in all the more majestic conceptions of the State – the temper that regards the main institutions of every great civilisation, whether it be property, or law, or religious custom, as necessarily, in some degree, divine and sacred. For man has not been their sole artificer! Throughout there has been working with him 'the spark that fires our clay'.[53]

Out of this Burkeian Conservatism, Beatrice Webb, a possible original for Marcella, was able to prise a commitment to social reform: 'I especially admire your real intellectual impartiality and capacity to give the best arguments on both sides, though naturally I am glad to see that your sympathy is on the whole with us on those questions.'[54] Feminist writers have also attributed independence and integrity to Mary Ward's heroines, despite their submissiveness in the ostensible plot. But both miss the main point. Mary Ward opposed female suffrage because she accepted Positivist élitism, modified it in a collective direction and radically curtailed whatever democratic content it had.

The issue which leads Marcella to break with Raeburn, the hanging of the poacher Hurd, was a metaphor for the politics of the 1880s. On the edge of starvation, with an ailing family, Hurd was goaded by Raeburn's keeper and when surprised by him and another keeper, fired in self-defence. The gang Hurd was with fatally wounded the other keeper, who still lived long enough to incriminate Hurd. Marcella is struck by Hurd's manner:

> He did not look afraid or cast down – nay, there was a curious buoyancy and steadiness about his manner for the moment which astonished her. She could almost have fancied that he was more alive, more of a *man* than she had ever seen him – mind and body better fused – more at command.[55]

In Trollope's *The MacDermots of Ballycloran*, Thady kills Myles Ussher, through a similar combination of impulse and maturing predisposition. Mary Ward depicts Hurd as a rebel rather than as a criminal, a man – half-Irish for a start – who reads Marcella's Venturist tracts and brews his grievances into a homicidal resistance, in which 'a life which was not merely endurance pulsed in him'.[56] Hurd, like Thady, personifies the Irish predicament, but Ward's empathy is more limited than Trollope's. Hurd is not just Ireland but democracy: misinstructed and dangerous; to be handled firmly and – for its own good – without sentiment. When Marcella petitions for his reprieve, Raeburn takes his father, Lord Maxwell's line: 'I should be not only committing a public wrong, but I should be doing what I could to lessen the safety and security of one whole class of my servants – men who give me honourable service – and two of whom have been so cruelly, so wantonly hurried before their Maker!'[57] Ward took her details from a double murder of gamekeepers which occurred at Stocks, the Buckinghamshire estate she bought in 1892, shortly before she moved there. She discussed the reprieve of the murderers with the Home Secretary, Henry Matthews, so Lord Maxwell's views are presumably his. Maxwell is, in this sense, an embodiment of the Conservative ideal of justice, akin to Robert Louis Stevenson's Lord Weir of Hermiston, taking shape, at the time that Ward wrote, in far Samoa. Much more directly, Aldous Raeburn is Arthur Balfour, the intellectual aristocracy's gift to politics as Chief Secretary for Ireland. Mary Ward had met Balfour when he reviewed a posthumous volume of T. H. Green, and was plainly bowled over by him: 'As I look back on those five dramatic years culminating first in the Parnell Commission, then in Parnell's tragic downfall and death, I see everything grouped round Mr Balfour.'[58] She went on to laud his rectitude and chivalry and insouciance:

> His nerve struck me as astonishing, and the absence of any disabling worry about things past. 'One can only do one's best at the moment,' he said to me once, *à propos* some action of the Irish government

which had turned out badly – 'if it doesn't succeed, better luck next time! Nothing to be gained by going back on things.'[59]

One wonders what the 'action' was. Mary Ward's husband was a leader-writer on *The Times*, which Balfour had deeply involved in the 'Parnellism and Crime' fabrications.[60] The Irish (who appreciated Arthur's brother Gerald as a sympathetic Chief Secretary) had another view of the man who suspended their civil liberties and tried to discredit their leaders. But she was not the last to make Balfour a philosopher-king of British Conservatism. Fictional Balfours were still being turned out in the 1970s: urbane, pragmatic, slightly world-weary, and probably a lot more attractive than the real thing.[61]

Mary Ward was clever enough about Westminster to guide Henry James around when he was writing *The Tragic Muse*, and both *Marcella* and its sequel *Sir George Tressady* show an ability – like that of Disraeli in *Sybil* – to present social problems while leaving the initiative with the establishment. In *Sir George Tressady*, Marcella, now Lady Maxwell, rescues a luckless coal-owning baronet from an extreme right-wing party run by Lord Fontenoy (Lord Randolph Churchill) and gets him to back Maxwell's anti-sweating bill. Tressady is swept away (like Robert Elsmere, but in his case by a mine disaster) before he can quite accept his creator's line, tactfully conveyed by Gwynn: 'The collectivist and authoritarian view has much to commend it to the instincts of a trained governing class: in a word . . . Tory socialism is a very defensible combination.'[62]

Ward's keynote is 'the new cleavage of parties . . . everywhere brought about by the pressure of the new collectivism'.[63] In *Sir George Tressady* there are now four, from left to right: Socialists, Conservatives, 'Old Liberals' and Fontenoyites, with the Conservatives, under Maxwell, buying off the socialist threat with *étatiste* reforms, and the Irish obligingly vanishing. One of the Fontenoyites grumbles, 'The hands are the hands of the English Tory, the voice is the voice of Karl Marx'[64] – an early appearance of the good doctor in an 'establishment' novel.[65] Again Ward reflects the grasp of Marxism shown by Balfour and his circle, and their willingness to use state power (as long as it was *their* state) to frustrate the left.

But was this what millions read her novels for? *Robert Elsmere* certainly chimed in with the shift away from revealed religion which Beatrice Webb noticed in 1884.[66] But Ward had also discovered the appetite of the English and American reading public for upper-class life and gave it what it wanted. Roy Foster's epithet, 'George Eliot with the literature left out', may be unkind but it does stress Mary Ward's relentlessness and her limitations. Gwynn, arguing that 'she would sooner found an influential sect than write a superbly good book', thought her spoilt undereducated marriage-market girls, like Letty Tressady, well done, but the rest merely animated points of view.[67] But her politics was seriously meant. Neither Disraeli's outrageous drama nor Eliot's psychological insight was apposite for a proconsular age, not noted for levity,[68] and Ward's house-parties (in real life and in her books) composed an otherwise undistinguished political generation into the image of a Platonic élite, infinitely satisfying to itself.

The victory of 1886 personalized establishment values in the image of the administrator as hero – Balfour in Ireland or Alfred Milner, Toynbee's friend and Morley's protégé, in Balliol, Toynbee Hall, the Civil Service and South Africa. Milner appealed not only to imperialists like Kipling and Buchan; his Bismarckian emphasis on 'national efficiency' made him the prototype of the scientific élite – the Samurai – which the socialist H. G. Wells saw as essential to reform: fusing the poetic quality of adventure to the claim of administrative competence. He practised what the Italian sociologist Gaetano Mosca set out in theory: the superior manoeuvrability of the small expert group. Milner fitted into a frame prepared by the likes of Ward, and the incense of the *religio Milneriana* drifted over to the centralist Fabian left.[69]

VI

Mary Ward's paternalism was not – given her numerous anti-suffrage interventions – supposed to be politics at all. She so infuriated Wells that he and one of his mistresses made love on top of a copy of *The Times* bearing one of her articles. But even in the 1900s her 'house-party' ethos, however reactionary, could obsess him, in the image of Bladesover, the great house at the beginning of *Tono-Bungay*. What, therefore, had happened to the radicals? Even Hale White belonged to the élite, as Director of Contracts at the Admiralty. Although his pacifist convictions revolted, and led to perennial depressions, he stayed until he retired. His problem was the recurrent one of divided loyalties: tactical affiliation to a state system in which no personal confidence was placed. But what alternatives were there?

John Morley, starting from the same middle-class provincial background as White and Gissing, took the direct way out of their dilemma. Gissing commented on his 'unscrupulous ambition', and there's probably something of him (besides the initials) in Jasper Milvain in *New Grub Street*: a recycled and domesticated Carlyle. Mary Ward derived the morality of *Robert Elsmere* from his *On Compromise* of 1874, where 'the coarsest and most revolting shape which the doctrine of conformity can assume' was the adoption of holy orders in the absence of belief.[70] As reader for Macmillan and editor of the *Fortnightly*, 1866–80, he was close to Harrison, Meredith, Trollope, Matthew Arnold and Leslie Stephen. He then made perhaps the most rapid political ascent of the century, entering Parliament in 1883 and Gladstone's Cabinet in 1886.

Here the resemblance to Carlyle ends. As a literary patron Morley turned down the first works of Hardy, Shaw and Yeats. No fricative force, he was the type of politician who ascends through his skill as a literary organizer – a homogenizer of party politics and the world of letters. His successors, C. F. G. Masterman, John Buchan, John Strachey, Richard Crossman, Michael Foot, were mainly to be found on the left; assiduously polishing the memory of the statesmen whom they helped create – Gladstone, Lloyd George, Aneurin Bevan – and thus editing their political principles. Morley ought, as home ruler, to have embodied republican decentralization. He did not. Deeply élitist, his earlier republican phase was simply, as Tom Nairn has pointed out, an inoculation against the real thing to provide parliamentary sovereignty with its imagination, applying the psychological insights of the mid-century novel, with all the energy of Disraeli.[71]

Morley opposed 'positive' programmes for the Liberals, as this threatened the party's broad base, which extended from manufacturers to trade unionists, from churchmen to nonconformists.[72] Instead he advocated 'great moral issues' and charismatic leaders, first Gladstone, and after 1894 the Earl of Rosebery (a protégé of Disraeli in his *Lothair* phase, married to a Rothschild). Rosebery was a failure, but Morley's superb biography, published only three years after Gladstone's death in 1898, powerfully aided the Liberal revival between 1900 and 1906. Morley on Gladstone is apologia rather than history,[73] conveying little trace of Gladstone's psychological complexity, religious pedantry and powerful sexuality.[74] When Carlyle wrote *Heroes and Hero-Worship* in 1840, he lamented that hero-worship had 'gone out': ' "He was the creature of the Time, " they say; the Time called him forth, the Time did everything, he nothing – but what we, the little critic, could have done too.' With an optimism beyond Carlyle, Morley restated the heroic as power-worship for the Liberals. The party was 'dry dead fuel, waiting for the lightning out of Heaven that shall kindle it'. The leader was the 'free force direct out of God's own hand' that would do the trick.[75]

Gladstone and Disraeli had dealt in epics, *and* centralized and systematized politics. Carlyle was ingested into this process of establishing the pilgrimages of the parliamentary career as the norm, creating Sidonias for the mass parties. There were more mundane reasons. State papers were closed to researchers; colleagues and families wanted commemorations; party machines could sell books. Serious analysis was left to foreign scholars, to Mosei Ostrogorski in his *Democracy and the Organisation of Political Parties* (1902) or Laurence Lowell in *The Government of England* (1908). The bones of British political instruction were the grand generalizations of Dicey and a few maxims from Bagehot (back in favour in the 1890s), and the flesh was Parker's *Peel*, Trevelyan's *Macaulay* and above all Morley's *Gladstone* – homily, practical instruction, and apotheosis of the adversary system.

VII

'The best people in every party converge', says H. G. Wells's fictional Balfour in *The New Machiavelli*, not wholly to the taste of Wells's hero Remington, who believes that 'there is no real progress in a country, except a rise in the level of its free intellectual activity'.[76] Where it could not co-opt it, the sheer wealth and organization of establishment political culture had pushed dissent to the margins, even though this was a period of remarkable intellectual innovation, in psychology with Freud, in anthropology with Frazer, and in politics with the rise of pluralist ideas associated with F. W. Maitland, J. N. Figgis and Ernest Barker.[77]

Checked from any access to power, the responses of the unrepresented fluctuated between fantasy, flippancy and pessimistic realism. In Ireland the revival of Celtic mythology – partly in reaction to the collapse of political initiatives on the fall of Parnell – evolved into the *Blut und Boden* of Patrick Pearse. The bleak pessimism of Somerville and Ross's *The Real Charlotte* coexisted with the humour of *The Irish RM* and the novels of George Birmingham, which paid. To someone inspired by Ibsenite social drama, like James Joyce, the result was the stasis depicted in 'Ivy Day in the Committee Room' in *Dubliners* (1914). His Nationalist organizers drink their warm stout and recite their awful poems, like servants setting the scene for some Nordic tragedy. But there is no tragedy. *Nothing is going on.*

Nonconformity immured itself behind Sunday-school prize books, churned out by Silas K. Hocking and W. E. Tirebuck, pietism spiced with only the faintest traces of Bunyan and Carlyle. In Scotland, Nicoll quickly captured intellectual discontent – notably the real, and politically–informed, talent of J. M. Barrie – for the rewards of the Kailyard. Catholicism proved more impervious. W. H. Mallock continued as an extreme conservative, even assaulting Mrs Humphry Ward, in *The Individualist* (1899) as a crypto-socialist; Frederick Rolfe's *Hadrian the Seventh* (1900) created a peculiar but in its own way convincing mixture of ritualism, homosexuality, clerical intrigue and *Weltpolitik*; and throughout the 1900s Hilaire Belloc shelled what he saw as an over-centralized political system with regular satires. Although hurriedly written and ephemeral in Belloc's hands, this critique gained coherence and plausibility in the fantasies of G. K. Chesterton, whose *The Napoleon of Notting Hill* (1906) combined a satire on centralized politics with an attack on monistic philosophy. But the idea of the small state remained metaphysical; the facts of Catholic politics were metropolitan.

The suffrage movement was more promising as, lacking access by definition to Parliament, literature had a vital function in structuring its activities. The Women Writers' Suffrage League, founded in 1908, was the first of many 'politicized' writers' groupings.[78] It followed the success of Elizabeth Robins, the Ibsen actress, in writing and producing the play *Votes for Women*, and then rewriting it as a novel, *The Convert*, in 1907. The drama is set in Mrs Humphry Ward's *milieu*, but its spirit is far more aggressive: a suffragist blackmails a cabinet minister into supporting the campaign by threatening to reveal that, ten years earlier, he had got her pregnant and she had had an abortion. *Votes for Women* is very tough-minded. Its broad social sweep stressed that women of whatever class were subject to a repression which was simultaneously sexual and social. In comparison, Barrie's *What Every Woman Knows* (1908) was clever pro-suffrage propaganda, effective in its portrayal of a successful politician who owes everything to a strong-minded wife, but inhibited by Barrie's avoidance of any sexual theme. Women's political literature made a real effort to cross class boundaries and reach a mass audience. If Gissing in the 1880s had lit on the commodification of literature, he was also aware of the commodification of women, and of the consciousness of alienation and exploitation which could unite the causes of middle- and working-class women. Moreover, since women were reasonably well represented on the stage, their 'consciousness-raising' sketches stole a march on the novel and anticipated political theatre as it developed between the wars.

VIII

The feminists were one portent, the growing number of socialists another. The latter had retreated into the Utopias of Bellamy and Morris in the 1890s, but now began to imitate the increasing confidence and articulacy of their Continental comrades, particularly in the revolutionary year of 1905. Besides Marx, Nietzsche, Kropotkin and Tolstoy contributed to what John Carswell has called 'a kind of Thebaïd filled with seekers and pedlars of new quasi-religious formulations', and required interpreters.[79] This was the period of Shaw's dominance in the Vedrenne–Barker seasons at the Royal Court, and Wells's shift from dystopic science fiction to social forecasting, of Blatchford's *Clarion* and Orage's *New Age* – boosted both by the Liberal landslide in 1906 and the sharp economic depression which succeeded it.

The results of this enthusiasm were ambiguous, its most significant bequest not being published until 1914, after its author's death, and then in a garbled form. Robert Tressell's *The Ragged Trousered Philanthropists*, written between 1906 and 1909, became 'the book that won the 1945 election for Labour', and indeed its sales in the interwar years were remarkable when compared with fiction written at the time – even compared with *The Iron Heel* or *News from Nowhere*.[80] Its mixture of didactics and accurate description of the life of skilled working men packed a powerful charge, although it was only half of a longer and more impressive work. Tressell – his real name was Robert Noonan, and he may have been from the Crokers', the Ascendancy family which provided Disraeli's Nicholas Rigby – has no time whatever for the political system the workers of Mugsborough are deceived as 'philanthropists' into supporting. Elections are a circus, local government and nonconformity are frauds, the unions are impotent. Tressell's view may have been affected by the fact that his health drove him from South Africa, where the skilled worker was in a seller's market, to Hastings, politically the most conservative town in Britain (the only one to shift to the Tories in 1906); nothing of his Irish nationalism survived, beyond an identification with the underdog. He had transferred his nationality to revolutionary socialism.

What precedents were there for Tressell's book? The didactic fiction of Chartism, the *Clarion*, Jack London's *People of the Abyss* (1903) and *The Iron Heel* (1907) – and perhaps the 'conversion' books published by religious bodies. Tressell can, however, be placed pretty accurately as an activist in the new wave of agitation, the generation which rejoined or expanded the militant socialist organizations, backed the campaigns of Victor Grayson, the 'lost leader' of the British left, and attended the Sunday-afternoon lectures of John MacLean in Glasgow. Not a group given to reading novels, which they considered as misleading as Cobbett had done sixty years earlier, they broke both with the 'literary humanism' of the older Labour activists and with bourgeois political systems of any sort.

A figure like Noonan's hero Owen would be instantly recognizable in the interwar Communist Party: enthusiastic, dogmatic, incorruptible and tied as firmly to the Kremlin line as his father might have been to papal infallibility. Joseph Conrad, reviving James's obsession with the subterranean currents of metropolitan life, must have had such extremism in mind as he wrote *The Secret Agent* in 1907. On one hand he noted the understated confidence of the British élite, embodied in the Assistant Commissioner who ushers the Russian *agent provocateur* out of the country; on the other he could identify with those who, like Mr Vladimir or the anarchist Professor, 'saw Europe from the other end' and like them took the streams of political mass-action seriously. In comparison with this reality, the political ease of the British was a diminishing asset.[81]

IX

Conrad dedicated *The Secret Agent* to H. G. Wells, at this point right at the centre of the English literary world – the friend of Bennett, James and Madox Ford, and the *enfant terrible* of the Fabians. In 1904, Meredith, no less, had tried to get him to write a novel about political life, 'The Knight-Errant of the Twentieth Century'. Meredith's Quixote was 'a man immensely rich, imbued with Herbert Spencer's ideas, full of the all-importance of the future and its problems, always dwelling in them, always working on them'.[82] The result appeared six years later. Wells's *The New Machiavelli* is still controversial. He regarded it as his best work to date, yet his publisher refused it, and Wells himself later disowned it. Most critics regard it as the first of many wordy reports on the great test match of HG versus the world. Yet, when much of the 'best' Wells is little read – social change having destroyed the environment of *Kipps* (1905) and *Mr Polly* (1910) – *The New Machiavelli* still looms up like one of those vast Edwardian buildings in Whitehall: a very good novel indeed, delivering a subtle critique of a politics which, while superficially healthy, was in fact heading towards a chronic crisis.

The New Machiavelli is a sequel to that other impressive panorama-novel *Tono-Bungay* (1908) as part of Wells's conscious attempt to emulate Dickens's succession of socially critical novels – *Little Dorrit*, *Bleak House*, and *Our Mutual Friend* – adding the consistency of Trollope's *The Way We Live Now*. Together, the two novels show a remarkable attempt to assess the 'fit' between political institutions and contemporary society. In *Tono-Bungay*, Wells presents his Merdle or Melmotte: a fraudster's career which exposes the social corruption which permits it. But Edward Ponderevo, the promoter of Tono-Bungay, 'slightly injurious rubbish at one and three halfpence a bottle', is attractive in comparison with the earlier villains; the society he exploits less predatory than catatonic. Wells's handling of this huge canvas, from lower-middle-class life in London suburbs to the Conradian environment of George Ponderevo's quest for Quap, is always assured. *Tono-Bungay*'s *polis* comprehends themes salient since 1886: science, wealth, 'enterprise', publicity. Politics seems both incidental and mystifyingly malignant. When, at the end of the novel, the inventor, George Ponderevo, steers his new destroyer down the Thames, 'passing all England in review', his meditations suggest a further series of hostilities: against Parliament.

Wells, hitherto somewhat authoritarian, was 'democratized' by the Liberal landslide in 1906 – seeing it as part of an international 'progress-ive' movement – and examining the British political system's adaptability in his Fabian 'New Heptarchy' project convinced him of the need for 'appropriate areas of government' – a 'civic humanism' very much on

Machiavellian lines.[83] But he also knew the power of nationalism and authoritarianism in an epoch of mass political mobilization. He knew the popular press and the effect of invasion-scare and socialist-scare novels. Indeed, he had contributed to both genres. *The War of the Worlds* echoes Chesney's *Battle of Dorking*, and many of the more hysterical productions of Le Queux and Ernest Bramah were triggered by the social and sexual radicalism of his own *Anticipations*. He also knew the authoritarianism latent in Fabian socialism, but acquired, through his friendship with Graham Wallas, something of the patient analytical quality of his *Human Nature in Politics* (1908).

Even the sexual theme of *The New Machiavelli* is implicated in politics, in the storm which surrounded the banning of Harley Granville-Barker's *Waste* in 1907. A radical politician is destroyed by a sexual scandal and betrayal by his cabinet colleagues: this theme was deemed by the censor too strong for the West End, already, like the politics of London in general, curdling into conservatism. Wells took part in a private protest performance, and the shadow of Henry Trebell lay long on the career of Richard Remington.[84]

X

The New Machiavelli got a bad press from the first. Henry James wrote in overwrought terms to Wells that he was 'riding so hard that accurst autobiographic form'. There could be 'no authentic and no really interesting and no *beautiful*, report of things on the novelist's, the painter's part, unless a particular detachment has operated . . .'.[85] Yet Wells's programme was as logical as Trollope's in the Palliser novels. *The New Machiavelli* is an inquiry into political institutions counterpointed by a love-plot. Remington states the problem at the beginning – describing the chaos of Bromstead – and then proceeds to narrate his own pilgrimage through the institutions of socialization and political life: the grammar school, Cambridge, industrial capitalism in the shape of his uncle's pottery firm, the Fabian Society, the Liberal and Conservative parties, elections, Parliament, and political journalism. Behind him he had, like Trollope, his American travels, and he had also Wallas's account of habitual and non-rational political behaviour – derived, ironically, from Henry James's brother William. Remington's love-life is, as 'human nature', integrated with this programme. The sexual drive collides with the political and deflects it – Remington abandons an intellectual walking tour with Willersley (Wallas) to have an affair at a Swiss hotel – but can also concentrate it, when a Russian prostitute tells him about repression in her homeland. Wells sees sexual openness as a gain to both men and women, but he allows Remington to be contradicted by Britten (Gissing), for whom sex remains, with chance and death, one of the eternal uncontrollables.

As autobiography, *The New Machiavelli* would be valuable for the picture it gives of the British élite, put over with great detail and wit, but Wells distances himself from his intrusive and opinionated narrator. Stevenson and James had played around with first-person narration in the 1890s to make the reader feel disquiet about what he's being told. And Remington seems by no means reliable. He tells us how feminist he is, and how intelligent his mistress Isabel is, but he hardly allows any of his women a word. He justifies his change of party in lofty terms -- 'love and high thinking' – and then records a Tory dinner party at which he is reviled by the Tory right: proof, if any were needed, of the hopelessness of his cause.

Such a dinner apparently happened, but Wells orchestrates it superbly into an episode which, like the Duke of Omnium's confession, justifies the genre. The upper storeys of the house are burning, the dinner-guests are drunkenly recounting the European sack of Peking, fire-men tramp about upstairs and dirty water drips from the ceiling. To Evesham (Balfour), Peking proves the fragility of civilization: 'a mere thin net of habits and associations!'; all Remington's insecurities surface in Freudian style as 'a break in the general flow of experience as disconcerting to statecraft as the robbery of my knife and the scuffle that followed it had been to me when I was a boy at Penge'. He is assaulted by his 'back-self' in the shape of a 'little shrivelled don':

'Got to rec'nize these facts,' said my assailant. 'Love and fine think'n pretty phrase – attractive. Suitable for p'litical dec'rations. Postcard, Christmas, gilt lets, in a wreath of white flow's. Not oth'wise valu'ble.'

I made some remark, I forget what, but he overbore me.

'Real things we want are Hate – Hate and *coarse* think'n. I b'long to the school of Mrs. F's Aunt —'

'What?' said some one, intent.

'In "Little Dorrit",' explained Tarvrille; 'go on!'

'Hate a fool,' said my assailant.

Tarvrille glanced at me. I smiled to conceal the loss of my temper.

'Hate,' said the little man, emphasising the point with a clumsy fist. 'Hate's the driving force. What's m'rality? - hate of rotten goings on. What's patriotism? – hate of int'loping foreigners. What's Radicalism? – hate of lords. What's Toryism? – hate of disturbance. It's all hate – hate from top to bottom. Hate of a mess. Remington owned it the other day, said he hated a mu'll. There you are! If you couldn't get hate into an election, damn it (hic) people wou'n't poll. Poll for love! – no' me!'[86]

This shatters Remington. He is as out of his depth as Stephen Blackpool in *Hard Times*, finding society 'aw a muddle' – or as Dickens himself was in politics. There is no political community, and his pilgrimage is over even before he takes flight with his Isabel.

Wells was completely removed from the nonconformist culture and the sexual sublimation of Hale White. To Wells hedonism and political engagement were compatible, but *The New Machiavelli* all but destroys his case. Remington panics and flees, and leaves the last word, and the argument for civic humanism, with his deserted wife: 'You remind me – do you remember? – of that time we went from Naples to Vesuvius, and walked over the hot new lava there . . . One walked there in spite of the heat because there was a crust; like custom, like law. But directly a crust forms on things, you are restless to break down to the fire again.'[87] The message of the novel is that 'love and high thinking' aren't enough. Remington is isolated not because of his affair but because neither his own nature nor the British two-party state gives him, and his ideas, any political purchase.

XI

The New Machiavelli ends ominously; the fire-and-water rebarbarization of Europe offstage. Evesham's 'thin net' and Margaret's lava echo Carlyle and Disraeli; we will meet them again in John Buchan. This ominous diction had been revived in the new edition of J. G. Frazer's *The Golden Bough* (1908), which was ransacked by the avant-garde as a symbolist treasure-trove. The anthropologist trembled at the advance of mass culture, as throughout Europe conservative institutions – the House of Lords in Britain or the Kaiser-appointed ministry at Berlin – came under assault from the Third Estate, just as the Dreyfus case in France and the Catholic–Monarchist reaction, exemplified in Barres, Maurras and Action Français, impinged on Proust's *A la Recherche du Temps Perdu*.

French 'Jacobinism' was centralist, as was British 'welfarism', old-age pensions and National Insurance, but home rule – now likely for Wales and Scotland – went some way to meet Chesterton and the decentralists. This accompanied an increase in provincial literary activity, both in the novel and in the theatre. The Abbey in Dublin, the Gaiety in Manchester and the Glasgow Repertory took over the torch from the Royal Court.[88] In Scotland the Kailyard was invaded by novels such as George Douglas Brown's *The House with the Green Shutters* (1901) and John MacDougall Hay's *Gillespie* (1914) which assaulted individualism not for muddle but for a demonic heartlessness, while Tom Johnston's *Forward*, published in cosmopolitan Glasgow from 1906, serialized much of the best socialist fiction and polemic from Europe and America. In Manchester, Stanley Houghton and Harold Brighouse satirized the northern bourgeoisie and set against them their newly confident daughters. In Ireland, Synge was not alone in confronting the sentimentality of Catholic nationalism; few writers ever dissected the Irish problem with such skill as Shaw in *John Bull's Other Island* (1904), and even more strength would come to the Irish theatre through Sean O'Casey, then an assistant to James Connolly and James Larkin in the Dublin trade union movement. Even in Wales, the home of radicalism at its most orthodox and nonconformist-penetrated, Caradoc Evans would shortly blast the pieties of Lloyd Georgite dissent.

Such writing dealt with 'local' politics: in families, chapels, newspapers and small towns, reviving the debates of the pre-Disraeli epoch. Douglas Brown had edited Galt with Andrew Lang; Shaw juxtaposed the Ruskin–Carlyleian 'madman' Keegan with his entrepreneurs Broadbent and Doyle in *John Bull's Other Island*; John Buchan subjected imperialism to the Peacockian *causerie* in *A Lodge in the Wilderness* (1908). With imminent decentralization of power went a shift from convention to ideas and radicalism. Practically all the provincial writers were socialists of some sort, supporters of female suffrage, unorthodox – or at least 'modernist' – in religion; their monstrous villains modulating Christian notions of sin and the devil into humanist gradations of greed and indifference to the rest of society.

If Wells, or Wells-Remington, found the Liberals unconvincing in power – brilliantly conveyed by his image of a Commons occupied by discarded hats – this was because they felt uneasy in such a centralized *polis*. Galsworthy attempted to animate this unease in plays such as *The Silver Box* (1906) or *The Mob* (1913) but never reached the centre of the party's dilemma: a Cabinet whose 'high politics' – its secret international alliances – bore no relation whatever to the programme of the rank and file. The Liberal élite had passed beyond the clash between ideals and actuality which produces either satire or tragedy; its 'corruption' would be conveyed by George Dangerfield's *The Strange Death of Liberal England* (1935) over two decades later, and in the 1940s and 1950s by Joyce Cary and William Cooper.[89] But the murderous element which Dangerfield discerned among the Tories was real enough.

Wells's dinner-party provides an engaging metaphor, but the same impression could come from reading the short stories that Saki (H. H. Munro) and Rudyard Kipling directed against their opponents. In the slapstick of 'The Village That Voted' (1913) or the venomous allegory of 'The Mother Hive' (1908) Kipling, as Orwell would later put it, was sulking – perhaps. But he was also fanning the extremism of the

Conservative Party under Andrew Bonar Law, which brought Britain to the verge of civil war in July 1914.

NOTES

1 Quoted in G. H. Bantock, 'The social and intellectual background', in Boris Ford (ed.), *The Pelican Guide to English Literature: The Modern Age* (Harmondsworth: Penguin, 1961), p. 29.
2 H. G. Wells, *Tono-Bungay* (New York: Scribner's, 1925), p. 522.
3 Justin McCarthy, *The Story of an Irishman* (London: Chatto & Windus, 1904), p. 226.
4 Brian Masters, *Now Barabbas Was a Rotter: The Extraordinary Life of Marie Corelli* (London: Hamish Hamilton, 1978), pp. 87, 122; Richard D. Altick, 'The sociology of authorship', *Bulletin of the New York Public Library*, vol. 66 (1962), p. 402.
5 See Norman and Jeanne MacKenzie (eds), *The Diary of Beatrice Webb*, Vol. 1 (London: Virago/London School of Economics, 1982), pp. 78, 291.
6 Auberon Herbert, *A Politician in Trouble with his Soul*, cited in Beatrice Webb, *My Apprenticeship* (Harmondsworth: Penguin, 1938), p. 213.
7 See Christopher Harvie, *The Lights of Liberalism* (London: Allen Lane, 1976), ch. 9.
8 John Lucas, 'Conservatism and revolution in the 1880s', in John Lucas (ed.), *Literature and Politics in the Nineteenth Century* (London: Methuen, 1971), pp. 173–221.
9 Henry James, *The Princess Casamassima* (New York: Scribner's, 1936), Vol. 2, p. 235.
10 Trilling in Walter Allen, *The English Novel* (Harmondsworth: Penguin, 1960), p. 269; James quoted in Lucas, 'Conservatism', p. 177.
11 Lucas, 'Conservatism', p. 216; Maxwell Geismar, *Henry James and His Cult* (London: Chatto & Windus, 1964), p. 69.
12 See Alastair B. Cooke and John Vincent, *The Governing Passion: Cabinet Government and Party Politics in Britain, 1885–6* (Brighton: Harvester Press, 1974), section 1.
13 Christopher Harvie, 'Gladstonianism, the provinces, and popular political culture', in Richard Bellamy (ed.), *Victorian Liberalism* (London: Methuen, 1989).
14 See J. Stuart Walters on Dicey in *Mrs Humphry Ward: Her Work and Influence* (London: Kegan Paul, 1912), p. 32.
15 Christopher Harvie, 'Ideology and home rule: James Bryce, A. V. Dicey and Ireland, 1880–87', *English Historical Review*, vol. 91 (April 1976), pp. 39–61.
16 Harvie, *Lights of Liberalism*, pp. 221 ff.
17 Neal Ascherson, 'Devolution diary', *Cencrastus*, no. 22 (Winter 1986), p. 53.
18 See Noel Annan, *Leslie Stephen: The Godless Victorian* (London: Weidenfeld & Nicolson, 1984).
19 Geoff Crossick, 'The emergence of the lower middle class in Britain', in Geoff Crossick (ed.), *The Lower Middle Class in Britain* (London: Croom Helm, 1978), pp. 19, 27.
20 Garnett worked successively for Unwin, Heinemann, Duckworth, Lane and Cape, and discovered Conrad, Ford Madox Ford, Galsworthy, T. E.

and D. H. Lawrence; see Linda Marie Fritschner, 'Publishers' readers, publishers and their authors', *Publishing History*, Vol. 6, pp. 50 ff.

21   Justin McCarthy and Mrs Campbell Praed, *Our Book of Memories* (London: Chatto & Windus, 1912), p. 83.

22   George Gissing, *Demos* (London: Smith Elder, 1886), p. 278.

23   Quoted in John Halperin, *Gissing: A Life in Books* (Oxford: Oxford University Press, 1982), p. 60.

24   Frederic Jameson, *The Political Unconscious: Narrative as a Socially Symbolic Act* (London: Methuen, 1981), p. 202.

25   Halperin, *Gissing*, pp. 40–55.

26   Gissing *Demos*, p. 384; see John Goode, 'Gissing, Morris and English Socialism', *Victorian Studies*, vol. 12 (December 1968), pp. 201–26.

27   ibid., p. 202.

28   Halperin, *Gissing*, p. 99.

29   Korg, *George Gissing: A critical biography* (London: Methuen, 1965). pp. 235–9.

30   George Gissing, *Denzil Quarrier* (Brighton: Harvester, 1979), p. 341.

31   Quoted in Halperin, *Gissing*, p. 216.

32   ibid., pp. 286, 288.

33   George Gissing, *Charles Dickens* (London: Blackie, 1897), p. 17.

34   Jameson, *Political Unconscious*, pp. 201 ff.

35   Mark Rutherford, *The Deliverance of Mark Rutherford* (London: T. Fisher Unwin, 1881), p. 4.

36   Mark Rutherford, *The Revolution in Tanner's Lane* (London: Trubner, 1887), p. 135.

37   Donald Davie, *A Gathered Church* (London: Routledge, 1978), p. 103; Valentine Cunningham, *Everywhere Spoken Against: Dissent in the Victorian Novel* (London: Oxford University Press, 1975), pp. 264 ff.

38   Stephen Koss, *Nonconformity in Modern British Politics* (London: Batsford, 1975), pp. 28 ff.

39   Edward Thompson, *John Arnison*, (London: Macmillan, 1939), pp. ix, 67.

40   See also Edwin Clayhanger and his problems with Methodists and the new theology, in Arnold Bennett, *Clayhanger* (Harmondsworth: Penguin, 1954), p. 128.

41   See T. H. Darlow, *William Robertson Nicoll* (London: Hodder & Stoughton, 1925), chs 7 and 9, and Christopher Harvie, 'Behind the bonnie brier bush: the Kailyard revisited', *Proteus*, no. 3 (June 1978).

42   Quoted in John Gross, *The Rise and Fall of the Man of Letters* (Harmondsworth: Penguin, 1973), p. 221.

43   Harvie, 'Behind the bonnie brier bush', p. 56.

44   See Carola Ehrlich, 'The "Dialectable Duchy": Regionalism in the Novels of Sir Arthur Thomas Quiller-Couch', Tübingen MA thesis, 1988; Robert Gittings, *The Older Hardy* (London: Heinemann, 1978), pp. 16–19; and Ian Gregor in Thomas Hardy, *The Mayor of Casterbridge*, ed. J. K. Robinson (New York: Norton, 1977).

45   *The British Weekly*, 9 July 1896.

46   Mark Rutherford, *Clara Hopgood* (London: T. Fisher Unwin, 1897), ch. 29.

47   See Irvin Stock, *Mark Rutherford* (London: Allen & Unwin, 1956), p. 220.

48   Rutherford, *Clara Hopgood*, pp. 270–1.

49 M. A. Ward, *A Writer's Recollections* (London: Collins, 1918), p. 8; Stephen Gwynn, *Mrs Humphry Ward* (London: Nisbet, 1918), p. 10.
50 Ward, *Writer's Recollections*, p. 178.
51 ibid., p. 170; Amiel, a neurasthenic professor of philosophy, in retreat from public life into his own *accidie*, later appealed strongly to Anthony Powell; see his *Faces in My Time* (London: Heinemann, 1980), pp. 186–7.
52 Gwynn, *Mrs Humphry Ward*, p. 52.
53 Mary Ward, *Marcella* (London: John Murray, 1915), pp. 554–5.
54 Quoted in Janet Penrose Trevelyan, *The Life of Mrs Humphry Ward* (London: Constable, 1923), p. 117.
55 Ward, *Marcella*, p. 230.
56 ibid., p. 131.
57 ibid., p. 285.
58 Ward, *Writer's Recollections*, p. 211.
59 ibid., p. 213.
60 See Leon O'Broin, *The Prime Informer* (London: Sidgwick & Jackson, 1971).
61 See Anthony Lentin, *Lloyd George, Woodrow Wilson and the Guilt of Germany* (Baton Rouge: Louisiana University Press, 1986), p. 125.
62 Gwynn, *Mrs Humphry Ward*, p.51.
63 Mary Ward, *Sir George Tressady*, p. 329.
64 ibid.
65 Characters in Mallock's *The Old Order Changes* and Gissing's *Demos* claimed to be translating *Capital*, see Lucas, 'Conservatism', p. 203.
66 Webb, *My Apprenticeship*, pp. 186–7.
67 Gwynn, *Mrs Humphry Ward*, pp. 119, 41; and see the acute analysis in Harold Williams, *Modern English Writers* (London: Sidgwick & Jackson, 1918), pp. 438–45.
68 A. P. Thornton, *The Imperial Idea and Its Enemies* (London: Macmillan, 1959), p. 88; see also Brian Harrison, *Separate Spheres* (London: Croom Helm, 1973), p. 154.
69 See G. R. Searle, *The Quest for National Efficiency: A study in British political and social thought* (London: Oxford University Press, 1971).
70 Gissing, quoted in Pierre Constillas (ed.), *London and the Life of Literature in Late Victorian England* (Brighton: Harvester, 1978), p. 124; Ward, *Writer's Recollections*, p. 182; Morley, quoted in D. A. Hamer, *John Morley: Liberal Intellectual in Politics* (London: Oxford University Press, 1968), p. 24.
71 Tom Nairn, *The Enchanted Glass* (London: Radius, 1988), p. 388.
72 Hamer, *Morley*, pp. 213 ff.
73 Seventy-nine Gladstone biographies were published between 1850 and 1914, as against twenty-one of Palmerston in the same period. The length of time taken by the Tories to publish the official life of Disraeli obviously disadvantaged them.
74 A. O. J. Cockshut, *Truth to Life: The Art of Biography in the Nineteenth Century* (London: Collins, 1974), pp. 175–6.
75 Thomas Carlyle, *Heroes and Hero-Worship* (Leipzig: Tauchnitz, 1916), pp. 20–1.
76 Wells, *The New Machiavelli* (Harmondsworth: Penguin, 1946), pp. 266, 255.
77 Ernest Barker, *Political Thought in England: From Spencer to the Present Day* (London: Williams & Norgate, 1915), pp. 179–83.

78 Elaine Showalter, *A Literature of Their Own* (London: Virago, 1978), p. 222.
79 John Carswell, *Lives and Letters* (London: Faber, 1978), p. 19.
80 See Alan Sillitoe, introduction to Robert Tressell, *The Ragged Trousered Philanthropists* (London: Panther, 1965), p. 7; and F. C. Ball, *One of the Damned* (London: Lawrence & Wishart, 1973), pp. 31 ff.
81 Harvie, 'Political thrillers and the condition of England from the 1840s to the 1880s', in Arthur Marwick (ed.), *Literature and Society* (London: Routledge, 1990), p. 229.
82 Viscountess Milner, 'Talks with George Meredith', *National Review*, no. 131 (1968), pp. 454–6.
83 H. G. Wells, *New Worlds for Old* (London: Constable, 1908), pp. 274 ff.
84 See C. B. Purdom, *Harley Granville Barker* (Westport, Conn.: Greenwood Press, 1956), pp. 73–6.
85 James to Wells, 3 March 1911, in Leon Edel and Gordon Kay (eds), *Henry James and H. G. Wells* (London: Hart-Davis, 1959), p. 128.
86 Wells, *New Machiavelli*, pp. 529–30.
87 ibid., p. 558.
88 cf. P. F. Clarke, *Lancashire and the New Liberalism* (London: Routledge, 1971), ch. 1.
89 Joyce Cary, *To Be a Pilgrim* (London: Michael Joseph, 1942); William Cooper, *Disquiet and Peace* (London: Macmillan, 1956).

7

In Time of Strife, 1914–26

I

You used to laugh at the books Miss Savage read – about spies, and murders, and violence, and wild motor-car chases, but dear, that's real life: it's what we've made of the world since you died. I'm your little Arthur who wouldn't hurt a beetle and I'm a murderer too. The world has been remade by William Le Queux.[1]

THRILLER-WRITERS had been prophesying war for over forty years. Chesney's *Battle of Dorking* was the first of many mass-psychology preparations for the real thing, marching in step with European mobilization plans, worked out like railway timetables and codified in the 'war books' of general staffs. When Britain began to catch up, with the Anglo-French *Entente* (1904) and the creation of a general staff, so did espionage as a literary theme. As information about military technology, secret treaties and war plans could affect a vast range of policies, *raison d'état* and its use against liberal values became an important weapon in the hands of the European right. Overplayed, as in the Dreyfus case, it could have near-revolutionary consequences.

The spy-story and its theme of corruption in high places seems to date from Conan Doyle's Sherlock Holmes story 'The Bruce-Partington Plans' of 1892; novels on this theme by William Le Queux and E. Phillips Oppenheim quickly followed.[2] The Holmes tale was another example of our hero's versatility, and Oppenheim was a talented entertainer, but Le Queux, a dreadful writer and probably a total fraud, became politically the most significant. The formula of Le Queux and Oppenheim was the 'future war' combined with Wildeian social melodrama: blackmail is almost *de rigueur*, locations are exotic, with plenty of coincidences, *femmes fatales*, and so on. Rubbish, in other words.

So who read them? Douglas Sladen, first editor of *Who's Who*, wrote that bishops and judges would brawl in the Athenaeum to get their hands on the latest, and Arthur Balfour said he regarded a Le Queux book as worth several thousand votes to the Tories in any election.[3] Such voters were presumably the clerks and small businessmen who might read Kipling or Wells, Harmsworth's *Daily Mail* (1896) or Pearson's *Daily Express* (1900). One person in eighty read a daily paper in 1850; one in five in 1901, largely white-collar workers, non-unionized, poorly paid, anxious about security. Robertson Nicoll's classic reprints and sentimental regional novels were didactic, preachy and aimed at nonconformists: the new suburbs, sketched graphically by Masterman in *The Condition of England*, inclined to 'sensational' literature. A generation reared on penny dreadfuls and melodrama now wanted the 'authenticity' of being taken into the confidence of diplomats, statesmen and spies, while its guides – Le Queux, Oppenheim, Conan Doyle, Buchan, Wallace, Childers – were often from provincial cultures, anxious to assimilate by appearing super-patriotic, even at the expense of their own community.[4]

Le Queux's *forte* was that, as news editor of the *Globe*, he knew enough about Foreign Office intelligence-gathering to impart pedantic details. But, if Balfour appreciated this stuff, it was not a throwaway flippancy; his murky Irish career was followed by close involvement in the Committee of Imperial Defence, which in 1909 set up MI5, the intelligence department dealing with domestic affairs. MI5, in turn, drafted the Official Secrets Act of 1911, in response to a spy scare, which greatly expanded the State's control over its employees and their contacts.[5] In this way the thriller-writers helped create an atmosphere in which limitations of individual freedom intolerable to the Victorians received consensus support.

II

Yet when the outbreak of war gave literature an unprecedented political *gravitas* they found themselves sidelined. British literary men, who had always kept independent of the State, even when – like Trollope or Hale White – it employed them, were suddenly nationalized. Britain had become embroiled because of secret treaties and agreements, yet the will to fight had to be created in a deeply divided society, in the absence of conscription or a war-aims programme. The Liberal government shrewdly recruited the writers, and put in charge of them Charles Masterman, Carlyleian, Christian Socialist, the friend of Wells and cousin (by marriage) of Buchan. A member of the Cabinet, who had lost his seat at a by-election, Masterman took over Wellington House, Park Lane, with a fat secret-service budget, offering his friends involvement and influence where *Waste* and *The New Machiavelli* had seen frustration and disorientation.[6]

Twenty years later Goebbels was to say that he had learned most of his techniques from the British. With reason: Masterman chose liberals with good transatlantic connections. Lord Bryce chaired the inquiry into German behaviour in Belgium which, fed with undiluted and unverified atrocity-stories, changed the German image from a bumbling pipe-smoking peasant to a ravening beast. Edward Marsh, Churchill's private secretary, turned a Rugbeian Fabian, Rupert Brooke, and his '1914' sonnets into the Sir Philip Sidney of the potential officer class. The sanction of major *littérateurs* – Wells, Galsworthy, Bennett – helped confine opposition to a small minority of Liberals, socialists and convinced pacifists.

The organization of enthusiasm for the war – still not fully explored – had greater barriers to surmount in Britain than in Europe. Although socialism wasn't strong, the habitual militarism inculcated by conscription didn't exist. But the likely break-up of the world economic order, with bankruptcies and associated unemployment, even if Britain didn't participate, demanded certainties which Wellington House was able to supply, if need be by co-opting working-class and socialist supporters of the war effort – Hyndman, Blatchford, even Edward Carpenter. Thus was engendered a literature persuasive and even original. *The First Hundred Thousand* by 'Ian Hay' and the anonymous *Spud Tamson VC* (1915) were good recruiting propaganda, venturing into a society – urban Scotland -that the 'serious' novel had neglected, and gave stiff competition to the didactic Marxism of the Red Clyde.[7]

The intellectual mobilization of 1914 affected more than propaganda. It slew the 'Germanic' philology which had pervaded the teaching of English in the universities, and replaced it with English literature as a value-system. The way was prepared for the literary-political *démarches* of T. S. Eliot and F. R. Leavis.[8] But Masterman's initial success was not sustained. He couldn't get back into the House, and even his ingenuity failed to sell the Moloch of the Western Front. H. G. Wells, one of his star performers, was, by *Mr Britling Sees It Through* (1916), lapsing into quietism, and those now facing conscription had, despite the censorship, a fair idea of what they were in for. The new power in government, the press lords who controlled the mass-print culture, demanded and got his replacement in 1916. His successor was Colonel John Buchan.

III

John Buchan, publisher, proconsul and latterly Commonwealth statesman, seems to embody an inhibited conservatism at odds with Wells's radical hedonism. Yet his immobile features conceal as mysterious an intellect as Disraeli's, and arguably the central key to the problems of British political imagination in the twentieth century. Buchan had launched himself into political fiction with as much enthusiasm as

Disraeli, whose biography he had wanted to write, but *The Half-Hearted* (1900) and *A Lodge in the Wilderness* (1908) are immature works. In some ways *The Power House*, which he wrote to entertain Balfour in 1913, is no better – its plot is clumsily coincidental – but the chase of the first and most autobiographical Buchan hero, Edward Leithen, after the charming but sinister establishment figure Andrew Lumley, hits one nail very hard on the head.

The lawyer Leithen, his motor broken down, finds himself face to face with Lumley in his country house. In age, appearance and conversation uncannily close to Balfour, and to that last mysterious creation of Disraeli, Lumley coolly dissects civilization: 'You think that a wall as solid as the earth separates civilisation from Barbarism. I tell you the division is a thread, a sheet of glass . . .'[9] Leithen realizes that here is the centre of a formidable intellectual conspiracy against civilization: 'The earth is seething with incoherent power and unorganised intelligence . . . All that is needed is direction, which could be given by men of far lower gifts than a Bonaparte. In a word, you want a Power-House, and the age of miracles will begin.'[10] Graham Greene and Janet Adam Smith have taken this as expressing a conservative apprehensiveness, but the story itself shows this reading as eccentric.[11] It is the anarchist who is on about diseased civilization, not Leithen, who resembles Conrad's Assistant Commissioner in his confident legal rationalism, and his extrovert ally the Labour MP, Harry Chapman, who together force Lumley to commit suicide.

Buchan had only confidence in the system which bore him from a Free Church manse (like Robertson Nicoll and Beaverbrook) to Oxford, Milner's staff in South Africa, marriage with a Grosvenor and the board of the publishing firm of Nelson. He held to his father's Conservatism (although his wife and most of his friends were Liberals), probably calculating, like Wells's Remington, that after 1906 the Conservatives were likely to be more open to new ideas. Yet Buchan himself became isolated in the extremism of the Bonar Law period, and Lumley, the Tory magnifico fanning revolution, must have seemed to him increasingly plausible. Shortly after *The Power House* was written Buchan the centrist was given his chance by the outbreak of war, in the course of which Richard Hannay, hero of perhaps the purest of thrillers, *The Thirty-Nine Steps*, was pressed into the service of political consensus.

Buchan said he held Oppenheim 'the greatest Jew since Isaiah', borrowed some of his techniques and eventually took him into his propaganda unit. Oppenheim was already, with some skill, putting across a 'national Labour' line in *A People's Man*, published in January 1915, in which a militant Anglo-American socialist is won over to a Conservative government headed by a Balfourian figure, Stephen Foley, on finding out that international socialism is run by the German secret service. A dash of Jack London and whiff of sulphur from the 1912 visit of the Wobbly leader Big Bill Haywood are dispelled by wartime consensus, and the socialists get mine and railway nationalization:

> 'Do away with the horde of money-bloated parvenus, who fatten and decay on the immoral profits they drag from Labour. We are at the parting of the ways. We wait for the strong man. Raise your standard and the battle is already won.'
> 'And you?' Mr Foley muttered.
> 'I'm your man,' Maraton answered.[12]

This consensus would dominate politics for the next eight years, during the hegemony of Lloyd George. Buchan, too, made Hannay expound it in *Mr Standfast* (1919). More diffuse and baffling than its predecessor *Greenmantle* (1917), in it Hannay set out, against the background of the German advance of March 1918, to explore the opposition in Britain to the war – from pacifists to the trade unionists of the Red Clyde. Where Kipling would have been vitriolic, Buchan 'understands' and co-opts. Pacifists die heroically; the Clydeside shop stewards, venomously attacked in the press, are seen as patriotic labour aristocrats forced into industrial conflict by an inept management. The last evil gambit of Moxon Ivery, Graf von Straubing, is frustrated by a grand coalition of left and right.

The notion – still, alas, current – of Buchan as tweedy clubman with crypto-fascist and anti-Semitic tendencies is not just stupid but an example of metropolitan literary sloth.[13] David Daniell's case that here is a major literary reputation, grossly undervalued, is one I accept. Buchan took himself seriously (rightly) as biographer, as a historical novelist, and (with less reason) as a politician. But his thrillers are important as articulating, almost subconsciously, the gentleman-parliamentarian and provincial patriot's doubts about the new state. Buchan created Carlyleian heroes but he was also a nonconformist democrat uneasily aware that secrecy and intrigue cut off those inside the system from those outside. Between the wars his friend Baldwin used the Special Branch and its spies as part of Conservative Party intelligence. Disraeli with his worship of intellect in politics would have approved; Buchan did not. Buchan's cosmopolitan villains – his Lumleys, Medinas and Moxon Iverys - are no more Jewish than Disraeli's Sidonia but they resemble Disraeli's supranational intellects. After the war, Buchan must have felt that the Lumleys had, in effect, taken over.

Greenmantle and *Mr Standfast* were not wholly fantasy. Buchan was a master of agents – not the only or the last literary man so involved, in a company which has included Somerset Maugham and Compton Mackenzie, Graham Greene, Malcolm Muggeridge, Ian Fleming and

John Le Carré. Kept by ill-health off the active list, he made the intellectual spymaster into an oddly resonant image, a wounded Amfortas-figure dispatching into peril the active agents whom he modelled on his friends killed in action. But Buchan did more. In 1916, trying to divert American attention from the Western Front, he sent the American journalist Lowell Thomas to Palestine to cover the operation of a young volunteer officer, T. E. Lawrence, with Arab forces. Buchan helped create a conquering hero for a war which badly needed one.[14]

IV

Buchan's misgivings were aggravated by the political consequences of the war. *The New Machiavelli* forecast an alliance between the most dynamic elements in the Liberal Party and the Conservatives. By 1917 this was a fact. The war had brought the traditional structures of adversary politics to an end. 'For thirty years I have lived among what the world has agreed loosely to call "the Governing Classes"', Stephen McKenna, nephew of Asquith's Chancellor of the Exchequer, Reginald McKenna, wrote in *Sonia* (1917): 'The title may already be obsolescent; sentence of proscription may, as I write, have been passed on those who bear it. At the lowest computation those classes will soon have changed beyond recognition in personnel, function, power and philosophy.'[15] The Easter Rising and its consequences had snapped the Anglo-Irish Union, and the fall of Asquith divided the Liberal Party. The Reform Act under way in 1917 would enfranchise women and more than double the electorate. The few surviving veterans of George Eliot's Sunday afternoons – Bryce, Dicey, Morley, Harrison – found themselves in a bewildering new world.

And a bewilderingly articulate one. Political fiction would pour out in the interwar years, ultimately even influencing theatre and film. Most of this output was poor, either remote from the huge social problems generated by the war, or panicked into extremism by the immensity of its impact and the rapid evolution of civil society into 'mass society'.[16] The Victorian novelist's readership (Mudie's subscribers, and so on) was reasonably close to the 'upper 10,000' who effectively wielded power. This type of focused élite, already failing fast, could not survive electoral expansion, Liberal collapse and the changing patterns of entertainment in a society which had more leisure and more cash. There was, or would soon be, a new 'mass media' of radio and cinema, but the book market's behaviour was also radical. Book sales (not to speak of loans from down-market libraries like Boots and W. H. Smith's) increased fivefold between 1914 and 1939.[17]

The sheer scale of change seemed beyond the interpretive ability of British creative artists. In 1916 the British tanks which first fought in the battle of the Somme (which with Verdun slaughtered and wounded over a million men) particularized a new type of industrialized conflict which eliminated the powers' unfitted to sustain it: the Russian and Austrian Empires and (very nearly) France. In 1917 the Russian Revolution confirmed that the war had destroyed the original aims of the participants and the whole notion of international stability. European intellectuals, used to large-scale wars and inoculated with some experience of Marxism, or at least Hegelianism, had at least a foothold on the new situation. The British, a hundred years away from their last major war, were adrift.

One *ex post facto* rationalization of this was 'modernism': Virginia Woolf deciding in 1926 that human nature changed in 1910.[18] In political terms 'modernism' was anything but modern; but, rather, an attempt by the élite to control – or at least comprehend – the mass society which had baffled James in 1886, not through empiricism, but through metaphors which would restore a pre-democratic, pre-industrial 'unity of feeling'. Advances in literary style – in particular the recovery of 'consciousness' - sanctioned a 'counter-enlightenment'. Where Meredith anticipated a growth of mental capability, 'modernist' writers argued that the dependence on habit and ritual detected by psychoanalysis and sociology limited the 'rationalism' of the novel, and thus helped to revive romance and the epic. Quite explicit in the Homeric–Virgilian structure of *Ulysses* and the Wagnerian *leitmotifs* of *The Waste Land*, symbolism and anthropology came to penetrate even supposedly realistic works.[19]

This shifted literary initiative to the provinces of the English language – Ireland, Scotland, the American Midwest and South - where pre-print capitalist modes were liveliest, but its conservatism meant that the policies of new communications technologies – radio after 1923, talkies after 1929 – were decided on crude commercial or conservative political criteria, with next to no intellectual input. Elite 'modernism' stressed the intimate and introspective; mass 'modernism' consisted largely of the technology-transmitted values of American business and entertainment. Wedding the two was a political issue in itself, with a new political geography – Hollywood patronage, Reithian broadcasting, Soviet agitprop and documentary – demanding a new cultural politics.

The new subjectivity could give the imaginative writer a prophetic rôle, but he or she could end trapped in a commercialized world as one of its most insignificant elements. The average novel, selling 2,000 copies, would earn its author no more than the dole. Storm Jameson's Hervey Russell in *Company Parade* (1934) is urged by her boss to become the Shakespeare of the advertising agency; George Orwell's Gordon Comstock dissects, in *Keep the Aspidistra Flying* (1936), the anatomy of the popular fiction which presses like a nightmare on his Hampstead bookshop.

V

The fall of the Lloyd George coalition in 1922 was a more convincing politico-cultural *Zeitbruch* than 1910. At the end of 1916 an intrigue of press barons and Conservatives had brought a man to Downing Street whom they had earlier reviled as a radical and an opportunist, if not (*pace* the Marconi scandal) an actual crook. But he had created the Ministry of Munitions in March 1915 and, with a scratch organization ranging from provincial businessmen to social workers, had relieved the shortage of war *matériel* (everything from boots to shells) and had squared – or crushed – trade unionists as deftly as he deflected opposition at Westminster. His press-magnate friends, Beaverbrook and Northcliffe, created a myth of dynamism, which his enemies duly supplemented.[20]

Lloyd George expressed the energy of dissent and the negation of its ethics. Critics saw politics under him as more centralized, more manipulative, case-hardened against real democracy. Defenders saw him as a radical innovator, impaled by an archaic establishment. His fall thus seemed one of those junctures at which, as a part of a common European crisis (the onset of Italian fascism, German inflation, the Ruhr occupation) British social evolution perversely slipped away on a line of its own. A powerful, if crude, bourgeois régime gave way to a moralistic version of the old two-party system.

Reasons for this can be seen in the literature which the war generated. The First World War left an indelible literary mark in the writing of Owen, Sassoon, Rosenberg, Mottram, Manning and Graves, yet much of this was only discovered and published – and, in the case of prose works, only written – afterwards: it is the literature of the lost peace as much as of the war. Stephen McKenna's *Sonia; or, Between Two Worlds* was, however, a wartime bestseller - seventeen editions between March and December 1917 – and has been cited as providing an insight into wartime politics. The first of a dozen novels on upper-class life, solemnly acknowledging Disraeli, which McKenna produced between then and the 1940s, *Sonia*'s subtitle is taken from Matthew Arnold's 'Stanzas from the Grand Chartreuse' –

> Between two Worlds,
> One dead, one struggling to be born.

– and it stands in the tradition of Compton Mackenzie's novel of public-school and Oxford life, *Sinister Street* (1913): silver fork revived, with a *roman à clef* element, was strong enough to appeal to the very profiteers and *arrivistes* it elegantly denounced.[21] Sonia is a 'bad girl' novel, a precursor of Michael Arlen's *The Green Hat* (1924), about a spoilt brewer's daughter, in and out of love with a string of Winchester-and-Oxford products making their way in politics. At the end these are mostly dead on the Western Front, and Sonia marries her first love, David O'Rane, a Kim-like figure from an (aristocratic) Irish rebel family. O'Rane, blinded in an attack, is crucified by his German captors but survives to return to his old school as a master and preach social reconstruction:

> There was deep silence as O'Rane paused. 'I – all of us who were out there – have seen it. We can't forget. The courage, the cold, heart-breaking courage . . . and the smile on a dying man's face . . . We must never let it be forgotten; we've earned the right. As long as a drunkard kicks his wife, or a child goes hungry, or a woman is driven through shame to disease and death . . . Is it a great thing to ask? To demand of England to remember that the criminals and loafers and prostitutes are somebody's children, mothers and sisters? And that we've all been saved by a miracle of suffering?'[22]

Sonia is only mildly ill-behaved, and the political narrative, provided by O'Rane's friend George Oakleigh, a Liberal backbencher, seems almost grotesquely limited. Few of the Liberal government's problems appear. Oakleigh may be an Irish landowner and O'Rane the son of a Parnellite MP, but there is no word of Sinn Fein, Larkin, Connolly, of the 1913 Dublin strike or even the 1916 Rising. Oakleigh and his uncle run a 'Little England' peace campaign, but they say little about it before they drop it in August 1914. The prewar labour unrest is (fittingly, perhaps) confined to a strike of dining-car attendants. Of the suffragette movement, nowhere a sign. *Sonia* becomes more interesting when faced by the slaughter. Here the 'lost generation' is framed in the intense homoeroticism of Edward Marsh's *Rupert Brooke* (1915) and Ernest Raymond's *Tell England!* (1922). Its sequel, *Sonia Married* (1919), conveys disillusion and the unpleasing backwash of profiteering and wartime politics, enhancing its sexual theme by contrasting Sonia's waywardness with the sacrifice of the men in her life.

The backgrounds of the greatest war writers were far from those of McKenna's young aristocrats: Blunden was a Catholic, Graves half-German, Sassoon half-Jewish, Rosenberg Jewish, Owen lower-middle class Anglo-Welsh. Rather a lot of *Sonia*'s young men in fact resemble the 'scarlet majors at the base' that Sassoon and Owen loathed. By the time the 'pals' battalions' of Kitchener's army were being mown down on the Somme, to be entombed for decades in 'Tipperary' sentimentalism, the freedoms they fought for were, in the name of efficiency, being curtailed. Conscription was being introduced; rationing imposed; news unscrupulously managed by the General Staff and a handful of war-correspondents. A new political leadership appropriate to such mechanisms was taking over, personified in *Sonia* by one Michael Bendix, 'the man who was going to win us the war'.

McKenna did not approve of Lloyd George. But his personality underlay two important literary assessments of the war, and later formed the centre of the most impressive novel of modern British politics: Joyce Cary's Chester Nimmo trilogy. In 1926, the year of the General Strike, and (effectively) of the Liberal collapse, two of the great Edwardian literary pedagogues summed up the war. Ford Madox Ford published the third volume of *Parade's End*, a meditation on 'the public events of a decade', and Arnold Bennett published *Lord Raingo*. Diagnoses differed and, ironically, the sceptical and isolated Ford seemed more sanguine than Bennett, who had paced the carpets of Whitehall with the great.

Ford was half-German, but his English grandfather was Ford Madox Brown, the painter of *Work* over sixty years before, and 'the English Tory' carried on the Erastian nationalist element in Christian Socialism.[23] As editor of the *English Review* Ford had printed *The New Machiavelli* in 1910 – he, too, was a friend of Masterman – yet he was also the collaborator of James and Conrad. His response to the war was neither Wells's determination to make the best of it nor the revulsion of 'progressive' socialists and pacifists. *Parade's End*'s hero was another 'English Tory': Christopher Tietjens, younger son of a great Yorkshire landowner, and emblematic, to Ford's mind, of the excellence of the élite – solid, honourable, responsible, kind and very intelligent. This Bolingbroke-like repertoire makes Tietjens a 'country' man, distrusting the metropolis and yearning for rural integrity, symbolized by the parish of George Herbert, the metaphysical poet, at Bemerton near Salisbury, where 'a man could stand up on a hill'. His competence takes him to a high position in the statistical office of the Civil Service, but his career – though not his personality – is destroyed during the war, partly for personal reasons, partly through the decay of politics.

Tietjens is pursued by the hatred of his Catholic wife Sylvia, whose determination to destroy him is only just greater than her sexual need of him. He finds relief in the friendship of Valentine Wannop, a socialist, pacifist and suffragette, the daughter of an academic who once wrote Disraeli's speeches. The two are discovered together by Tietjens' godfather, General Lord Edward Campion, and he and Sylvia spread rumours of adultery which drive his father to suicide. Refusing a government demand to falsify statistics, Tietjens also loses seniority to his ambitious pliable Scots colleague Vincent MacMaster. Campion has him sent to a section of the front where he has a good chance of being killed.

His solidity enables him to take over command of his battalion when his seniors, a promoted-ranker and an Oxford prizeman Scots-Cockney latinist, crack up, and he applauds Campion's assumption of supreme command. When he returns to London and Valentine on Armistice Day, Tietjens is in much better shape than Sir Vincent MacMaster, guilt- and hag-ridden by his *salonnière* wife.

Parade's End was written after *Ulysses* (1925), and follows an innovative 'stream of consciousness' narration. Ford's political argument is, however, conservative in a sense even deeper than Disraeli. Tietjens' integrity of perception and behaviour, like the Great Tree at Groby, is being overthrown by the mechanics of wartime government. The statistical incident was, for example, based on the 'Maurice affair' of 1918. General Maurice, whose predicament mirrored Tietjens', was the son of F. D. Maurice, portrayed alongside Carlyle in Madox Brown's *Work*.[24] MacMaster expresses the deracinated opportunistic provincial, bending politics to his own selfish ends: Lloyd George – or Buchan? – writ small. By contrast Father Consett, Sylvia's confessor, is an honest enemy, prepared to martyr himself in the Irish cause. Tietjens' survival endorses similar, English decencies.

Parade's End came out to respectable reviews; *Lord Raingo*, written at a Trollopian lick between May 1925 and January 1926, to a well-orchestrated furore. Bennett had served Lord Beaverbrook at the Ministry of Information in the last months of the war, and Beaverbrook aided him with details and criticism: 'It is *marvellous* to me that I have been able to do all these complicated politics without once getting off the rails,'[25] Bennett wrote. Beaverbrook ran *Raingo* as a serial in the *Evening Standard* and spent £5,000 advertising it. Placards asking 'Who is Lord Raingo?' sprouted throughout London – 'Very vulgar', commented the author, by now £1,100 to the good. Other friends from the coalition and the Club clustered round. Winston Churchill (Tom Hogarth in the book) gave praise. Lord Birkenhead, Attorney-General in the war government and always after ready cash, denounced *Raingo* as a *roman à clef*, giving Bennett a useful chance to reply. To good effect. *Raingo* sold nearly 20,000 copies in its first fortnight, the opening shot in the battle over wartime strategy which was fully joined when Lloyd George published his *War Memoirs* in 1930.[26]

Lord Raingo's humdrum all-but-first-person diction masks a plot of satire, allegory and formal tragedy. Sam Raingo, a semi-invalid Lancashire millionaire, is summoned by the premier, his former fellow-townsman Andrew Clyth, to the Ministry of Records, a front for the propaganda department. Warned off elections because of his heart, Raingo insists on a peerage. This brings disaster on the two women in his life. His feckless wife Adela, dreaming coronets, crashes her car and is killed. His mistress Delphine, shattered by the death of a former lover at the front, commits suicide. Raingo, trapped in Whitehall intrigues, with ministries fighting each other more than the Germans, has to defend himself in the Lords. He does so ineptly, but to save face relates a confidential report about a German mutiny at Brussels – the first sign of total collapse. The effort overtaxes him, and he contracts pneumonia. Although he recovers from it, the strain is too much for his heart and, on the last night of the war, he dies.

At the allegorical level, Sam Raingo *is* Liberal Britain, shifting from provincial industry to finance and the City. This is not the elegant Liberalism of the Asquiths, but the 'solid' acumen of the provinces, which commits itself to the war effort, partly out of patriotism, partly out of pride in its own capabilities. Sam is 'a man of push and go', a sort of humanized Gradgrind. And therein lies the metaphor of Britain's economic decline, starkly apparent by the time Bennett wrote in 1926. The specialist explains to Raingo the nature of his malady:

> The lungs are engorged – congested with blood. At least, one of them is, in your case. The air has to make room for the blood, and so the lung is put partially out of action. This means that the part that isn't out of action has to work harder. That's why you're breathing quicker. And it's the heart that has to bear the strain. That's about all there is to it.[27]

The blood in the lungs, the deaths and waste of resources on the front, has to be pumped out by the heart, the economic power of the country. When Raingo enters the Government, Clyth is carrying a bill to extend conscription to the middle-aged and to Ireland. Much of Sam's work at the Ministry consists of organizing a visit to London by American editors, the power-brokers of Britain's new financial master. Sam's recovery from pneumonia but death from an overstrained heart symbolize the unreality of Britain's victory over Germany, in comparison to its huge social and economic costs.

Sam's son, disoriented by the gulf between civilians and fighting men, tries to beautify Raingo's gloomy mansion. Expensive antiques stand in shabby rooms. The wealthy are able to 'get round' controls, just as the 'hard-faced men who have done well out of the war' could buy their peerages and country estates. Raingo takes to a huge bed from the time of the first Napoleon, but not to make love to Delphine. The bed becomes an imperial catafalque. But, if the young are victims of war, women have rôles which are both practical and symbolic, reflecting advances in status and economic activity. Raingo is surrounded by female bureaucrats, drivers and typists, at their apogee the prime minister's secretary Miss Packer (directly modelled on Lloyd George's secretary and mistress Frances Stevenson). The implication is not only that women can realize themselves in such new occupations, but also that failure so to do can be – as with Adela and Delphine - fatal.

Bennett, to Virginia Woolf, was a worthy plodding realist, one of modernism's predestined victims. Ford was much more explicitly innovative. Yet Bennett, in his *New Age* days, had sponsored the avant-garde and, even in *Lord Raingo*, used a 'modernist' narration similar to that of Ford: a 'third-person-subjective'; he was the liberal, where Ford was the romantic conservative. Ford's civil society was still implausibly aristocratic. Although the Tietjens family was modelled on the Marwoods, Yorkshire baronets, Tietjens-like figures were unlikely in the Civil Service, and Field-Marshal Haig, a Scots career officer, was socially closer to Vincent MacMaster than to Lord Edward Campion. Ford implies that the old élite was felled by the intrigues of Whitehall *arrivistes*; Bennett sees the opposite. Raingo becomes a peer because he thinks it a technicality, and is trapped. Like Tietjens he is an innocent, but an innocent from a business community puzzled and adrift in government, and driven to death by war.

As businessmen had supplanted the landowners in the Conservative Party, this may have seemed unduly gloomy. The progressive Bennett ended almost as a German 'cultural pessimist'. In 1926, although he called himself a socialist, he condemned the General Strike, which he saw as a revolutionary act directed at a collapsing economy. Ford was more composed. In *Last Post*, he had Tietjens marry Valentine and, on his brother's death, inherit a life-interest in Groby, albeit a Groby entailed on his Catholic son by Sylvia, and desecrated by Sylvia's final act of venom: the cutting-down of Groby Great Tree. Yet the Ford tetralogy ends with almost Disraelian optimism. Tietjens keeps Groby and marries the future, in the shape of a socialist and feminist.

VI

These two novels emphasize the massive paradox of postwar Britain. In Wellsian, republican, bourgeois terms, the war had been fought and won to make the world safe for democracy; militaristic Germany, imperial Austria and tsardom were no more. President Wilson's world view, seconded by British liberals, would create an international order rooted in seventeenth-century notions of divided sovereignty. Was not the League of Nations grounded in a covenant? Yet liberal values were at a low ebb. The whole project of home rule had failed; the Irish had left the Commons, and the electoral system had swiftly and efficiently throttled the Liberal Party and replaced it with an immature and inexperienced Labour Party.

As a result, there was a retreat to another seventeenth century, reflected in *Parade's End*. T. S. Eliot's essay 'The Metaphysical Poets' appeared in 1921, rehabilitating George Herbert and his contemporaries, and setting their 'unity of thought and feeling' against a greedy, vain, unstable age with plausible parallels to the early twentieth century. A year later came *The Waste Land*. In both Eliot followed the line of Bergson, Sorel, Freud, and Jung that the habitual and ritual kept civilized life from falling apart, something echoed by more orthodox Conservatives, who regarded Newtonian physics as unable to provide certainties on which to construct the natural, let alone the social sciences.[28]

This was a restatement of the Kiplingite 'Law', and the hierarchy of Christian Socialism, in a paternalistic continuity. Later applauded by Continental refugees like Schumpeter and Popper, it 'moralized' the Tory reaction to the Lloyd George coalition. Although in trouble by 1922, this had been crudely successful in imposing the Versailles settlement, carrying out some industrial reorganization, and getting out of the Irish mess. It had also amassed considerable business support. Yet its atmosphere, in Lord Blake's words, 'hard, glittering, sophisticated . . . heartless and insincere', provoked the same sort of revulsion that Disraeli, confronted with Liverpool and Peel, had displayed, in the shape of another literary-minded romantic, Stanley Baldwin.[29]

VII

Baldwin (like Kipling and Ford, of Pre-Raphaelite descent: he was Burne-Jones's nephew) wanted a return to adversary politics, with Labour as the 'loyal opposition'. Yet his cabinets were elderly, he failed to secure economic reconstruction (which Lloyd George could have managed), and he retained the coalition's strong-arm techniques, apparent in the Home Office under Joynson-Hicks, the Zinoviev letter affair, or Winston Churchill's heroics in the General Strike. 'Uncle Stan' personified a curious *entente* between modernism and conservatism, between the *ingénu* and the adept (he managed to be both), the cosmopolitanism of the City and the fetishizing of England.

Martin Green, one of those in the 1960s preoccupied with the arrested development of Britain, argued in *Children of the Sun* (1977) that upper-class youth developed in the 1920s a game in which it took its rôles – Harlequin, Columbine, Pulcinello – from the Italian *commedia dell' arte* and superimposed these on politics.[30] Games, mysteries, imaginary countries, the simple life of the German *Wandervögel* or of the gangs of American kids who turn up in Richard Hughes's *The Wooden Shepherdess* (1973): all these were celebrations of the child in a great age of children's literature. Barrie, Kenneth Grahame and A. A. Milne were still going strong, and Richmal Crompton's William, Enid Blyton and innumerable comics first appeared. Disraeli excepted, there are few childhood themes in Victorian political fiction but, with infant mortality dropping by 70 per cent after 1900, childhood became, at last, a cheerful confident time, and Wells deals at length with Remington's boyhood in *The New Machiavelli*. Wells had little time for immature theatricals – Remington was a state-builder from the word go – but the notion of dressing up for the theatre (or perhaps for the church) and the demand for 'instructors' were as strong in the interwar years as they had been a century earlier.[31]

The Carlyle figure was Eliot. W. H. Auden later wrote: 'Whatever its character, the provincial England of 1907, when I was born, was Tennysonian in outlook; whatever its outlook, the England of 1925, when I went up to Oxford, was *The Waste Land* in character.'[32] Eliot dominates the social criticism of the inter-war élite, in odd symbiosis with Disraeli. Evelyn Waugh's *Vile Bodies* (1930), a generic production of the 'bright young things', combines much *Waste Land* patter with the moralism of the ubiquitous Father Rothschild, SJ (Sidonia Redux?), lecturing the Prime Minister:

> I know very few young people, but it seems to me that they are all possessed with an almost fatal hunger for permanence. I think all these divorces show that. People aren't content just to muddle along nowadays . . . And this word 'bogus' they all use . . . They won't make the best of the bad job nowadays.[33]

Eliot, too, represented a literary response to a Europe-wide cultural crisis; but, while Carlyle had ultimately helped create the individualistic culture of the Victorian state, Eliot's 'world as text' remained that of the child: a chaos of objects with different sounds and purposes and textures – like the tray with which Lurgan Sahib confronts Kim in Kipling's novel – which could only be given order through belief. As liberal industrial 'civilization' decayed, Eliot offered the innocent the chance to reify society. His quotation from Verlaine's sonnet 'Parsifal' – 'O ces voix d'enfants, chantant dans la coupole' – refers to the moment when Wagner has a choir of children accompany Parsifal's healing of Amfortas, and the lifting of the curse from the waste land. His mystagogery takes us back, not just to the millennial 1880s, but to the Arthurian tradition of political renewal.

Elitist 'modernism' made Ford interesting and Bennett boring. Yet Bennett, and later on Cary, were attempting to probe a real tragedy, which disrupted not just political ideas but generations: the attempt of the former liberals to locate themselves in a politics and an imagination controlled by the conservative enemy. A. A. Milne, for once out of the nursery, wrote one political drama, *Success*, about the corruption of childish innocence into the selfishness of a Conservative MP. Galsworthy's *Swan Song* (1928) has his Forsytes similarly imprisoned: Michael Mont, MP, Soames Forsyte's son-in-law, sees his class as in command of the machinery of government. Revolution was interdicted because 'Brains, ability and technical skill, were by nature on the side of capital and individual enterprise, and were gaining ever more power'.[34] Yet with 'a directive sense in the country which really settles things before we get down to them in parliament', power lay with those who had slain their children in the war. In the General Strike of 1–9 May, 1926, Galsworthy spurned a plea from Winifred Holtby to support the strikers, but in *Swan Song* he acidly compared the frivolity of the younger Forsytes 'playing trains' with the doubts of the Victorian Conservative Soames Forsyte, when he sees a tank rumbling along the Embankment: ' "No *body* in the strike!" These great crawling monsters! Were the Government trying to pretend that there was? Playing the strong man! Something in Soames revolted slightly. Hang it! This was England, not Russia, or Italy! They might be right, but he didn't like it! Too – too military!'[35] His daughter Fleur Mont has an affair with Jon, the son of Soames's first wife Irene by his cousin Jolyon, after they meet as strike-breakers at Paddington Station. After they part, Soames dies saving the suicidal Fleur from a fire she has caused in his picture-gallery. The children's game has destroyed the stern parent.

The images of dissent were those of childhood. Harold Nicolson's *Public Faces*, written just after a close encounter with fascism, in the shape of Oswald Mosley, whose New Party magazine Nicolson edited, has the bad children, the politicians headed by the British Air Minister, starting an atomic war, while the Foreign Secretary tries to escape from a world he finds unreal to an island on a lake on his estate where he was happy as a child. In the anthropologist Geoffrey Gorer's *Nobody Talks Politics* (1936) the communists are brother-and-sister martyrs in a society brutalized by 'parliamentary' politicians. Although Auden's famous summing-up of the 1930s, as he reverted to Christianity, suggests certain Calvinistic reservations, his tone rings true:

> All the conventions conspire
> To make this fort assume
> The Furniture of home;
> Lest we should see where we are,
> Lost in a haunted wood,
> Children afraid of the night
> Who have never been happy or good.[36]

VIII

The General Strike dramatized most of these ambiguities. The King rejoiced that it had 'passed off so well', and while it emphasized class, as labour-movement localism dissolved in solidarity with the miners, it showed Baldwin, whose manoeuvrings were less than straightforward, that Labour was a reputable opponent, which would always lose. At Oxford it politicized W. H. Auden, who joined Hugh Gaitskell, Richard Crossman and John Betjeman in driving courier cars for the Trades Union Congress, and met Tom Driberg, homosexual and communist, who introduced him to *The Waste Land*.[37] In the 1920s European socialists made their accommodation with the nation states and their political cultures. Most successful in the small Scandinavian liberal democracies, in Britain accommodation and even 'modernism' were on Tory terms.

Few attempted consciously to investigate the political community, using the 'modernist' repertoire, but two who did were D. H. Lawrence and John Buchan, in the first version of *Lady Chatterley's Lover* and in *A Prince of the Captivity* (1933). It might seem odd to juxtapose the prophet of 'phallic tenderness' with the proconsul, but both identified as a key issue the liberation of labour through a new politics, and both observed Britain from a standpoint at once provincial, tradition-conscious and cosmopolitan.[38]

Preoccupation with the sexual theme in *Lady Chatterley* has tended to evict (and in Lawrence's own case ultimately evicted) the ethical–political theme, conveyed by metaphor. In *The First Lady Chatterley* Oliver Parkin, the gamekeeper, embodies the Carlyleian 'soul' – expressed both in his affinity to nature and in his sexual identity. By becoming a communist trade union organizer he represents a working-class bid to reform a state whose élite is decaying. Its embodiment is the 'rationalizing' coalowner Clifford Chatterley, a Fabian intellectual – impotent and confined to a motorized wheelchair – who takes on the challenge of large-scale industrial organization, only to become even more 'mechanical in hand and heart'. Parkin brings to Constance Chatterley, another prewar Fabian, and Scottish as well, equilibrium through physical fulfilment; sex rather than Buchan's mountain climbing. Yet in the first draft sex isn't an end in itself, nor is the male dominant over the female; it is a sort of sacrament of union with the rest of mankind and nature.[39]

Behind both Buchan and Lawrence stood, besides Carlyle, Disraeli and the vision of 'two nations'. In the fourth section of his novel Buchan reruns *Sybil* in a Midlands industrial town, Birkpool, in which a Young England movement, faced with the challenge of the General Strike, corrupts Joe Utlaw, a 'decent' union leader. Constance Chatterley's car journey through South Yorkshire is a meditation on the decline of the social influence of land, the Duke of Coningsby included. Buchan is in fact the more critical: his Young Englander seems close to Sir Oswald Mosley, and he is rightly unconvinced about his democratic beliefs. The second influence was more immediate: Wells's *The New Machiavelli*. Lawrence was immediately affected by Wells's plea for openness about sex, while to Buchan the 'Machiavellian' element is reflected in his hero Adam Melfort's search for a ruler with the qualities necessary to cope with first the British and then the international crisis. The third element is the common use of the Hegelian dialectic: thesis proceeding through antithesis towards synthesis.[40]

It is evident, though, that Lawrence's final synthesis is different from what he originally intended. In the last version of *Lady Chatterley* the gamekeeper has advanced in social class (owning up to a wartime commission); he slips at will in and out of his working-class identity; and sexually he exerts his will on Constance in a dominant, not a partner-like way. It is possible to see a political statement here: *The First Lady Chatterley* was written during the long miners' lockout in 1926, when Lawrence had revisited Nottinghamshire and still had hopes of a socialist outcome to the industrial action; the later revisions were undertaken as he moved closer to an anthropologically influenced authoritarianism. Sympathetic though Lawrence was to the miners, he had no political *locus* for them. Buchan's 'Clifford' figure is Warren Creevey – an expert, unscrupulous economist, not unlike Keynes. Ultimately he is captured for a humane democratic politics by the lean super-athletic Melfort, who undergoes the nearest Buchan ever got to describing sexual intercourse – with the wife of the Young England baronet – before achieving his martyrdom (and apparent merging with Creevey) in protecting the latter against a Nazi attack. By the time the novel came out, however, the Nazis were in power.

The strike ended whatever appeal to the working classes the Liberals had, and was succeeded by huge swings to Labour in local elections and by-elections. But its failure also ended the 'millennialist' appeal of the Independent Labour Party. Writers close to the action, such as Storm Jameson in *Company Parade* and Ellen Wilkinson in *Clash* (1929), eschewed metaphor to comment on the polarization of forces and the weakness and confusion of the Labour leadership. Where the strike was at its most intense, in mining areas in Scotland and in Wales, it generated a radical and popular fiction – Lewis Jones's and Harold Heslop's novels, Joe Corrie's plays and poems – and a strong debate about the nature of political community.

For many activists, ethical socialism had been an alternative to the cultural poverty of urban life. In Edwin Muir's novel *Poor Tom* (1934) his hero Mansie Manson experiences a mystical sense of unity with all humanity when he takes part in a May Day march, only to find this fade when he returns to the misery of a household transplanted into Glasgow from what seemed a paradisal life in the Orkneys. Other Scots experienced such disillusion in the strike's failure. In his epic poem *A Drunk Man Looks at the Thistle* (1926), Hugh MacDiarmid symbolized the workers changing the thrawn thistle into the 'braw flooer' of the rose – only to see the cowardice of their leaders shrivel it up. In his friend Lewis Grassic Gibbon's *Cloud Howe* (1933), Chris Colquhoun loses her child when her husband, a parish minister, tries to stop strikers derailing a blackleg train. The dead child, like the shrivelled rose, is the symbol of a revolution which was aborted. This led to an increasing split between class and regional politics, exemplified on one side by the development of British communism and on the other by the foundation of Plaid Cymru in Wales and the National Party of Scotland.

IX

At the end of *Cloud Howe* Grassic Gibbon's minister deserts social democracy and calls for 'a faith that will cut like a knife'. Chris Colquhoun's son Ewan goes on in *Grey Granite* to personify a new communist élite.[41] Buchan, too, looked for a leader-figure, but in a more psychoanalytical sense. In the twenties, like many other writers and public figures, he was attracted by the other Lawrence, T. E., and believed that, biographically or fictionally presented, he could restate humane values in a world increasingly inclined to gospels of mechanism or force, and somehow compensate for the moral squalor of the war. In Germany the 'stab in the back' conferred a corporate heroism on *Frontsoldaten* of all ranks which the Nazis subsequently exploited. In Britain the élite didn't have this alibi and, dismayed by the collapsing reputation of the military leadership, had to project heroism into the margins of the war, operations outside Europe or in the secret service. T. E. Lawrence became the centre of a cult whose devotees included, besides Buchan, Churchill, Shaw, Robert Graves, E. M. Forster, Winifred Holtby, C. Day Lewis – and even the Oxford exotics Harold Acton and Brian Howard. The first major study was written by Liddell Hart himself.

What was Lawrence's attraction? An individual still effective in a mechanistic age? A patriotic élitist, all the more significant for 'going native' in Arabia and the RAF? An intellectual active in politics? Lawrence's Arabism reflected the preoccupations of Victorian foreign affairs, the Byronic itinerary, politics and mysticism of *Tancred*, not to speak of such later figures as Gordon, Doughty and Scawen Blunt. Arabism implied a return to the Disraelian preference for cultivation over civilization, while Lawrence's degradation and recovery chimed in with homoeroticism, an establishment recoiling from revolutionary experience, and a revival of the pilgrimage ethos of Bunyan's radicalism.

Buchan's *A Prince of the Captivity* was probably the most elaborate Lawrence fiction, in which an adventure-story frame acted as a report on the present discontents of the world. Degraded for a crime he didn't commit, Adam Melfort becomes a British secret agent in the First World War, rescues an American explorer, Falconet, in the Arctic in 1919, almost provides the Labour movement with a new leader in 1926, saves the Weimar Republic from the communists and Nazis, and finally redeems Creevey in the Alps. Lawrence himself was baffled by the book:

> He takes figures of today and projects their shadows on to clouds, till they grow surhuman and grotesque: then describes them! Now I ask you – it sounds a filthy technique, but the books are like athletes racing: so clean-lined, speedy, breathless. For our age they mean nothing: they are sport only: but will a century hence disinter them and proclaim him the great romancer of our blind and undeserving generation?[42]

Melfort seems impossibly heroic, yet he is framed in an intricate code of references, literary, philosophical and political, and functions in a realistic context. In this sense he fits into Buchan's interest in leadership in *The Path of the King* (1930). Throughout the novel there are references and allusions to Disraeli, Kipling – *Kim* in particular – Bunyan, Frazer, Jung. Melfort's ultimate incorporation into Creevey is out of the folk-tale elements – the Fisher King or Adonis–Attis–Osiris myths – which Buchan like Eliot had culled from *The Golden Bough*.

This ambiguity could be put down to two things. One was Buchan's continuing relationship with Scotland, symbolized by Melfort's semi-mystical affinity with the mind of his dead son, and a Hebridean island, Eilean Ban (the Island of Youth), whose shape continually changes in his dreams. The idea of the cultivated leader appealed to him, but he could never shake off the alternative, local community of Scots Calvinism. His major work of 1932, a remarkable biography of Walter Scott, must have intensified this, and in the same year he made an impassioned defence of Scottish nationality, which cut right across the absolute sovereignty which underlay the ideal of the leader as hero.[43]

Buchan's 'clubland hero' style coexisted ill with such complexity. Modernism could fuse with conservative politics to restate a heroic ideal, but the formal policy of the State had to be worth it. In 1933, Buchan was counselling Ramsay MacDonald, the illegitimate son of a Morayshire farm labourer. The successful careers of both had ended in a moral murk. In 1931, MacDonald – supported by Buchan – had, like Utlaw, 'gone back on' his class, and badly damaged the conventions of adversary politics, while Buchan had found out that Balfour/Baldwin 'Englishness' had many Lumley/Balfour qualities: infiltration, *agents provocateurs*, forgery, media manipulation. Appeals to patriotism can become double-edged when the devotee – particularly the *provincial* devotee – looks behind the curtain. Erskine Childers, the Anglo-Irishman whose *Riddle of the Sands* (1903) created the precedent for Buchan's shockers, reacted against British 'betrayal' and died before an Irish Free State firing squad in 1923 as an irreconcilable republican. Just as Graham Greene later wrote that Elizabethan England incubated determined and, by their lights, patriotic recusants who would go to the stake for Catholicism, Buchan must have realized the appeal of such responses.[44] In his last novel, *Sick Heart River* (1941), he deserted Britain altogether for the multiculturalism of Canada.

X

The Auden generation had no such scruples about sovereignty; although their élitism led to communism, Valentine Cunningham has pointed out that many of its aspects were compatible with various sorts of semi-mystical authoritarianism, fascism not excluded. In May 1933 Auden wrote in the *New Statesman*: 'We live in an age in which the collapse of all previous standards coincides with the perfection in technique for the centralised distribution of ideas; some kind of revolution is inevitable, and will as inevitably be imposed from above by a minority.'[45] Eliot and Auden, and for that matter Lawrence and Leavis, slipped into the semi-vacuum left by the expulsion of Germanism and left-wing socialism's total absence of ideas about the State: a situation favourable to a man as handy with the *Führerprinzip* as Auden. But the limitations of his impact are as significant as his successes. Harold Nicolson may have borrowed the title of *Public Faces* (1933) from an Auden poem, and Naomi Mitchison got some of the fantasies in *We Have Been Warned* (1935) from him as well as from *The Golden Bough*, but he had little connection with actual politics, or even (although Mitchison's brother was J. B. S. Haldane) with the most purposive strand of 1930s Marxism, the research scientists.[46] Instead, a self-consciously schoolboy element of mystery, conspiracy and adventure, coupled with hero-worship and homoeroticism, made Auden and his friends a curiously archaic and English avant-garde.

In the 1600s, the dynamics of English Protestantism ran either to millenarianism or imperialism, while Scots 'covenant theology' thought in terms of the smaller civic unit. English Marxism was similarly ambitious and its élitism was the 'ascriptive' élitism of those born to power. Stephen Spender's father was the editor of the *Westminster Review*, John Strachey's was the *Spectator* editor who had fulminated against *The New Machiavelli*; Harold Laski and Victor Gollancz were disillusioned Liberal crown princes. There was in the 1920s no radical Bohemia to build on like that of the Surrealists in France or the *avant-gardes* in the various German cities, and the British periphery was restating, not negating, its nationality. The young Australian Jack Lindsay regarded himself as a radical, and inhabited the same sort of Fitzrovian *milieu* as that frequented slightly later by Anthony Powell – whose early novels suggest an atmosphere of overbearing middle-aged stuffiness – but even he reflected how most of his London associates were themselves Australian: 'We remained at root . . . an Australian explosion in the English scene, which politely ignored the noise, held its nose, and went on with its own business.'[47] Eliot's continuing influence showed that the establishment could still domesticate rebels. Its historical perspective took it back, *through* the 1789–1848 epoch – via the liberal Anglicanism which had confronted godless revolution – to the sixteenth century, and the imaginative world of the younger writers remained framed by its constructs: the public schools, gamesmanship, the ideal of trusteeship, the reconciliation of science and belief. The graveyard of Liberalism – the desolation of Arnold Bennett's provincial industrial towns – was to be the starting-point of Auden's topography of British society, but the metropolis was the goal.

The plays that Auden wrote for the Group Theatre – *The Dog beneath the Skin* (1935), *The Ascent of F6* (1936) and *On the Frontier* (1938) – were pervaded by the millennial and the Manichaean: all saw innocent or duped protagonists encountering an evil world. In this, was the courage of the hero an escape from moral choice, or a positive response to it? In *The Ascent of F6*, Auden and Isherwood differed on the position of their mountaineer hero, modelled on T. E. Lawrence. Isherwood saw him as a weak man in flight from moral choice; Auden, perhaps mindful of his beloved Norse sagas, was more positive. Even so, between the Carlyleian tradition of the hero as maker – which found it easy to assimilate the images of Soviet films and propaganda – and the all-enduring martyr figure of the front-line soldier, current in the flood of war novels and memoirs in the early 1930s, the idea of non-metaphorical politics in a pluralistic community simply disappeared.

W. B. Yeats argued in his introduction to *The Oxford Book of Modern Verse* (1936) that the humanist realism of the war poets was incapable of handling the scale of the conflict: 'When man has withdrawn into the quicksilver at the back of the mirror no great event becomes luminous in his mind; it is no longer possible to write *The Persians*, *Agincourt*,

Chevy Chase: some blunderer has driven his car on to the wrong side of the road – that is all.[48] 'The quicksilver at the back of the mirror' alludes to Stendhal's realism which Yeats, seeking a political culture to vitalize the leaders of 1930s Ireland, had to reject. Catastrophes on such a scale could not be allowed to distort the practical politics - 'theatre business, management of men' - which he had largely derived from his understanding of Renaissance Italy. His own career included an embarrassing dalliance with the putative leaders of Irish fascism, but he was ultimately constrained by the new Irish *polis*, which he had served as Senator.[49] The statement of E. M. Forster that he would put friendship above patriotism might make sense in a conservative imperial power, but not in a new small nation.

Beneath the bucolics of Baldwin, confidence in England had diminished. The 'métèque' element which had been super-patriotic in the 1900s now became 'collapsible': the most susceptible to other patriotisms. Guy Burgess was part-American, Anthony Blunt from the family of that Sidonia-like Irish-Arabist gadfly Wilfred Scawen Blunt, Donald MacLean the son of Buchan's Liberal opponent in Peebles-shire. In 1934, Graham Greene published *It's a Battlefield*. It begins like a Buchan story in Clubland – Conrad, James, Balfour are flickering presences – as an elderly Assistant Commissioner at Scotland Yard investigates the case of a communist bus-driver condemned for murdering a policeman. Greene stressed that the novel was ironic, not a political tract, although he treated his communists with sympathy. But Greene's Clubland is a crust: beneath it is the trackless city of Conrad's *Secret Agent*, and his Assistant Commissioner has no longer any of the confidence in his cause that his predecessor had in that novel. Approached by an elderly relative, now a communist, pressing for a reprieve, he admires her enthusiasm, and wonders why he persists with his own job:

I am a coward, he told himself; I haven't the courage of my convictions; I am not indispensable to the Yard; it is the Yard which is indispensable to me . . . If I had faith, he thought wryly; if I had any conviction that I was on the right side; Caroline has that; when she loses it, she has only to change her side.[50]

A couple of years later a young upper-class Englishman read a passage about communists from Greene's *The Confidential Agent* – ' "No, of course not," he replied, "But I still prefer the people they lead – even if they lead them all wrong." "The poor, right or wrong," she scoffed. "It's no worse – is it? – than my country right or wrong. You choose your side once and for all – of course, it may be the wrong side. Only history can tell that" '[51] – and used it to justify a political decision: his name was Kim Philby and he was joining the KGB.

NOTES

1   Graham Greene, *The Ministry of Fear* (London: Jonathan Cape, 1943), pp. 68–9.
2   See Harvie, 'Political Thrillers and the condition of England from the 1840s to the 1880s', in Arthur Marwick (ed.), *Literature and Society* (London: Routledge, 1990), pp. 226 ff.
3   Douglas Sladen, *Twenty Years of My Life* (London: Constable, 1915), p. 294.
4   David T. Stafford, 'Spies and gentlemen: the birth of the British spy novel, 1893–1914', *Victorian Studies*, vol. 24, (1980–1).
5   Leon O' Broin, *The Prime Informer* (London: Sidgwick & Jackson, 1971), pp. 38–70; and see Christopher Andrew, *Secret Service* (London: Constable, 1985).
6   David Wright, 'The Great War, government propaganda and English "men of letters" 1914–1916', *Literature and History*, no. 7, (Spring 1978), pp. 70–100.
7   cf. Paul Fussell, *The Great War in Modern Memory* (London: Oxford University Press, 1975), p. 28.
8   Baldick, *The Social Mission of English Criticism* (London: Oxford University Press, 1981), ch. 4.
9   John Buchan, *The Power House* (n.p.: Blackwood, 1916), p. 64.
10 ibid., pp. 80–1.
11 Graham Greene, 'The last Buchan', in *The Lost Childhood and Other Essays* (Harmondsworth: Penguin, 1962), p. 119; Janet Adam Smith, *John Buchan* (Oxford: Oxford University Press, 1985), p. 253.
12 Oppenheim, *A People's Man* (London: Methuen, 1915), pp. 247–8; *The Pool of Memory* (London: Hodder & Stoughton, 1941), pp. 37 ff.
13 David Daniell, *The Interpreter's House* (London: Nelson, 1975), pp. 1–37; I have a copy of a Nazi publication, *Who's Who in Britain* (Frankfurt, 1938), in which the relevant entry is: 'Tweedsmuir, Lord: Pro-Jewish activity.'
14 Smith, *Buchan*, p. 212.
15 Stephen McKenna, *Sonia* (London: Methuen, 1917), p. 2.
16 cf. the reputation of Ortega y Gasset's *The Revolt of the Masses* (London: Allen & Unwin, 1932).
17 See John Stevenson, *British Society, 1914–45* (London: Allen Lane, 1984), pp. 398–9.
18 Virginia Woolf, 'Mr Bennett and Mrs Brown', in *Collected Essays*, Vol. 1 (London: Hogarth Press, 1966), p. 320.
19 Malcolm Bradbury, *The Social Context of Modern English Literature* (London: Blackwell, 1971), pp. 65 ff.
20 Still the best thing on Lloyd George and his entourage is A. J. P. Taylor, *English History, 1914–45* (Harmondsworth: Penguin, 1975), pp. 30, 103 ff.
21 See Max Beloff, *Wars and Welfare: Britain 1914–45* (London: Arnold, 1984), p. 38.
22 McKenna, *Sonia*, p. 404.

23 For Ford's career, see Arthur A. Mizener, *The Saddest Story* (London: The Bodley Head, 1971), pp. 365–81.
24 For the Maurice incident, see Taylor, *English History*, pp. 146–7, 172–3.
25 *Arnold Bennett's Journal*, ed. Newman Flower (London: Cassell, 1933), entry for 11 November 1925; and see Andrew Mylett, *Arnold Bennett: The Evening Standard Years* (London: Chatto & Windus, 1974), pp. xviii–xvix.
26 Birkenhead in *Daily Mail*, November 1926, quoted in James Hepburn (ed.), *Arnold Bennett: The Critical Heritage* (London: Routledge, 1981), pp. 475–83.
27 Arnold Bennett, *Lord Raingo* (London: Cassell, 1926), p. 285.
28 Walter Elliot, *Toryism and the Twentieth Century* (London: Philip Allen, 1928), p. 95.
29 Robert Blake, 'The Right', in John Raymond (ed.), *The Baldwin Age* (London: Eyre & Spottiswoode, 1960), p. 35.
30 Martin Green, *Children of the Sun* (London: Constable, 1977), ch. 1.
31 Valentine Cunningham, *British Writers of the Thirties* (Oxford: Oxford University Press, 1988), pp. 143–4.
32 Humphrey Carpenter, *W. H. Auden* (London: Allen & Unwin, 1981), p. 57.
33 Evelyn Waugh, *Vile Bodies* (London: Chapman & Hall, 1930), pp. 126–7.
34 Galsworthy, *Swan Song* (London: Heinemann, 1928), p. 88.
35 ibid., p. 31.
36 W. H. Auden, 'September 1, 1939'.
37 Carpenter, *Auden*, p. 135.
38 Catherine Carswell, Lawrence's first biographer, was a close friend of both men, and elements of Constance Chatterley seem derived from her. See John Carswell's introduction to Catharine Carswell, *The Savage Pilgrimage* (Cambridge: Cambridge University Press, 1981).
39 See the introduction by Roland Gant to D. H. Lawrence, *The First Lady Chatterley* (Harmondsworth: Penguin, 1973), p. 5.
40 D. H. Lawrence to Arthur MacLeod, 1913, in *The Letters of D. H. Lawrence*, ed. J. T. Boulton (Cambridge: Cambridge University Press, 1979), p. 544. For Buchan, see 'Gods are kittle cattle: J. G. Frazer and John Buchan', in R. Fraser (ed.), *James George Frazer* (London: Macmillan, 1990).
41 See Angus Calder, 'A mania for self-reliance', in Graham Martin and Douglas Jefferson (eds), *The Uses of Fiction* (Milton Keynes: Open University Press, 1983).
42 Quoted in Smith, *Buchan*, p. 280.
43 Speech in Commons of 24 November 1932, in *Hansard*, Vol. 272, cols 235–360.
44 Graham Greene, preface to H. A. R. Philby, *My Secret War* (London: MacGibbon & Kee, 1968).
45 Quoted in Carpenter, *Auden*, p. 135; and see Cunningham, *British Writers of the Thirties*, p. 236.
46 See Gary Werskey, *The Visible College* (London: Allen Lane, 1977).
47 Jack Lindsay, *Fanfrolico and After* (London: Bodley Head, 1962), p. 182.
48 W. B. Yeats, introduction to *The Oxford Book of Modern Verse* (London: Oxford University Press, 1936), p. xxxiv.
49 Conor Cruise O'Brien, 'Passion and cunning', in T. N. Jeffares (ed.), *In Excited Reverie* (London: Macmillan, 1965).
50 Greene, *It's a Battlefield* (London: Heinemann, 1970), pp. 216–17.
51 Quoted in Philby, *My Silent War*, p. xviii.

8

Class? Nation?
Commonwealth?

I

IN CONTRAST TO postwar indirection, our perception of the 1930s
is sharp. Politics is important and literature foregrounded; the output of
political fiction higher than it would be for another couple of decades;
the literary historiography dense. Yet a closer inspection of the period is
less reassuring: a survey of a territory subjected to an almost totalitarian
Anschluss, resulting in a rewriting of history and a new chronology. The
problem is Auden.

Auden is a *fact* of 1930s literature, as Hitler or Stalin were facts of
1930s politics – to be explained by academic literary historians, not
these days much concerned about 'value', in empirical terms. Was
Auden as a poet more than middle-ranking? On a level with Edwin
Muir? Inferior to MacNiece or MacDiarmid? Time has not dealt kindly
with his *entourage*, with Spender or Day Lewis, but there can be no
doubting his literary-political significance. But a monument on the
scale of Valentine Cunningham's *British Writers of the 1930s* suggests
parallels with Morley's *Life of Gladstone*: literary politics of a particular
sort – metropolitan, male, declaratory, authoritarian – is sanctioned;
other approaches, more intimate, more humane, are excluded. It isn't
just that one looks in vain in Cunningham for Saunders Lewis or Neil
Gunn or Seán O'Faoláin, and realizes that literary historians in Scotland
or Wales would regard his incursions into their fields as capricious. A
whole structure of literary sensibility has somehow got lost.

To discard the notion of 'value' invites the substitution of alternative
social assessments, yet the ruling interpretation is no more helpful here,
social history only figuring where it seconds some literary symbol or
tendency. Carlyle fits such treatment, because he affected practically all
of his contemporaries who mattered. But an account like Cunningham's
must be suspect, if Sir Oswald Mosley appears frequently but not
Clement Attlee; if Henry Williamson figures much more prominently

than J. B. Priestley, and Joyce Cary doesn't figure at all. One senses a skewing, all the more telling because completely unconscious, towards the paradigms of the metropolitan élite - something as valid for the 1980s as for the 1930s. This approach also distorts chronology. Auden's annexation of the decade *as such* is taken for granted, even when, in culture-politics terms, it ought to divide into two longer periods, one extending from around the General Strike to 1935, and the second from 1935 to 1955. The first is marked by 'anti-bourgeois' experimentalism, provincialism, feminism and revolutionary ideas; the second by a more specific, less radical, defence of British political practice against the Nazi threat.[1]

Or is this unfair? Does the counter-case give minor talents undeserved significance? Cary, Priestley, Winifred Holtby, Howard Spring and Eric Linklater were more than 'good reads' and reached a bigger public than, say, Harold Heslop or James Barke. The bestseller had moved on from Marie Corelli and Dornford Yates, with its readers demanding enlightenment about technical and social change. If many authors of Left Book Club selections and early Penguins are now obscure, this doesn't mean that they were *then* insignificant. The important thing is to establish the questions to which they were supposed to provide answers.

Many of the old pedagogues were still active. Notably Wells and Shaw. Late Shaw – praising Stalin and Mussolini in his polemics - is not respectable. But *Too True to Be Good* (1931), *The Apple Cart* (1929) and *On the Rocks* (1933) mattered to the politically alert, as his dramatic skill could still animate ideas and pose ethical dilemmas – some quite unexpected. Private Meek (T. E. Lawrence) doesn't turn out the hero of *Too True to Be Good*; Shaw's own position is projected by Aubrey Blount, clergyman-burglar, as awkward as madman Keegan, a potential Carlyle-figure for the decade:

Nature never intended me for soldiering or thieving: I am by nature and destiny a preacher. I am the new Ecclesiastes. But I have no Bible, no creed: the war has shot both out of my hands. The war has been a fiery forcing house in which we have grown with a rush like flowers in a late spring following a terrible winter. And with what result? This: that we have outgrown our religion, outgrown our political system, outgrown our own strength of mind and character . . .[2]

Shaw's characters reject Mosley, Mussolini and both of the Lawrences as enthusiasts for Louis MacNeice's 'shooting straight in a crooked cause'. Arguments dense with allusion and ingenuity explain why Shaw remained important to the non-Oxbridge and non-metropolitan left, the readers of *Forward* and *Tribune*, the members of the Left Book Club. His economics remained acute. *The Apple Cart*'s Britain, living off the luxury goods and service industries, dominated by multinationals and the United States, with the monarchy more salient than the politicians, was closer to the real 1984 than Orwell, who never got beyond J. A. Hobson's *Imperialism* of 1901. In *On the Rocks* a Labour government modernizes Britain through a New Deal more drastic and effective than anything the Independent Labour Party had ever advocated. But behind this ingenuity there is also a humane confusion at the horrors of the post-1914 world, and an attempt to analyse and control them.[3] Wells also regained his status as a prophet, boosted by modern technology, in the 1935 filming of *Things to Come*, in which he publicized the supremacy of air power. Both remained Victorians – *The Battle of Dorking* still echoed in Wells, Comtist élitism in Shaw – but perhaps they contributed more than their juniors to the popular front, the documentary movement and the growth of support for socialist ideas during the war.

Popular culture is not just about innovation but about dissemination, and in the 1930s this was particularly energetic. Most homes got radios, talkies took the cinema to its zenith; regular holidays, personal transport and daily newspapers filtered down to working people – as long as they *were* working. Orwell grabbed at some of these developments, as Wells had earlier done, but without Wells's synthesizing skill. He was weak on films, commerce and sport, but he gave the 1930s two vivid Bromstead-like images: Wigan, the run-down northern industrial town, and Lower Binfield in *Coming Up for Air* (1938): old England corroded by the rapid industrialization of the South-East. On one hand the 1930s ethos was centralized, methodized, standardized – the semi-D, the Morris 8, Ovaltine, Truby King babies. More people were better off. But in Scotland, Wales and the North conditions had worsened; while the Irish Free State and Britain were at economic war. Even this prosperity carried its paradoxes. Politically the North was inert, the South radical; the North was also more fearful of the menace Wells had forecast: the bomber.[4]

What would Trollope or Disraeli have made of the condition of this England? Ireland – central to Trollope's idea of Britain – had gone its own way. Israel was, thanks to the Balfour Declaration, a practical possibility. Hugh MacDiarmid – another Carlyle redux? – was trying to tear the 1707 Union apart. Ford and Bennett had shown the battering that war and Lloyd George had given the conventions of Westminster *and* the novel of high politics. So one aspect of political writing after the General Strike was about defining the British *polis*: seeing by what fictional strategies it could be nailed down.[5] In this the novel was side-tracked. Instead, Orwell saw stereotypes out of the cinema, sent up by the American writer Elmer Rice in *A Voyage to Purilia* (1935), as significant 'from an anthropological point of view'.[6] Rice was certainly a prototype for an outbreak in 1933 of semi-scientific investigations of the British 'image'. A. G. MacDonnell's *England, Their England*, Winifred Holtby's *The*

Incredible Island and Harold Nicolson's *Public Faces* painted a frieze of elderly politicians muddling away, a tranquil dull landscape receding behind them, and 'England Destroyed' on the news-stands meaning a follow-on at Trent Bridge. These writers tended to be mildly reformist, patriotic, arch and cosy (although Holtby scratched a little in the feminist cause), even when, as in Nicolson's ponderous diplomatic game, his cast start a nuclear war.

Complacency didn't last. In 1936, Winifred Holtby ended *South Riding* by anticipating bombing raids; MacDonnell (to be killed in one) savaged the Conservative arms manufacturers in *Lords and Masters* (1936); while Orwell's friend Geoffrey Gorer ended his *Nobody Talks Politics* (1935) with his hero Freddy Green (after a decade's sleep) on the run from a British fascist government. Tossed from Labour to the Mosleyites to sandalled progressives, Green opts for the revolutionary left. Where he would doubtless have joined Cyril Connolly's Comrade Cris Clay, sometime Oxford aesthete, now cultural commissar, keeping discipline with his tommy-gun: 'I stand no nonsense. Remember, my dears, a line is being drawn. Tatatat. See you at the Mass Observatory. Something is going to go, baby, And it won't be your stamp collection. Boom!'[7]

II

The Communist Party polled 0.1 per cent of the vote in the 1935 election, although it returned Willie Gallagher in West Fife. Labour polled nearly 38 per cent, and had around 400,000 individual members; and, although Eng. Lit. can do without it, it was in the 1920s, after the eclipse of the German and American movements, *the* social-democratic prototype. Between the wars the Labour Party inspired over thirty plays and novels, their authors including some senior MPs and ideologists: G. R. Mitchison and his wife Naomi, Mary Agnes Hamilton, Barbara Wootton and Ellen Wilkinson. Two – Winifred Holtby's *South Riding* (1935) and Howard Spring's *Fame Is the Spur* (1940) – became enormous successes among party members, while J. B. Priestley – for Beatrice Webb in 1941 'the dominant literary personality of England today . . . owing to his superlative gift for broadcasting' – played a major rôle in Labour's 1945 victory, though more as commentator and playwright than as novelist.[8] 'Labour Party' fiction tells much about the mobilization of activists, while some of it – particularly Storm Jameson's *Mirror in Darkness* sequence (1934–6) – is of remarkably high quality. So why, then, was the net result a Labour ideology centralized, Parliament-fixated and (as post-mortems on the 1945–51 government suggested) almost fatally lacking in its own imaginative power?[9]

Labour didn't fit into the old paradigms of high politics (while the class-position and the élitism of the *communisants*, of course, did). The movement was grounded in the provincial working-class community; its élite reflected the politicization of women through the suffrage movement; and it suffered throughout from the calculated intervention of international communism with its deliberated strategies for intellectual politics. All of these factors, which were to diffuse the literary image of the party, can best be analysed in three separate stages: the fiction of the Independent Labour Party, the fiction of 'revolutionary disillusionment with parliamentarianism', and the 'Popular Front' fiction of 'democratic anti-fascism'.

The 'soul of the Labour movement', the Independent Labour Party, was formed in Bradford in 1893, and most of its branches were in Scotland and Yorkshire, with in 1927 about 60,000 members, organized like much of nonconformity in 'gathered churches', rather than in constituency parties. Its ethos was grass-roots, regionalist, and strongest in the North. Its links with the 'party of power' of the 1920s were limited, as its sudden expansion into the vacuum caused by the Liberal collapse fitted no Marxist pattern of class struggle. To Egon Wertheimer, a German Social Democrat journalist, Labour was still the 'trade union' wing of the old Liberal alliance. Yet he was amazed at how it ingested and promoted members of the old governing class: 'Where I had come from a Mosley would have had to serve for years in the outer darkness because he was Curzon's son-in-law. The party statutes would have kept him far away from any position of influence.' Labour might be flexible, but was it at all radical?

Even at this stage a 'parliamentary consensus' of trade unionists, centre-left reformers and metropolitan intellectuals had evolved, visible even to a Tory like Buchan in his *causerie, The Island of Sheep* (1919), and extending to ex-Liberals from the suffrage movement or the Union of Democratic Control. In *Follow My Leader* (1921) a journalist and future Labour MP, Mary Agnes Hamilton, had her suffragette heroine marry a dependable union leader, who meets her capitalist father on equal but reassuring terms. Ellen Wilkinson, in *Clash* (1929), was less persuaded, contrasting the febrile 'Bloomsbury circle . . . who bestowed fame on themselves by writing reviews of each others books' (while living off coal shares) with the northern trade unionist William Royd 'a man who had put his feet upon a rock that was under the shifting sands of modern life'. Buchan had written that even the Clydesiders, the most intransigent of MPs, would come into line as parliamentarians, but by 1933 was dismayed by the rapidity with which any constitutional radicalism evaporated.[10]

Ethical socialism as dissenting religion found little outlet here, while the mining industry, the largest single source of ILP support, was beset by the triangular conflict between the owners, the union hierarchy and the communist 'Minority Movement'. The Scottish coalfield, whose 'Little Moscows' radiated a highly literate consciousness, captured this in Joe Corrie's play *In Time o' Strife* (1927) and James Welsh's novel *Norman Dale MP* (1929). Corrie's play was published by *Forward*, toured with a miners' drama company, was staged by the Workers' Theatre Movement, and even managed an expressionistic performance (somewhat disconcerting to the author) in Leipzig. Set at the end of the 1926 lockout, it shows a community at the limits of its endurance. The older miners grumble about the lockout, curse the socialists and communists, but stay out. Their women are resolute, even when facing death or rejecting a lover who blacklegs. Government is alien and hostile: the police protect the blacklegs; the parish council cuts off relief. Resistance ends, but the community stands firm, waiting for its next challenge, the last words with the archetypal collier's wife:

> Jean: That's the spirit, my he'rties! sing! sing! tho' they hae ye chained to the wheels and the darkness. Sing! tho' they hae ye crushed in the mire. Keep up your he'rts, my laddies, you'll win through yet, for there's nae power on earth can crush the men that can sing on a day like this.[11]

Corrie was certainly influenced by O'Casey's *Juno and the Paycock* (1924) and like O'Casey presents a distanced but still sympathetic account of militancy. Fife, where he had been a miner, had seen strikers issuing their own money in 1920 and in 1926 (albeit briefly) taking over local government. Corrie probably also drew on Welsh's *The Underworld*, about a trade unionist's struggles and his death in a pit disaster, which sold 50,000 copies after publication in 1922, and was translated into German, Dutch and Japanese. Welsh became a Labour MP in 1922 but, moving rightwards like so many union officials, made his next novel, *The Morlocks* (1926), a polemic against the communists. *Norman Dale MP* reverts to the condescending integration of the Kailyard. A young miner finds an abandoned baby whom he christens Corrie (oddly enough), brings up as his sister and sends to university, while he ascends to Parliament via the union, the county council and the ILP. Welsh conveys the biblical covenanting spirit of Scottish Labour – the commitment to education, and even the suspicion of Westminster: 'To Norman, accustomed as he was to the breeze of the moor, the place was suffocating. He perspired freely, and a constriction of the throat made him uncomfortable as he became conscious of the quiet feeling of tension which pervaded the place.'[12] Dale falls – literally – into the aristocratic embrace, and his constituents have it in for him. But Welsh solves everything by bringing Dale to the rescue at a pit disaster, which kills off the titled vamp and Dale's rival in love, and marries Dale and Corrie off.

Norman Dale MP is interesting mostly for its evasions and its central cliché: the MP and his constituency split by his London affairs. It also shows the breach between the first generation of Labour MPs and their juniors whose outlook was formed by the materialist 'revolution' of 1906–14 and the Labour Colleges. To this challenge Dale has *no* social democrat answer. His Tory opponent tells him: '". . . I wish you would drop the class cant, Dale, and talk about men and women as human beings or people, or something less liable to stir up the hatred you're so anxious to avoid." Norman did not know what to reply, and stood still thinking.'[13] Even Buchan, realistic about class, never tried this one. Welsh reacted to the setback of 1926 with unconditional ideological surrender. Although he remained an MP until 1945, he never wrote again. Joe Corrie's reaction was different, but almost equally depressing: he left the pits to make a living as a writer for the Community Drama movement which swept Scotland in the early 1930s, and his pawky 'kitchen comedies' sustained him until his death in 1968. Welsh accepted the *polis* of Westminster, Corrie settled – reluctantly – for the continuing popularity of the Kailyard.

The General Strike and unemployment blocked the development of the local Labour community – strong though inarticulate in Corrie's miners. Labour had either to compromise with Parliament or withdraw from democratic politics. It took the former course, and the dismal consequences in 1931 are foreboded in *Norman Dale*, whose social and sexual troubles in London expressed both personal alienation and the failure of a vision of social justice which was essentially local and pluralist. Fictive affairs between Labour MPs and upper-class women – perhaps wish-fulfilment – were an aspect of this. Both had gained new prospects through the war, only to find conventions hardening again. Constance Chatterley was not alone. But the left's weakness meant that this theme – suggesting new strategies for tackling a society created by the male upper class – relapsed into sticky cliché.

III

In 1936, Vera Brittain, a bestseller-writer on the strength of *Testament of Youth*, published *Honourable Estate*, a worthy trudge through feminist and socialist history since 1900. She ended it in 1929, with her heroine a Labour MP, and noted that to stop there gave the book shape: '. . . so much has changed since.' Indeed it had. Labour MPs fell from 288 to 52 in the 1931 election, when the Liberals – Lloyd George excepted – threw themselves in with the Tories, and Snowden and MacDonald deserted ethical socialism for the National Government. Few followed them into the ranks of National Labour, but within the Labour Party divisions with the ILP grew and in 1932 it disaffiliated.

By 1936, thanks largely to communist subversion, ILP membership had collapsed, while the Communist Party of Great Britian, 3,200 strong in 1930, rose to 11,700 members. Was native radicalism being under-mined by a foreign power, or could the ILP simply not cope? The CPGB of the 'third stage', between 1928 and 1935, was uncompromisingly hostile to 'social fascists'. Disastrous in Germany, this still managed to attract many British socialists fed up with parliamentarianism, and it made a real attempt at an alternative, revolutionary culture. Many of the Cambridge scientific élite enlisted, besides such upper-class rebels as Philby and Claud Cockburn. The *Daily Worker* appeared in 1930, the Workers' Theatre Movement thrived, and in 1933 came the *Left Review*.[14]

The Soviet commentator Dmitri Mirsky argued in 1933 that the British intelligentsia would go fascist, except for lower-middle-class groups whom the Communist Party could radicalize. Given the intellectual support Mosley got in his early days, there was some logic to this, and as a result the Communist Party welcomed non-party radicals in the Workers' Theatre Movement, which produced Corrie's *In Time o' Strife* and adapted agitprop ideas derived from Germany. Few writers were communists, not even Harold Heslop, whose novel of the General Strike, *The Gate of a Strange Field*, was first published in Russia in 1929. When Heslop went as a delegate to the World Council of Socialist Writers in 1934, the other British delegate was Amabel Williams-Ellis, sister of John Strachey. The latter, only three years earlier adviser to Mosley, was now about to become the voice of intellectual communism. The British intelligentsia had protean qualities which would have baffled Mirsky – had Stalin allowed him to survive.[15]

This was aided by a number of ideological mediators. Grassic Gibbon and the Marxist historian Gordon Childe were anthropological dif-fusionists, their ideal of a pre-agricultural golden age tallying imagi-natively with Marx's notion of post-capitalist society. Science was rep-resented not only by the research élite, but also by the neo-positivist popularizers Olaf Stapledon and Gerald Heard, influential on such as Naomi Mitchison and Auden.[16] In fact 'establishment' culture, under pressure of the liberal nationalism of the Newbolt Report of 1921, the threat of mass-unemployment, and various schemes for imperial devel-opment, was more open than the left thought, notably to innovators like John Grierson in the documentary film.[17] Commercial publishers moved away from massaging middle-class *Angst* with the likes of Warwick Deeping to encourage a more Dickensian blend of entertainment and concern – J. B. Priestley's *The Good Companions* (1929) was read aloud by Attlee to his family – and allowed some astute commercial poaching on areas which could otherwise have been claimed by the left. A. J. Cronin's reworking of *The House with the Green Shutters*, *Hatter's Castle* (1931), sold 3 million copies in twenty years.[18] No wonder that, in return, the Communist Party suspected naturalism and documentary. The Workers' Theatre Movement declared in 1932: 'The naturalistic form, namely that form which endeavours to show a picture on the stage as near to life as possible, is suitable for showing things as they appear on the surface, but does not lend itself to disclosing the reality which lies beneath.'[19] But it was unable to sustain an alternative, let alone incubate an English Brecht.

Common to CPGB and non-CPGB writers before 1936 is an anticipation of violence: the Condition of England is expressed by the forces of order laying into legitimate protest – as when mounted policemen rode into communist-led hunger marchers in Hyde Park in September 1932. Such conflicts mark Gibbon's *Grey Granite*, Walter Greenwood's *Love on the Dole* (1935), Graham Greene's *It's a Battlefield* (1935). In Naomi Mitchison's *We Have Been Warned* (1936) a young communist – called, intriguingly, Donald MacLean – kills a Tory newspaper proprietor, and is then smuggled to Russia by the heroine. The novel presents alternative endings: the election of a socialist government, something anticipated in her husband G. R. Mitchison's *The First Workers' Government* (1935); or fascist troopers and the police terrorizing North Oxford. *We Have Been Warned* started out as an exercise in collective writing, but became a highly personal statement, part documentary, part fantasy. John Sommerfield's *May Day* (1936), on the other hand, welded documentary to a panoramic view of London's society, with its story centring on two brothers, one killed by the police in a demonstration, the other politicized by the experience. Stuart Laing argues that Sommerfield uses the demonstration to clarify the class-confrontation theme, while Greene's treatment of a similar situation shows it fragmenting into the incompatible perceptions of isolated observers. But the interesting thing is the intelligentsia's lack of confidence in the rule of law: something which stands in direct contrast to 1848. Representative institutions, in Britain as in Europe, seemed to be dissolving in the naked reality of social confrontation.[20]

The most perceptive literary study of this polarization was Storm Jameson's *The Mirror in Darkness*, a sequence intended to explore the relationships between literature and politics, province and metropolis, in the postwar years. Certain influences make themselves felt: the lucidity and radicalism of Mark Rutherford, the social *nous* of Stendhal, whose 'mirror in the roadway' epithet is latent in Jameson's title, and something of the feel for English society of Ford Madox Ford. This is a novel that Valentine Tietjens could have written. Jameson's *alter ego* Mary Hervey

Russell, grand-daughter of a Yorkshire shipbuilder, mediates between the progressive literary and political life of London and the economic changes which are throttling freedom and social reform. An intelligentsia parted from its social roots, deprived even of the bonding induced by the war, is increasingly at the mercy of a reorganized, cartelized and authoritarian capitalism, personified in Thomas Harben. Harben's empire stretches through shipyards and mines to banks and newspapers, with Labour MPs and fascist street-fighters in his pay. Neither he nor the sympathetic centrist Jewish businessman Marcel Cohen seems a particularly English figure, but both would be instantly recognizable in the Weimar Republic, which Jameson knew well through her husband, the historian Guy Chapman. By *None Turn Back* (1935), which centres on the General Strike, we are almost certain that Cohen will share the fate of Walter Rathenau and be murdered by the right.

Edwin Muir reviewed *None Turn Back* in *The Listener*. Although he praised Jameson's writing, he attacked her characterization: 'All these people are seen as conditional responses to society; with the result that they must remain conditional, and that they can never speak to us. Society is their ventriloquist.'[21] Jameson took the hint and quit the sequence for the documentary movement. Although she was not a communist, *The Mirror in Darkness* still reflects a 'third stage' scenario of big business and fascism versus the working class. But by 1936, with the Nazis on the attack, she – like the Communist Party itself – recognized that the authoritarian menace was so great that the liberal centre had to be strengthened.

IV

The Popular Front began at the Soviet party congress in 1935, when Stalin, appalled at where his strategy had got him in Germany, made overtures to Western democratic movements and confirmed Russia's membership of the League of Nations. Centre-left governments were elected in Spain in February and in France in June 1936, and the Front was cemented by Franco's nationalist rebellion in Spain in the summer. It was soon endorsed by activists in British opposition parties, frustrated by the opportunism of Baldwin, who had campaigned for collective security through the League in 1935 and dropped it once confirmed in power. Liberals, whose vote fell by half from 1931 to 1935 - ending at only 6.5 per cent – were as frustrated as Labour, whose 38 per cent of the poll brought them only 154 seats. The adversary system had broken down so drastically that literary politics to a great extent became opposition politics.

The Popular Front had a direct and decidedly negative impact on political fiction. Titles published or produced in the few years 1933–6 totalled thirty-four, all but five coming from the left; 1937–9 brought only eighteen, with twelve from the left. The Front ditched revolutionary writing to swing the literary establishment to the 'democratic' side. Anthony Powell neatly captures this in *The Acceptance World* (1955), when the ancient bestseller-writer St John Clarke is mobilized as a man of the left by his satraps Mark Members and J. G. Quiggin. Powell's friend Orwell took a much more bitter view, later telling Arthur Koestler, one of the numerous German communists drafted in to run the Front, that for him 'history stopped in 1936' – in the sense that the communists betrayed their claim to historical congruence for *Realpolitik* ends – and he wrote at the time to Geoffrey Gorer that:

> . . . the Popular Front boloney boils down to this . . . Fascism, not of course called Fascism, will be imposed on us as soon as the war starts. So you will have Fascism with Communists participating in it, and, if we are in alliance with the U.S.S.R., taking a leading part in it. This is what has happened in Spain.[22]

Orwell maintained this line in *Homage to Catalonia* and as late as 1940 in *The Lion and the Unicorn*, yet the Front brought him his first substantial sales. *The Road to Wigan Pier*, commissioned in 1936 by Victor Gollancz and published in his new Left Book Club in 1937, sold 30,000 copies. Most studies of the LBC have stressed the pro-Sovietism of the ruling Troika of Gollancz, Strachey and Laski, but it was also part of a revolution in marketing – along with book clubs, book tokens (1930), and Penguins (1935) – which sent sales up from 7.2 million in 1928 to 26.8 million in 1939.[23] By 1938, when *Coming Up for Air* acidly treated the cosy tedium of an LBC meeting (one of the few times Orwell describes actual political activity), the book business of *Keep the Aspidistra Flying* (1934) was unrecognizable.

'Revolutionary' literature had stressed the autonomy of socialist life and consciousness; the Popular Front put 'defending democracy' against fascism first, and its main instrument was the documentary, which portrayed (and even celebrated) society as it was, rather than as it could be. This had two effects on the activists: it made them appreciate the complexity of British social organization, regional diversity, religion and traditional literary culture; but it also diminished the sense of historical change in class and economic relationships, and the religious-radical tradition of millennial protest.

Perhaps we see this best in the 'working-class novel'. Lewis Jones's *Cwmardy* (1937) and its sequel *We Live* (1939) take a Welsh mining valley from the 1900s to the Spanish Civil War. Jones's own Mardy, in Rhondda, was one of the 'Little Moscow' fortresses of the Communist Party, but Jones presents Cwmardy as *typical*: communism and autodidact materialism take a back seat to *Gemeinschaft.* There is little difference between *We Live* and the social-democratic attitudes of Gwyn Jones's novel about 1926, *Times Like These* (1936); if anything, Lewis Jones is more sentimental about the mineowner Lord Cwmardy and in making the main tragedy of *We Live* the suicide of a small shopkeeping couple ruined by the strike. The purpose is, ultimately, to compose a community, united against fascism, sending its son, Len Morgan, off to fight in Spain. The Scottish communist James Barke was similarly remodelled. His *Major Operation* (1936) had ended with a 'demonstration death' – that of an employer, converted to the workers' cause by the arguments (painfully didactic) of the communist in the next hospital-bed. *The Land of the Leal* (1939) presents instead a 'cross-class' Scottish democracy, misled by the pressures of capitalism, but uniting against fascism. Barke's martyrs, like Jones's, die in Spain.[24]

The *plus* of the Popular Front was that radical writers had to respect their cultural context. Jones's and Barke's main vernacular characters – Big Jim Morgan and Jean Ramsay – have a unifying presence which, like that of Chris Guthrie in Grassic Gibbon, gives their fictional society authenticity. What revolutionary Marxists would have called a 'deficiency in consciousness' meant an advance in realism. The minus was that, as Orwell noted, they surrendered their radicalism and their sense of history to a print-capitalism whose control didn't change. As far as democracy was concerned, the Popular Front was all loss.

V

The Communist Party didn't present the only options. Regional economic depression reacted with Britain's own *Gleichschaltung* in 1931 to discredit centralism and re-create political writing in the provinces. There, a greater range of cultural expression developed, although the necessary political institutions were weak. As Liberal Britain fell apart, even Bennett in *Lord Raingo*, like Ibsen in *Rosmersholm*, shaded towards symbolism, something which the Celtic myth-kitty had in abundance. This could mean a regrouped dissenting radicalism, but it could also mean the anti-Jacobinism emphasis on 'rootedness' of Spengler, Maurras and Barres, mediated through the Welshman Saunders Lewis and even through the Scot Hugh MacDiarmid.[25]

This ambiguity can be seen in the ideological traverse of perhaps the major socialist novel of the decade: Lewis Grassic Gibbon's *Scots Quair* – *Sunset Song* (1932), *Cloud Howe* (1933) and *Grey Granite* (1934). The *Quair* takes Chris Guthrie, born in 1890 to an Aberdeenshire crofter, through the experience of her people – and three marriages – to end in the same place forty-five years later. John Guthrie's is a 'thrawn' radicalism, of liberal independency - capable of co-operation, incapable of obedience – a social doctrine destroyed, along with the crofters, by the war. This is symbolized by the execution for desertion of Chris's husband, Ewan Tavendale: 'I couldn't believe it was me that stood in the trench, it was just daft to be there. So I turned and got out of it.'[26] 'The last of the old Scots people' cannot survive the machine age. The theme could have come from Carlyle and like him Gibbon seems to find no stopping-place.

Cloud Howe is a critique of social democracy, as the Reverend Robert Colquohoun tries to replace greed, competition and gossip with class co-operation in the factory-town of Segget. He fails. The 'traditional intellectuals', like the schoolmaster, dismiss him cynically or, like the local manufacturer, reformulate co-operation as a sort of Scottish fascism. Chris loses her child in the General Strike, and the equally symbolic death of another baby, gnawed by rats in a pigsty where her unemployed parents have taken shelter, a savage inversion of the Christmas story, drives Colquohoun to demand 'a faith that will cut like a knife'.[27] He dies with this materialist revelation on his lips, but in *Grey Granite* it is carried into action in urban Scotland by Chris's son Ewan, who schools himself as a scientific materialist and is spurred into politics by police brutality. Ewan ends up as the leader of a column of hunger marchers, *en route* to London where he will become a communist organizer.

Liberalism – social democracy – communism; Scots village – Scots city – British revolution. This seems like a copybook evolution of materialist consciousness, but it isn't shared by the central figure, Chris. At the end of *Grey Granite*, having married, and parted from, a Segget radical of the old sort, she moves back to her father's croft and starts to farm again. Does her death prove the hopelessness of any 'back to the land' programme, or as 'Chris Caledonia' does she fuse with the land whose evolution her story has symbolized?[28] Gibbon never resolved this ambiguity (he died in 1935), but it was critical for the interwar 'progressive' novel. How was a 'scientific' account of social change to be squared with the experience of the actors themselves – and the actual impact on the reader?

The provincialism of the 1890s had been socially and stylistically conservative, the interwar movement kept the political arena 'open' while invading modernist domains like time and memory. Third-person narration gave way to 'involved' presentation, along with collective evocations of memory and patterns of local speech, communicating directly with the ordinary reader's thought processes. Gibbon's narrative in *A Scots Quair* shifts from a 'voice of the land' in *Sunset Song* to a protagonist-chorus pattern in *Cloud Howe* and a range of individuated urban voices in *Grey Granite*. The stilted diction of the provincial in the metropolis is avoided, because it is no longer attempted.

The removal of Ireland meant that the Scots had to cope with a more centralized and conservative polity. They had been the complaisant consorts of British politics, the 'heids o' depairtments'. Charles Lever had noted in the 1870s that Scotland 'had no national absurdities: she neither asks for a flag nor a parliament. She demands only what will pay.'[29] Fictional Scots had been competent, if mercenary and psychologically rather maimed (think of Mrs Proudie and Lady Glencora – or the unscrupulous Undecimus Scott in *The Three Clerks*). They continued useful in productions such as J. M. Barrie's *The Admirable Crichton* (1902) and Ian Hay's *The Right Stuff: Episodes in the Career of a North Briton* (1909); the message – strident enough to provoke T. W. H. Crosland's counterblast *The Unspeakable Scot* (1901) – was that in the Union the Scots were the masterful Figaro-like servants who took the real decisions. War, slump and literary renaissance articulated and expanded the Scottish Question. The National Party of Scotland was – like Plaid Cymru which slightly pre-dated it – a party of literary men: Lewis Spence, MacDiarmid, Compton Mackenzie, Neil Gunn and R. B. Cunninghame-Graham were all members from its earliest days. The literary impulse did not last long: after several disappointing election results the NPS was merged into the more orthodox, politician-led Scottish National Party. But the political issues and activity which it provoked contributed to a renaissance in fiction as impressive (though not as well recognized) as that in poetry.[30] Under the aegis of Gregory Smith's 'Caledonian Antisyzygy', this had two incompatible inputs: One: language, myth and imagery. Two: science.

The first implied a reversion to traditional storytelling, of the sort Buchan commended in his 1931 English Association address: the resumption of the saga, in which the hero sets out from, and returns sadder or wiser to, his home community.[31] Just as Adam Melfort 'returned' to Eilean Ban, the saga form can be found in the *Scots Quair*, in Mitchison's *We Have Been Warned*, in Linklater's *Magnus Merriman* (1934) and in Gunn's *The Serpent* (1943). Chris Guthrie returns to her father's croft in Aberdeenshire; Dione Galton sets out from Auchanarnish to voyage through English politics and Russia and to end again in Argyllshire. Magnus Merriman begins and ends in the Orkneys; Gunn's Tom the Philosopher departs from Sutherland to the city and the socialist movement and returns to die.

Douglas Gifford has argued that these voyagers return to isolation in a society which ignores them: Magnus's epic 'The Returning Sun' unfinished, Chris Guthrie dead on the Barmekin, Tom snake-bitten.[32] All end remote from Scotland's teeming cities. And enough careers sank in exile or discouragement to make this stick. Such pessimism discounts, however, a compensating quasi-individualistic theme: a reassertion of the 'will to understand' that marked the Enlightenment. The figure of the scientist - MacDiarmid's Lenin - stands behind Gunn, Gibbon, Grierson and Bridie, just as Frazer the anthropologist looms over Buchan and Mitchison. The scientist was the new, fully conscious man who could create a humane order out of the wasteland of industrial Scotland. Yet he could also, as psychologist – Jungian rather than Freudian – validate the human satisfaction of life in small nations and small communities. The hero of Neil Gunn's *Highland River* (1937), the most symmetrical of the 'sagas', in which the boy's growth matches the life-cycle of the salmon, the Gaelic image of knowledge, explains to a colleague in his nuclear laboratory:

> An old woman in the old days in my country knew the nature of what grew around her quite precisely. She gathered her roots and her lichens and out of them made the vivid dyes you see in tartans. That was what happened in fact. It is clear, too, that they achieved a very tolerable community life, and worked to the rhythm of their own music and that sort of thing. In fact if a Scot is interested in dialectical materialism or proletarian humanism, it seems to me he should study the old system in order to find out how the new system would be likely to work amongst his kind.[33]

In a culture scarred by the emigration ethos, rediscovering childhood and the rituals of socialization had a distinctive importance. The Popular Front concentration on the local and the vernacular aided a later radicalism. Young Scottish communists like Norman Buchan and Hamish Henderson were to become both crucial figures in the folk-song revival – the latter Gramsci's first translator – and patrons of the sustained cultural revival of the 1960s.

More immediately, Grierson's efforts paid off. The Second World War and after saw, in films like *The Shipbuilders*, *Whisky Galore*, *I Know Where I'm Going* (all 1945), an ironic but perceptive commentary on the strengthening of Scottish identity, through the wartime régime of Tom Johnston as Secretary of State. This was to be outpaced by the centralization of the coalition and Labour governments, even after a postwar petition gained 2 million signatures for a home-rule covenant. But three works stimulated by it presage the later revival. In 1948, Robert Kemp and Tyrone Guthrie restaged Sir David Lyndesay's *The Thrie Estaitis*, a political play against misgovernment and religious hypocrisy first staged in 1540 – a vivid re-creation which was to have a profound effect on the young John Arden. In 1954, J. D. Scott's *The End of an Old Song* had his economist 'lad o' pairts' laying waste the symbols both of romantic nationalism and British identity. The future of Scotland, if it had one, would not be presented by documentary, but by decoding myth and nightmare.

James Bridie, as successful an Anglo-Scottish dramatist as Barrie had been, was no great enthusiast for nationalism, satirizing its authoritarian aspects in *Storm in a Teacup* in 1935. But his strange last play, *The Baikie Charivari* (1951), showed a Scotland 'lit by the dying fires of Empire', both mundane and surreal. Bridie's imperial governor Pounce-Pellot – Punch – Pontius Pilate, returns to his Firth of Clyde bungalow and his old enemies. Punch slays them, left and right, and forces a stay of execution from Auld Nick. Only by returning to his small country, Walter Elliot commented in his introduction, could the Scots Peer Gynt save himself in the modern world, but Pounce-Pellot's 'madness' could be Keegan's in *John Bull's Other Island*: a theme of cultural dislocation later to be made much of by R. D. Laing.[34] The power and originality of the *Charivari*, and the magnificence of Bridie's Lord of Misrule, contrast with the well-bred vacuity of Eliot's verse-plays:

The tarnished swords, the battered sceptres,
The immemorial things,
Were waving in the hands and roond the heids o' the new kings.
The meek had inherited the earth.
What would they dae wi' it?[35]

Bridie made his Clown, Joey Mascara, ask. It was not a question which would be much raised in the Britain of the 1950s.

VI

Cunningham deals with 1930s provincial fiction like Grimm's brave little tailor with his flies. Cronin, Howard Spring, Winifred Holtby and Richard Llewellyn are swatted in four lines, for (maybe) having 'excessively soft hands'.[46] Yet their products had a huge impact – Kim Howells records miners breaking down in tears watching John Ford's film of Llewellyn's incredibly reactionary *How Green Was My Valley* (1939) – and were themselves complex and highly literate works. Film adaptation, however, introduced a new economic dimension, and a new political problematic. Most novelists would be lucky to sell more than 2,000 copies, mostly to lending libraries; adoption by Penguin or the Left Book Club would boost sales, but did little enough for income. Penguin's initial royalties were 1 per cent on 6*d* (2 $1/2$p) a copy.[37] By the 1930s, however, the cinema had replaced the church or chapel as the collective weekly experience of most families. Urban adults went at least once a week, often to 'modernistic' super-cinemas owned by chains which had bought into production firms and in turn had been penetrated by American capital. Films were overwhelmingly American, but the Cinematograph Films Act of 1927 tried to improve funding via a levy on film imports, and set a quota of British films which had to be shown. 'Quota quickies' – which Anthony Powell among others helped script – were abysmal efforts to fulfil the letter of the law, but by 1935 the British film industry had studios near London, its own stars and directors and a gradually rising prestige.[38]

In contrast to the incestuous world of publishing and politics, the film men ought to have been remote from the Establishment: the Ostrers and Deutsch were Jews, J. Arthur Rank a Methodist flour-miller; Sandor Korda had been a member of Bela Kun's Budapest Soviet in 1919. But their desire to assimilate outdid the nonconformists of the 1880s, and devised the comically reactionary self-censorship which in 1936 banned *any possible film adaptation* of Walter Greenwood's *Love on the Dole*. Meanwhile Korda, now Sir Alexander, advised the Conservative Party on its film propaganda.[39] Some writers quickly muscled in. Priestley adapted *The Good Companions* in 1933, and went on to script films for Gracie Fields in which she rescued whole industries and proved that all sorts could co-exist in MacDonald's Britain. Later, as Grierson's pupils moved into feature films, standards improved, but the outright sale of rights still meant that the movie could be quite different from the original novel.

Such was the fate of Winifred Holtby's *South Riding*. Martin Wiener writes that 'Stanley Baldwin's favourite reading was this tale of an impoverished landowner trying to save his estate from unscrupulous developers' and chalks up another run for English rural reaction – obviously on the strength of Victor Saville's film of 1938, in which everyone ends up singing 'Land of Hope and Glory'.[40] Was this the novel that the Kailyard veteran Annie S. Swan found 'full of pain even to savagery'? It was not. Yet, although the novel sold 70,000 copies in two years, the film - still reckoned a classic - was to be seen by millions.[41]

Thus ended an attempt by one energetic radical to harness the scope of the great Victorian novelists to the contemporary predicament. Winifred Holtby, socialist, pacifist and feminist, admired Virginia Woolf (a feeling not exactly reciprocated) and produced the first English study of her work. Writing in this of the suffragettes, she admitted that her own political involvement inhibited her from 'maintain[ing] that equilibrium and concentration which are necessary for an artist, in order that the form may burn up and make incandescent all the matter of her work'.[42] Yet the artist who had political purpose had to try to communicate. Holtby was aware, even before Orwell, both of the social and economic context of reading, and of the claim of popular fiction. Cheap romance novels, she wrote, 'contain the raw material of human drama, unchanged by the transmutations of art, uncriticised by intellectual reflection . . . Together with the cinema, the popular press and the radio, they must be accepted as the common basis on which the popular imagination feeds.'[43] In *South Riding* she tried to fuse the popular genre and a 'progressive' message, adapting the theme of *Jane Eyre*, fount of thousands of women's magazine serials, to the almost Galtian 'theoretical history' of a Yorkshire local authority.

If not incandescent, the story of Sarah Burton's attempt to reform the local girls' school and its effects is remarkably ingenious. Robert Carne, her opponent, is a gentleman-farmer dragged under by an unprofitable estate and an insane aristocratic wife. As with Rochester, Sarah sets her cap at him, by involving herself in the education of his daughter. But wish-fulfilment ends when her attempt to start an affair leads to Carne's collapse under a heart-attack. At the end of the book Carne is dead in a cliff fall, and Sarah barely reconciled to carrying on her task as a teacher. Yet such individual tragedies – a grimness in part stemming from Holtby's own incurable illness – are sublimated to a commitment to the community. Around the love-story, Holtby weaves the politics of the county and the lives and futures of its people.

Statistics and agenda items, as Raymond Williams would later write in *Border Country*, 'get up and walk'. In book 2, 'Highways and Bridges', Holtby uses a debate over a new road to exploit motifs of transport and movement. Carne's prize hunter, his last chance of solvency, is felled by the entrepreneur Alderman Snaith's fencing wire; he misses the vital meeting. A bus carries Councillor Huggins, Methodist and fornicator, to confront a pregnant girl – and put himself further in Snaith's power. The socialist Alderman Astell (and him tubercular!) walks to the hospital fancy-dress ball, where he wins Sarah Burton over to the road-scheme as a means to improve her school. Lydia Holly, Sarah's prize pupil, cycles to her rural slum to find her mother pregnant (as it turns out, fatally) and her future threatened. Finally, during a school hare and hounds chase, Sarah is confronted by Robert Carne on horseback, which, to 'her irreverent and educated mind', suggests the first meeting of Rochester and Jane Eyre – both 'frozen' in a snow-covered landscape against the leaden sea, like one of Jane's strange paintings. It is here that Carne will have his last vision of Sarah, before his horse carries him down to his death.

Sarah's social ideal enables her to survive. While Astell ruins his health organizing unions on Clydeside, she is taken up in a plane on the jubilee of George V and shown the Kingdoms of the World. The plane swoops over Carne's mansion, now roofless and about to be replaced by a home for mentally retarded children (thus does the twentieth century deal with Mrs Rochester!). Sarah sees from above the bedroom of Carne's wife, emblematic of a sexuality forever closed to her. Then the plane stalls and, in the instant of real danger, Sarah chooses the world, rejecting death *and* romance; as if Jane Eyre turned down both St John Rivers and

Rochester in favour of schoolteaching. The tragedy that still bites – also symbolized by the plane – isn't personal, but comes from the looming prospect of war.

South Riding doesn't create a 'national', deferential identity, but is as radical as *A Scots Quair* (which obviously influenced it). It succeeds as documentary; the scenes before the public assistance committee are arguments for the welfare state as effective as anything in *Picture Post*. But it also purges the abasements of romance. The man on the big horse ends, not a paterfamilias sans eye and arm, but dead, his estate sold up, his house demolished. Nor is Sarah absorbed like Chris Guthrie into some semi-mystical world order: she stays and fights.

When a 500-page book with 150-odd characters is reduced to a 1½-hour film in thirty-six scenes, something has to give. Yet Ian Dalrymple's script completely reversed the thrust of the book. The Sarah–Carne romance never reaches the bedroom (in the book Sarah loves Carne but knows he only wants to sleep with her), but Carne's mad wife dies, so, presumably, he can marry Sarah, after the duo have turned detective, exposed the wicked Snaith and recruited Astell to their side at the vital council meeting. The complex personalities of the novel, who need the community of the Council to survive – Snaith, calculating but also psychologically maimed by sexual assault while a boy; Huggins, randy but also reforming and devout; Mrs Beddows, unhappily married – become Muir's 'conditional figures', while Carne (superbly played by Ralph Richardson) ends triumphant.

Chamberlain's fall and the coalition with Labour eased censorship – and documentarists moving into feature films brought much more critical attitudes. Pen Tennyson's *Proud Valley* (1940), starring Paul Robeson and set in South Wales, both managed to be liberal on the colour question and – presumably with coal-supplies in mind - held out an olive branch to the miners. In 1943, *Love on the Dole* was at last filmed, and Churchill made an ass of himself trying to suppress Michael Powell's *The Life and Death of Colonel Blimp*, based on David Low's Turkish-bath ultra.[44] Yet, although there was a greater interest in locality, reforming ideas, and respect for ordinary people, the old political order was put back on its legs with productions like Thorold Dickinson's *The Prime Minister* (1941) starring John Gielgud as Disraeli, and the Boulting brothers' 1947 version of Howard Spring's *Fame Is the Spur*, which composed the Labour Party member's view of its history, from the working-class protest of the Industrial Revolution to the 'great betrayal' of 1931.[45]

Spring had been a political journalist, travelling from the Cardiff slums via the *Manchester Guardian* to succeed Bennett on the *Evening Standard* in 1931, and his eye for the details of Labour politics was that of someone who knew their heartlands: Manchester, Bradford,

South Wales, London.[46] His hero, Hamer Shawcross, resembles the 'traitor' Ramsay MacDonald, but as an old man, reminiscing on the verge of senility, is insecure enough to prompt sympathy. Compared with the friends of his youth – a decent dull trade unionist and an opportunistic businessman – he is a Faust, deceived by his own ability and self-confidence. His fate as an old man is to observe, cocooned in his literary world, combatants infinitely nastier than any of his old opponents.

Shawcross's politics is symbolized by the cavalryman's sabre which struck dead his grandfather's girl at Peterloo in 1819. 'On the Wall', 'In the Hand', 'In Velvet': the sabre gives title to the novel's three books. On platforms it is part of Shawcross's Tennysonian vision of himself as a liberator, yet it is also a symbol of sexuality and – having killed a woman – of sexual tyranny. The most harrowing part of the book describes the ill-treatment of the suffragettes – including his wife Ann – whose cause he ostentatiously rejects. Yet his career is sustained by the sacrifices of women, just as his feckless son Charles is kept going by the detective-stories of his communist wife Alice. *En route* to Spain, Alice takes out the sabre and flings it overboard, telling Charles: 'There's no job now for romantics. We, on our side, have to be as dispassionate as a sanitary squad, cleaning up a dirty smell. And we've got to be quick, because it's spreading, and soon it'll poison and suffocate every decent thing and instinct.'[47] Less than an hour later their ship is torpedoed and Charles killed. The sword begins and ends as the symbol of ages 'when no evil, no bestiality, no treason or treachery seemed incredible'. Alice returns from Spain and leaves the Communist Party over the Nazi–Soviet Pact. The novel ends on a note of liberal agnosticism. Shawcross's final words – 'Three things were immortal: good and evil and the hope in men's hearts that evil would be overcome by good' – are Spring's own, and his rejection of Communism close to that of Auden in 'September 1, 1939':

> I and the public know
> What all schoolchildren learn,
> Those to whom evil is done
> Do evil in return.

The 1947 film, made after a huge Labour victory, had the radical figure of Michael Redgrave in the central rôle of Hamer Radshaw. (Sir Hartley Shawcross was a Labour minister.) In this, Radshaw became a vain MacDonaldite demon, last seen failing (highly symbolically) to draw the rusted sabre from its sheath. In contrast to the broad humanism of the original novel it re-created the Labour myth – the 'great betrayal' of 1931, the metropolitan corruption of the ambitious representative.

Film had become both the custodian of the old political conventions and - as authors tried to maintain control of the interpretation of their writing - a new sort of politics. At its best, it had the bite of Disraeli at his most impudent, as in Robert Hamer's symbolic assassination of the English establishment in *Kind Hearts and Coronets* (1949) or Sandy Mackendrick's scathing picture of industrial decrepitude in *The Man in the White Suit* (1951), but both found it impossible to square an individual social critique with the demands of an entertainment industry.[48]

VII

The wartime government didn't repeat the emotional stampede of 1914. Propaganda satirized the Nazi leaders as clowns and stressed Britain's rôle in preserving the culture of Europe. Myra Hess performing Mozart in Humphrey Jennings's *Listen to Britain* documentary (1942) typified this sober self-justification. With broadcasting cut to one channel, newspapers shrunk to a single sheet, and millions forced to spend day after day in camps, shelters, crawling trains, the demand for reading increased enormously. The number of titles tumbled - from 14,904 to 6,747 - but low-priced paperbacks made reading books more important than owning them, readers being encouraged to leave them in buses or trains, or to give them to servicemen.[49] Literature about reading expanded, with figures like Cyril Connolly in *Horizon*, John Lehmann in *Penguin New Writing* and George Orwell in *Tribune*, performing the same public didactic rôle as Harrison or Nicoll sixty years earlier. The problem was that of publishing original work. 'Serious creative talent', Angus Calder has written, 'was in the position of a host at a crowded reception with a sore throat and doctor's orders not to drink.'[50]

Political fiction, however, dwindled. Fifty-six titles appeared in the 1930s, only twelve in the 1940s. To paper shortages was added the incineration of Paternoster Row, the centre of British publishing, in August 1940, and in a time of worry and inconvenience tastes ran to nostalgia rather than to commitment - much to the benefit of Trollope.[51] Angela Thirkell, yet another of the Baldwin–Kipling–Burne-Jones cousinhood, chronicled a revived Barsetshire in a series of howlingly conservative novels. If Lloyd George had betrayed reconstruction in the First World War, now an élite-led gradualism smothered the democratic revolution which some, Orwell included, had forecast. Paul Addison and Angus Calder have stressed the influence of wartime political culture on the 1945 election, yet by then many reform impulses had oddly evaporated, much to the relief of anxious Americans monitoring 'Britain's socialist experiment'.[52]

This was partly because of subtler propaganda. According to Ian

Hamilton, 'the heroic or the fiercely anti-propagandist note' gave way to a documentary style better fitted to the 'dreary, pointless and brutal interruption of the personal allegiances that really mattered'.[53] Yet even documentary, rising to a heroically hard-bitten resignation in Richard Hillary's *The Last Enemy* (1942), could be as loaded as Rupert Brooke. The image of the airman-hero was used to sanction the saturation-bombing of German civilians and the death of 50,000 aircrew, potential managers and technicians who would be difficult to replace. The decencies of Humphrey Jennings's documentaries masked a surrender by the left to the incantatory *Realpolitik* of the old order. 'A gentle, pragmatic form of international socialism', John le Carré later wrote, was abandoned for a system 'constipated with slogans, archaisms and compromise' which enveloped both the Establishment and its communist subversives.[54] Few things demonstrate the resulting intellectual stasis more than a comparison between the major fictions of the war: Joyce Cary's triptych *Herself Surprised* (1941), *To Be a Pilgrim* (1942) and *The Horse's Mouth* (1944), and Evelyn Waugh's *Brideshead Revisited* (1944).

The anticipated destructiveness of the war seems to have concentrated meditation on the fabric of England. Both *To Be a Pilgrim* and the main part of *Brideshead Revisited* end in the lull between Munich and the invasion of Poland, and impending conflict provokes the central characters to reassess their England. The disconcerting thing is how mutually hostile those reassessments are, despite the apparently common environment of the landed order, politics, time, change and love. Not only the mental worlds of Cary and Waugh, but also those of their critics and biographers, are so separate as to suggest opponents in a civil war.[55]

Though the origins of both writers were provincial – Cary's forebears were Anglo-Irish, Waugh's Scots – their central figures are deeply English. The Marchmains, 'barons since Agincourt', are obviously Whigs: 'the larger honours came with the Georges';[56] for Cary's Tom Wilcher, another Whig, 'abroad' means Edinburgh and Cardiff.[57] At first glance, too, the image of England is that conveyed by the great house: Cary's Tolbrook on the edge of Dartmoor; Waugh's Brideshead in the Cotswolds, but modelled on Castle Howard in Yorkshire, which Harold Macmillan described as 'the perfect Whig habitat'. Both Waugh and Cary were trained as artists, and the 'picture' of their houses is important. Yet Brideshead is realized purely in the architectural terms of Waugh's narrator, Charles Ryder, while Wilcher's Tolbrook, its exterior dismissed as 'an irregular house; a three storey block with one long east wing and on the west an absurd protrusion, one storey high, ending in a dilapidated greenhouse',[58] is explored room by room until we realize that it is in a symbolic sense an extension of Wilcher's skull. Wilcher shares Ryder's fixation with the tangible evidence of the retreating landed order, but his Tolbrook is, in the literal and metaphorical sense, a stage on which and through which history is created by individuals.

The Wilchers' pursuit of what Cary called 'positive freedom' leads them to challenge their order in various ways and with partial success; just as, in the other wings of Cary's triptych, Sara Monday orders her world as a great kitchen and Gully Jimson as a studio. Edward, the elder brother, rises in Liberal politics until he enters the ministry of 1906. Bill, the middle brother, an 'idiot' in the Greek meaning of private citizen, eschews politics for the life of a professional soldier. Lucy goes on the road with her field-preacher husband Puggy Brown. The 'indeterminacy' of the situation which results comes from the interplay between such personalities, their family responsibilities and divergent ethics, as well as from the impersonal forces of social change.[59] Tom is held in tension between Edward's politics – a radicalism sapped by cynicism and irresponsibility – and Lucy's Bunyan-like sense of mission. His narrative is punctuated by extracts from Edward's pasquinade against England, as well as by denunciation of his own failure to become a missionary. As the goals of his own generation dissolve, he makes a religion of Tolbrook.[60]

Redemption comes, however, not with preservation but with change. Ann, Edward's daughter, takes Tom back to Tolbrook, and marries Robert, Lucy's son. Robert gets the estate back into cultivation, installing a threshing machine in Tolbrook's chief architectural glory, its Adam saloon. Tom is horrified but, at the end of a marvellous passage, like a rendering of a Hogarth painting, comes to accept it:

I sit in the armchair, a tattered bergère, in white and gilt, last of the drawing room furniture; and the very ruin of this beautiful room is become a part of my happiness. I say no longer 'Change must come, and this change, so bitter to me, is a necessary ransom for what I keep.' I have surrendered because I cannot fight and now it seems to me that not change but life has lifted me and carried me forward on the stream. It is but a new life which flows through the old house; and like all life, part of that sustaining power which is the oldest thing in the world.

Tolbrook, so Jaffery says, is losing value – it is already not much better than a farm house. But is it not a fall back from death to life. . ?

Robert has brought it back into the English stream and he himself has come with it; to the soft corn, good for home-made bread; the mixed farm, so good for men, to the old church religion which is so twined with English life, that the very prayers seem to breathe of fields after rain and skies whose light is falling between clouds.

That was Sara's religion which served her like her pans, her rolling pins, her private recipes for clearing soup and saving a burnt stew; a wisdom and a faith so close to death and life that we could not tell what part of it was God's and what was man's sense; the sense of the common English, in a thousand generations.[61]

The similarity of the content of this to Lord Marchmain's deathbed oration in *Brideshead Revisited* is so close that Waugh must have read it. With evident distaste. As determinist as any Marxist, Waugh concludes that Brideshead is doomed. Julia Flyte, who rejects Ryder for the Catholic faith which, at the last moment, gives her father grace will never have a son to inherit. The army of the common man will smash the place up.

Brideshead's redeeming function is to provide an agency for the continuity of Catholic dogma: this is the ultimate consolation of Ryder and of Waugh, who wrote in his 1960 preface that the book exhibited a 'distasteful' degree of indulgence, but 'It seemed then that the ancestral seats which were our chief national artistic achievement were doomed to decay and spoliation like the monasteries in the sixteenth century. So I piled it on rather.'[62] In this set-up the political element of the novel – represented by the bounder Rex Mottram, who marries Julia – is treated with effective satire but without irony. Mottram, modelled on Brendan Bracken (an Irish adventurer in the Barry Lyndon mould who claimed at one stage to be Churchill's illegitimate son), makes Brideshead into a centre of political conspiracy, rendered in splendid Waste Land staccato:

'Ribbentrop told me that the army just kept Hitler in power so long as he was able to get things for nothing. The moment anyone stands up to him, he's finished. The army will shoot him.'
'The liberals will hang him.'
'The communists will tear him limb from limb.'
'He'll scupper himself.'
'He'd do it now if it wasn't for Chamberlain.'
'If it wasn't for Halifax.'
'If it wasn't for Sir Samuel Hoare.'
'And the 1922 Committee.'
'Peace Pledge.'
'Foreign Office.'
'New York Banks.'
'All that's wanted is a good strong line.'
'A line from Rex.'
'And a line from me.'[63]

Waugh had had, through Randolph Churchill, an earful of his father's entourage, Bracken included, and this sounds authentic enough. But politics was the *raison d'être* behind the building of places like Brideshead, where the early Churchills, the 'violent, bitter men' of Yeats's 'Ancestral Houses', had orated and intrigued. Ryder seems by contrast only a tiny barnacle on the 'marvellous empty sea-shell' of the great house once power and creativity had gone from it.[64] The Anglo-Irish Cary was far better placed to sense this than the internal exile Waugh.

Cary's technique was also innovative. *To Be a Pilgrim* was his 'Proustian' novel, moving along Tom Wilsher's stream of consciousness; but it also used a sequence of brief visual 'shots' instead of conventional chapters.[65] Cary was intrigued by film-making, and its atmosphere has the provisionality of Jennings's *Listen to Britain*: the mixes from servicemen on a stalled train, to schoolchildren playing, to workers in aircraft factories: the sense of a mobilization for purposes greater than winning the war – all the more vivid because conveyed by a falible lonely eccentric. Tolbrook's Devon was appropriate, too. Wartime reform may have been élite-led, but the popular pressure for it owed more to provincial radicalism than to its socialist successors, and its organizers were, disproportionately, Devon men – Foots, Aclands, Temples. Cary's fiction is the imaginative equivalent of the Common Wealth Party which generated much of the momentum for reform after 1942: patriotic but also decentralist and, as its name would suggest, emotionally puritan and republican.

Waugh's ultimate truths are not English but Catholic. Grace comes to Marchmain through a dull Scots-Irish priest. After the war Waugh came close to quitting Attlee's England for Ireland: republican but still Catholic. He would never have approved of Graham Greene's equation of the recusants with the communists, but he would have understood it. Cary, painter, soldier, administrator, was fourteen years older, and mentally rooted in the 'new liberal' world of Wallas and Wells. Edward Wilsher could be Remington, observed less indulgently and in the context of liberalism's 'strange death'. But this also meant that Cary's liberalism had no postwar locus. The Labour government of 1945–51 was efficient and exhortatory, but élitist and centralist, ensuring Brideshead's survival as an antipode to the 'planner's vision'. The irony was that the people who benefited, politically, from the contrast between its grandeur and Labour's 'drab uniformity' were not the Charles Ryders but the likes of Rex Mottram and his friends.

VIII

The political landscape of postwar Britain would be dominated by one book, rather as the London of *Nineteen Eighty-Four* lay in the shadow of the white pyramids of Miniplenty, Minitruth, Minipax and Miniluv. Its horrors and ingenuities seem apart from the normal pabulum of political novelists, and Orwell took little interest in their concerns. And yet 'the book' was a political event – 'worth a cool million votes to the Conservative Party', Orwell's publisher Fred Warburg wrote – and its images and concepts have proved indelible.[66]

'I ballsed it up rather . . . being so ill', Orwell wrote to Julian Symonds, 'but I think some of the ideas in it might interest you.'[67] There are aspects of *Nineteen Eighty-Four* which one longs to get away from: the tedium of Goldstein's treatise on 'Oligarchical Collectivism', the *Boy's Own Paper* quality of the torture scenes. Yet one can't really do without them: 'the book' – whether the *Communist Manifesto*, *Mein Kampf* or *The Thoughts of Chairman Mao* – being such an important part of any apparatus of belief, and torture being similarly indispensable in the totalitarian state. The *density* of *Nineteen Eighty-Four* can be seen by setting it against another contemporary dystopia: Fred Pohl and Cyril Kornbluth's *The Space Merchants* (1953). Pohl and Kornbluth invert Orwell's authoritarian collectivism to produce a predatory capitalism which has devoured the State, exploits 'consumers' and underclass workers, and is run by an élite of advertising agents. This is not only ingenious; it's in some ways more perceptive than Orwell, but there's not a lot to be said about it compared with the conceptual richness of *Nineteen Eighty-Four*.

The immediate political impact of *Nineteen Eighty-Four* owed much to awareness of the grubby social reality that Orwell described: unmaintained buildings, gritty bread, Victory Gin. He also hit off the complacency of the bureaucracy, its obsession with technical details, and the condescension of much of the 'progressivism' of the time. This echoed loudly in somewhat dismal propaganda fiction: the overt élitism of J. B. Priestley's pro-Labour *Three Men in New Suits* (1945) competed with a troop of Tory publicists pouring out an endless litany of complaint, sometimes directly subsidized by the press magnates.[68]

More telling, given the essentially administrative victory of collectivism, were low-key reports from the bureaucracy front, such as Graham Greene's short story 'Men at Work' (1940) or Nigel Balchin's *The Small Back Room* (1942). Greene had worked at the Ministry of Information – 'we are one of the fighting services' - housed in the Senate House of London University (the Minitruth building in *Nineteen Eighty-Four*), and growing 'like a kind of fungoid life – old divisions sprouting daily new sections which then broke away and became divisions and spawned in turn'. He observed the frivolous and callous careerism of the intellectuals:

> The committee as usual lasted about an hour – it was always, to Skate, an agreeable meeting with men from other divisions, the Religious Division, the Empire Division and so on. Sometimes they co-opted

another man they thought was nice. It gave an opportunity for all sorts of interesting discussions – on books and authors and artists and plays and films. The agenda didn't really matter: it was quite easy to invent one at the last moment.

Orwell would agree with Greene's deadpan concluding sentence in which Skate looks up to see white lines in the 'pale, enormous sky' which 'showed where men were going home after work'.[69] In Balchin's novel an experimental unit, destroyed by ministerial intrigue and individual ambitions, plainly mimicked the struggle over science policy between Sir Henry Tizard and Churchill's reactionary magus Viscount Cherwell, which C. P. Snow was later to document in *Science and Government* (1961). But even this is overshadowed by the technical problem of dismantling a booby-trap bomb. Henry James had chided Kipling in 1897 for '[coming] down steadily in subject from the simple to the more simple – from the Anglo-Indians to the natives . . . from the fish to the engines and the screws.[70] Machinery and procedures impose a presence denied to Balchin's people. The obsession with dismantling the bomb paralleled the scientists' abstention from any moral judgements about preparations for mass destruction.

A war of technology and paperwork, punctuated by horrific violence: this overshadowed the democratic gains, the increased trade unionization, the enforced equality of treatment and attempts at economic planning. Fascism, wrote Orwell in 1943, rebuking Yeats, 'will not be ruled by noblemen with van Dyck faces, but anonymous millionaires, shiny-bottomed bureaucrats and murdering gangsters'.[71] By 1945, under Marlborough's descendant, the bureaucrats had arrived, and the fruits of collective gangsterism could be tasted. Dresden, Hiroshima and Nagasaki vied with the Final Solution to suggest that the capacity for destruction had become universal.

Orwell lit on the old Carlyleian metaphor of the machine, not just in politics. Through his enthusiasm for Gissing, particularly *New Grub Street*, he sensed how the politics governing literary production could distort and destroy the integrity of the writer within any mass-culture, whether capitalist, as in Gissing's day, or collectivist. But the political symbolism of the machine, however socialized, haunted Labour, and would allow the right wing to proclaim its decency without forsaking 'realism'. Waugh's *Sword of Honour* (1952–61) and Anthony Powell's *The Military Philosophers* (1968) could afford a rather self-righteous sense of disenchantment and betrayal: of crimes committed by 'welfare state' bureaucrats against the old military code and Britain's *ancien régime* allies. Orwell attacked from the left the managerialist theories of James Burnham, now one of the noisier Cold Warriors; but, as Bernard Crick has pointed out, he was so used to arguing *within* the left that he failed to see the party political use to which his satire would be put.[72]

Nineteen Eighty-Four is a Chinese box of ironies, possibly even including a happy ending (could it have been written if Newspeak had, in the logic of the Appendix, triumphed?). Not the least of these is the mickey-taking of the documentary style. Winston Smith's descent into proledom, for instance, appears at first glance tragic:

> Within twenty years at the most, he reflected, the huge and simple question, 'Was life better before the Revolution than it is now?' would have ceased once and for all to be answerable. But in effect it was unanswerable even now, since the few scattered survivors from the ancient world were incapable of comparing one age with another. They remembered a million useless things, a quarrel with a workmate, a hunt for a lost bicycle pump, the expression on a long-dead sister's face, the swirl of dust on a windy morning seventy years ago: but all the relevant facts were outside the range of their vision.[73]

Such useless things, Orwell tells us elsewhere – in *Coming Up for Air*, for example – are a private 'real' history which, as well as real language, the proles still have. The joke is on Winston, the incompetent Mass Observer forcing his own opinions down his interviewee's throat, being too far gone in intellectual degeneracy to understand him.

One can see here what Orwell was reacting against: a sense of human alienation attributable as much to imperialism as to the arrogance of the intellectuals. But what was he *for*?

> 'England . . .' Not your England, Archer said to himself, not the petrol-flogging CQMS's England, not the major's England or Cleaver's England or the Adjutant's or the Colonel's or Jack Rowney's or Tom Thurston's England, but to certain extent Hargreaves' England and absolutely my England, full of girls and drinks and jazz and books and decent houses and decent jobs and being your own boss.[74]

Are these the Orwellian verities? What Winston believes keeps the proles human, in that brief moment of optimism before the thought police move in on him and Julia? The quote is from a short story by Kingsley Amis describing a soldiers' mock parliament expelling the regiment's Tory CO in the last weeks of the war. Knowing where Amis ended up, the image – although sympathetic – isn't reassuring. But it highlights Orwell's central inadequacy, one which he shared with Carlyle, Dickens, Gissing and D. H. Lawrence. He was never able to translate his sympathies into the patience with institutional democracy which was necessary for collective decision-making.

Orwell made virtually anyone voluntarily involved in politics a modernized Slackbridge, or a pathetic clown like Ted Parsons, with his shorts, forced cheerfulness and body odour. Orwell could strip himself of imperial or intellectual preconceptions and analyse how a dominant group manipulated history and language, but he recoiled from collective involvement. No one could be further from the radical–puritan, or Wellsian, ideal of civic humanism. So that while *Nineteen Eighty-Four* is an advance from the Gissing-like pejorum of the early novels to a biting Swiftian satire, in terms of practical politics Orwell ends as isolated as Swift. 'Imagine a boot stamping on a human face' is O'Brien on the political sanction of Ingsoc: simply an extension of the Benthamite calculus of compelling obedience by the threat of pain. Although *Nineteen Eighty-Four* is European in its reckoning with the horrors of mass-history, it remains stubbornly English in its concept of power.

NOTES

1   See Valentine Cunningham, *British Writers of the Thirties* (Oxford: Oxford University Press, 1988), passim, and Samuel Hynes, *The Auden Generation* (London: Bodley Head, 1976); John Lucas's symposium, *The 1930s: A Challenge to Orthodoxy* (Brighton: Harvester, 1978), and Frank Gloversmith's *Class, Culture and Social Change: A New View of the 1930s* (Brighton: Harvester, 1980), pay particular attention to socialist and provincial fiction, while Jon Clark *et al.*, *Culture and Crisis in Britain in the Thirties* (London: Lawrence & Wishart, 1979), is strong on the Communist Party contribution.

2   George Bernard Shaw, *Too True to Be Good* (London: Constable, 1933), p. 106.

3   I am grateful to Margot Kettle for a survey she made of the reading matter of a sample of 1930s activists. See also Kuno Schuhmann, 'Shaw und die parlamentarische Demokratie', in Paul Goetsch (ed.), *Englische Literatur und Politik im 20. Jahrhundert* (Wiesbaden: Athenaion, 1981).

4   See Martin Ceadel, 'Popular fiction and the next war', in Gloversmith, *Class*.

5   See Peter Widdowson on Patrick Hamilton in 'The saloon bar society', in Lucas, *The 1930s*, p. 119.

6   In George Orwell, *Collected Essays, Journalism and Letters* (Harmondsworth: Penguin, 1966), Vol. 1, p. 252.

7   Cyril Connolly, 'Where Engels fear to tread', in *The Condemned Playground* (London: Routledge, 1935), p. 153.

8   Vincent Brome, *J. B. Priestley* (London: Hamish Hamilton, 1988), p. 255.

9   cf. the general conviction in *New Fabian Essays* (London: Turnstile Press, 1952), that Labour had 'run out of ideas'.

10   See Smith, *Socialist Propaganda in the Twentieth-Century British Novel* (London: Macmillan, 1978), pp. 40–3; and Gustav Klaus, 'Silhouettes of revolution', in *The Socialist Novel in Britain* (New York: St Martins Press, 1982), pp. 103–6; Ellen Wilkinson, *Clash* (London: Harrap, 1929), pp. 17, 64; John Buchan, *A Prince of the Captivity* (London: Nelson, 1933), pp. 294 ff.

11 Corrie wrote that his main influences, apart from his own community, were O'Casey, O'Neill and Ibsen. See Linda Mackenney (ed.), *Joe Corrie: Plays, Poems and Theatre Writings* (Glasgow: 7:84 Publications, 1985), pp. 80, 183.

12 James Welsh, *Norman Dale MP*, pp. 176, 200; and see H. Gustav Klaus, 'James C. Welsh, Major Miner Novelist', *Scottish Literary Journal*, vol. 13, no. 2 (1986), pp. 65–86.

13 Welsh, *Norman Dale*, p. 205.

14 Alan Howkins, 'Class against class: the political culture of the Communist Party of Great Britain, 1930–5', in Gloversmith, *Class*, pp. 240–57.

15 Dmitri Mirsky, *The Intelligentsia of Great Britain* (London: Gollancz, 1935), p. 41.

16 Cunningham, *British Writers of the Thirties*, p. 95; and see Douglas F. Young, *Beyond the Sunset* (Aberdeen: Impulse, 1973), for Diffusionism and Gibbon.

17 See Erik Barnouw, *Documentary* (London: Oxford University Press, 1974), pp. 83 ff.

18 P. N. Furbank, 'The twentieth century best seller', in Boris Ford (ed.), *The Penguin Guide to English Literature*, Vol. 7 (Harmondsworth: Penguin, 1961), is dismissive, but see Brome *Priestley*, pp. 85 ff., and A. J. Cronin, *Adventures in Two Worlds* (New York: McGraw-Hill, 1935), pp. 264 ff.

19 Workers Theatre Movement, 1932 Conference statement, reprinted in *History Workshop*, no. 4 (Autumn 1977), p. 131.

20 Stuart Laing, 'Presenting things as they are: John Sommerfield's *May Day*', in Gloversmith, *Class*, pp. 142–60; and see John Stevenson, 'The politics of violence', in Gillian Peele and Chris Cook (eds), *The Politics of Reappraisal, 1918–39* (London: Macmillan, 1975).

21 Cited in Storm Jameson, *Journey from the North*, Vol. 1, (London: Collins, 1969), p. 342.

22 Orwell, *Collected Essays*, Vol. 1, p. 317.

23 Stevenson, 'Politics of Violence', p. 398.

24 See Dai Smith, *Lewis Jones* (Cardiff: University of Wales Press, 1983), pp. 70 ff.; Cunningham, *British Writers of the Thirties*, ch. 9; I also acknowledge the help given by my MA students Helmut Schröder and Brigitte Wall.

25 See A. R. Jones and G. Thomas, *Presenting Saunders Lewis* (Swansea: Gomer Press, 1973); P. H. Scott (ed.), *The Age of MacDiarmid* (Edinburgh: Mainstream, 1980).

26 Lewis Grassic Gibbon, *A Scots Quair* (London: Jassolds, 1946), p. 235.

27 Gibbon, *Cloud Howe*, in ibid., p. 156.

28 For Grassic Gibbon, see Angus Calder, 'A mania for self-reliance', in Graham Martin and Douglas Jefferson (eds), *The Uses of Fiction* (Milton-Keynes: Open University Press, 1982); Douglas Gifford, *Gunn and Gibbon* (Edinburgh: Oliver & Boyd, 1984); and Ian Campbell, *Grassic Gibbon* (Edinburgh: Scottish Academic Press, 1985).

29 Charles Lever, *Lord Kilgobbin* (London: Downey, 1899), Vol. 2, p. 18.

30 H. J. Hanham, *Scottish Nationalism*, (London: Faber, 1969), ch. 7; Christopher Harvie, *Scotland and Nationalism* (London: Allen & Unwin, 1977), ch. 3.

31 John Buchan, *The Novel and the Fairy Tale* (London: Oxford University Press, 1932), p. 8.

32 Douglas Gifford, 'In Search of the Scottish Renaissance', *Cencrastus*, no. 9 (1982), pp. 26–30.

33 Neil Gunn, *Highland River* (London: Arrow, 1982), p. 229.

34   Walter Elliot, introduction to James Bridie, *The Baikie Charivari* (London: Constable, 1953).
35   ibid., p. 58
36   Cunningham, *British Writers of the Thirties*, p. 321.
37   J. E. Morpurgo, *King Penguin* (London: Hutchinson, 1979), p. 89.
38   See Jeffrey Richards, *The Age of the Dream Palace* (London: Routledge, 1984).
39   ibid., pp. 119–20.
40   Wiener, *English Culture and the Decline of the Industrial Spirit, 1880–1980* (Cambridge: Cambridge University Press, n.d.), p. 102.
41   Annie S. Swan, *Letters* (London: Hodder & Stoughton, 1945), p. 177; and Vera Brittain, *Testament of Friendship* (London: Fontana, 1981), p. 307.
42   Winifred Holtby, *Virginia Woolf* (London: Wishart, 1932), p. 28.
43   Winifred Holtby, 'What we read and why we read it', in *Left Review*, vol. 1, no. 4 (1935), p. 113.
44   See Jeffrey Richards and Anthony Aldgate, *The Best of British* (Oxford: Blackwell, 1983).
45   See Nigel Mace, 'British historical epics in the Second World War', in Philip M. Taylor (ed.). *Britain and the Cinema in the Second World War* (London: Macmillan, 1988), pp. 101–20.
46   See Howard Spring, *In the Meantime* (London: Constable, 1942).
47   Howard Spring, *Fame is the Spur* (London: Collins, 1940), p. 632.
48   See Charles Barr, *Ealing Studios* (Newton Abbot: David & Charles, 1980).
49   F. A. Munby, 'The production of literature', in Alan Sinfield (ed.), *Society and Literature, 1945–70* (London: Methuen, 1983), p. 123.
50   Angus Calder, *The People's War* (London: Granada, 1971), pp. 590–2.
51   See J. B. Priestley, *Three Men in New Suits* (London: Heinemann, 1945), p. 23.
52   cf. Theodore H. White, *Fire in the Ashes: Europe in Mid-Century* (New York: Sloane, 1953), pp. 189–233.
53   Ian Hamilton, introduction to *The Poetry of World War II* (London: New English Library, 1972), p. 10.
54   John Le Carré, introduction to *The Philby Conspiracy* (London: André Deutsch, 1968), p. xvii.
55   For the background to both, see Alan Bishop, *Gentleman Rider: A Life of Joyce Cary* (London: Secker & Warburg, 1988), and Christopher Sykes, *Evelyn Waugh* (London: Collins, 1975).
56   Evelyn Waugh, *Brideshead Revisited*, p. 317.
57   Joyce Cary, *To Be a Pilgrim* (London: Michael Joseph, 1942), p. 99.
58   ibid., p. 11.
59   cf. Robert Bloom, *Joyce Cary: The Indeterminate World* (Philadelphia: University of Pennsylvania Press, 1962), pp. 90 ff.
60   See Giles Mitchell, *The Art Theme in Joyce Cary's First Trilogy* (The Hague: Mouton, 1971).
61   Cary, *To Be a Pilgrim*, p. 328.
62   Waugh, preface to *Brideshead Revisited*, 1960.
63   Waugh, *Brideshead Revisited*, p. 280.
64   cf. Yeats's 'Meditations in Time of Civil War', in *The Tower* (London: Macmillan, 1928).
65   Cornelia Cook, *Joyce Cary: Liberal Principles* (London: Vision Press, 1981), p. 116.
66   Bernard Crick, *George Orwell* (Harmondsworth: Penguin, 1982), p. 567.

67   Orwell, *Collected Essays*, Vol. 4, p. 535.
68   One example of which is Beaverbrook's apparent commissioning of the popular novelist Sir Philip Gibbs's *Both Your Houses* (London: Hutchinson, 1949), loosely based on Trollope's *Prime Minister*, as an instrument in his attempt to revive the Liberal Party.
69   Graham Greene, 'Men at Work', pp. 185, 189, 191.
70   Quoted in Charles Carrington, *Rudyard Kipling* (London: Macmillan, 1955), p. 344.
71   'W. B. Yeats', in Orwell, *Collected Essays*, Vol. 2, p. 314.
72   Crick, *Orwell*, p. 567.
73   George Orwell, *Nineteen Eighty-Four* (London: Secker & Warburg, 1949), pp. 96–7.
74   Kingsley Amis, 'I Spy Strangers', in *Collected Short Stories* (London: Hutchinson, 1980), p. 75.

9

The Fall and Rise of British Political Fiction

I

AT THE HEIGHT of the Westland crisis in 1986, Michael Heseltine stormed out of the Cabinet. 'It had been a pleasure to work with Mrs Thatcher', he told the waiting journalists, 'while in cabinet she had been first among equals.' Now she had become an autocrat, and cabinet responsibility did not function. Convinced about Westland, and knowing that bureaucracy and the mass party had long given even the most incompetent premier a privileged position, Heseltine still grabbed at the title of Jeffrey Archer's Westminster soap-opera, published in 1984 and by 1986 selling its millions in paperback and being serialized on television. Twenty years earlier, when politicians wanted to make a literary point, they would quote from Trollope or Disraeli, sources which suggested the mahogany conventions of Westminster and Whitehall. Now the dynamism of a prime minister to whom convention was alien was being fought with the aid of a quick dive into the supermarket dump-bucket.

Archer's book was a fact of publishing and public relations. As such, it helped make its author deputy chairman of the Conservative Party and enriched his literary agent, Mrs Deborah Owen, whose husband had his ambitions. As inept about political practice as it was leaden in style, its success still commented on the surviving conventions. If ever there was a precise moment when the grand structure really did fall to bits, then Heseltine's mouthings captured it. Convention no longer provided useful generalizations about how the 'flexible constitution' worked; it peddled untruths about an over-centralized and authoritarian system, justifying them with a quote from a piece of hack-work.

When Asa Briggs in 1957 compared Trollope to Bagehot as an exponent of the constitution he implied that this situation still obtained, that English politics still showed that sureness of grip which impressed

European exiles. More benign than Robert Michels's 'iron law of oligarchy', the conventions of Parliament and the party system removed authority from the enthusiasts and deposited it with the moderate and competent. Even in a desperate crisis like 1939–45, government and opposition amicably collaborated, and the system was rapidly set back on an even peacetime keel.[1] Perhaps this expertise was too boring to make for worthwhile political fiction – 'a lunar landscape' as Paul Johnson, then a man of the left, called the likes of C. P. Snow and Maurice Edelman in 1961. Now, the French Fourth Republic, that *was* the sort of politics you could write a novel about . . . He had, of course, done so.[2]

II

In 1963 the *Observer*'s Beirut correspondent defected to the Soviet Union, and it was revealed that 'Kim' Philby had enjoyed a long career as a Soviet agent in British intelligence, while the Profumo affair gave politics a lasting element of sensation if not of paranoia. From this perspective, the political fiction of the 1950s and 1960s, complacently secure and conservatively realist in style, can exhibit other, more disconcerting characteristics.

In 1986 the Conservative Chief Whip in the Lords, Bertie Denham, published a spy thriller, *Two Thyrdes*, in which one Lord Frost was unveiled as a Soviet agent. The disguise was thin, but the days when C. P. Snow had been an oracle, as novelist and 'scientist in politics', had ended long before his death in 1980.[3] In the 1960s, Snow's *roman fleuve*, *Strangers and Brothers*, had seemed to chronicle the transition from liberal capitalism to welfare corporatism. Snow on 'science and government' or the 'two cultures' commanded the respect Wells had always sought; his acceptance of office under Harold Wilson in 1964 endorsed Labour's strategy of harnessing 'the white heat of the technological revolution' to economic policy.[4]

Snow, then a young research scientist, had started *Strangers and Brothers* in 1935, a good year for left-wing fiction; the first and title-novel was published in 1940. As his models were the Edwardians – Wells, Galsworthy and Francis Brett Young – the enterprise was conservative, compared with Cary or Jameson, whose *Mirror in Darkness* has settings similar to Snow's early 'autobiographical' volumes.[5] Like his school and Civil Service colleague, William Cooper, Snow wanted to 'run experimental writing out of town', an ambition shared with 'the Movement': disgruntled rather than angry young men, penned up in provincial universities, eyeing London with envy, to whom both men stood as patron-figures. Equally of the period was their empiricism, their distrust of historicism and of any philosophical system which offended against the no-nonsense epistemology of the ruling logical positivism.[6]

Snow, like Mrs Humphry Ward, was an earnest guide to the arcana of administration. Cooper, a sprightlier but more self-satisfied performer, shows the style in *Memoirs of a New Man* (1966), set in a nationalized industry, when one scientist grades the 'Ks' of the civil servants and board members assembled round a Whitehall table.[7] Such a *tour d'horizon* had been Trollope's purpose in the Palliser novels; but, while he blended this with the 'epic' of Phineas Finn, Snow was 'scientifically' descriptive. Lewis Eliot's progress from the provincial lower middle class to the heart of the Establishment via the law, Cambridge and the Civil Service exemplified the 'rise of the meritocracy', while Snow's empathy even with his more unprepossessing characters showed its liberal virtues. In contrast to the tetchy Carlyleian moralizing of his chief opponent, F. R. Leavis, Snow combined Matthew Arnold's human sympathy with his desire to 'co-order' a civil society grown archaic and disordered.

Snow's *annus mirabilis* was 1964: a Labour minister with a former premier as publisher. He held at Macmillan John Morley's post of literary adviser, and his reputation, on closer reading of his novels, seems every bit as ambiguous. Lewis Eliot is too wide-ranging a civil servant to be plausible in a clannish profession; Snow's empathy seems at times an unwarranted exercise in mind-reading. Far from overhauling Wells and Trollope, let alone the great European realists, Snow's most successful novels – *The Masters* (1951) and *The Affair* (1960) – resemble 'well-made plays' of a rather old-fashioned sort (both were, in fact, dramatized by Ronald Millar, later speech-writer to Mrs Margaret Thatcher). His treatment of party politics, in *Corridors of Power* (1964) – which injected a timely phrase into the language – was almost devoid of *ideas* about government: merely personality-studies within an élite. To John Halperin, 'many of the problems, issues and quandaries Lewis Eliot faces are those of sentient modern man; the parade of them in the novels traces his evolution from a relatively hopeful creature to an increasingly pessimistic one'.[8] To claim this degree of universality is pushing it. 'Yes, Minister' without the jokes might, alas, be closer to the point.

In fact *Corridors of Power* was derived from the novels a shrewd but frustrated Labour MP had been writing for several years. 'I would like to prowl around the House with you', Snow wrote to Maurice Edelman in 1964. 'I hate to be a nuisance but I very much want to get everything right.'[9] Edelman obliged, and was really the more interesting of the duo. He wrote his first parliamentary novel, *Who Goes Home*, in 1952 and soon was as much a master of this genre as Ian Fleming was of the exotic spy thriller. All other writers venturing into this *milieu* – besides Snow, William Clark, David Walder and Wilfred Fienburgh – emerged with elements of Edelman adhering to them; even Richard Crossman, taking up cabinet office in 1964, felt he was 'living in a Maurice Edelman novel'.[10]

For Edelman, the rules of the parliamentary game still held. There might be sexual and financial entanglements, malign foreign powers and press barons, but the two-party system, and the devotion of good men to it, would overcome them. The Cardiff-born son of a Jewish socialist from Russia, Edelman revered Disraeli, and wrote his last two novels about him, from a flat in Hughenden. As in Disraeli, the didactic was never absent, whether conveyed at dinner-parties or, symbolically enough, at cricket-matches, by figures half Sidonia and half Crossman:

> As an undergraduate Morrow had learnt that the quickest way of attracting an audience was to affirm the opposite of an accepted idea, to claim that all who held it were outdated, and if the argument became too involved, abandon it as if it had never been advanced. His rumbling voice soon subdued the conversations around the table.
>
> 'Oh, no,' he said, 'There's no East and West any more.'
>
> 'China?' said Miss Felton.
>
> He ignored her.
>
> 'Among the sophisticated peoples, there are only the ideas men and the technique men. The problem of politics is to keep the technique men from getting ideas . . . Once you have parties, you get government by caucus. The democracy thing is as dead as Gladstone. What we've got in Britain is a kind of Venetian oligarchy, and it runs right through the democracy.'[11]

South Wales also produced Gwyn Thomas and Howard Spring, but neither followed Edelman into the Oxbridge élite or shared his fascination with the Tories and the way their leaders chivvied a progressive social and colonial policy out of them. This he personified in Harold Macmillan – who appears early in the Edelman canon in *A Trial of Love*, after Edelman had encountered him as Minister-Resident in Algeria during the war. Edelman saluted the self-control with which Macmillan overcame a tormented personal life, and such tensions figure in his portraits of Conservative ministers: '. . . the contrast – indeed the conflict – between the private and public personalities of politicians who must present a certain standard face to the world, whatever their private inner conflicts.'[12]

A Westminster in which psychology mattered more than centrist ideology – most political fiction of the 1950s or 1960s fitted into this mould. In 1953 the left-winger Edward Hyams became so depressed about its solidity that he invented in *Gentian Violet* an opportunist who, with the aid of a false beard but little change in his politics, got elected for two separate constituencies as a Labour and a Conservative MP. Such discourtesy was merited. With the migration of authority to the Cabinet and the Civil Service, parliamentary prestige became a carapace for insecure representatives. Edelman's later novels are more disenchanted with Parliament, more concerned with the isolation of a Jew in British society. By *All on a Summer's Night* (1969) the prognosis for a Britain weakened by a decadent and anti-industrial élite is all but despairing.

The concentration of power increased disquiet. William Clark, a journalist and publicist with wide and important contacts – he had been Eden's press officer at the time of Suez – used novels of a heavily documentary type to caution against national egoism and the selfishness of the 'developed' world.

> It seems to me the PM is mad, literally mad . . . My mood towards him is extraordinary. I never see him, worn, dignified and friendly, but a surge of deep and almost tearful compassion surges up in me; I leave him, and my violent bitter contempt and hatred for a man who has destroyed my world and so much of my faith burns up again. Then I long to be free as a journalist to drive this government from power and keep the cowards and the crooks out of power for all time. God, how power corrupts.[13]

When this sort of thing occurs in a diary (as it does), not a novel, then the system is in trouble. *Number 10* (1967) and *Special Relationship* (1969) bear comparison with Edelman, but essentially they convey the migration of power, both within the British political structure and from Britain to America.

III

This sense of airlessness was contagious. Wilfred Fienburgh, a young Labour MP who had been a Transport House official, wrote *No Love for Johnny* shortly before his accidental death in 1958; serialized in the *Daily Mirror* and later filmed, it scandalized even an old parliamentary hand like Crossman – 'I was nauseated by it . . . an extremely compelling novel with a uniquely unpleasant combination of peep-hole sex and career politics'.[14] In fact Fienburgh's plot, about an opportunist Labour MP, debarred from office by a communist wife, attempting to lead a left-wing revolt and having an affair with a much younger woman, slewed between prurience and melodrama, while remaining reverential towards Westminster. What redeemed it was Fienburgh's awareness of the insecurities of the meritocracy into which Johnny Byrne had climbed:

'Then, having carefully learned the grammar of table manners, you know, which knife and which spoon to use when, I started to unlearn the careful "Don't make a noise when you're eating", "Eat with your mouth shut" stuff my mother had taught me.'

'But why on earth?' asked Ray.

'Because I had noticed that only the lower middle class takes pains not to give offence at table. The true well-born sloshes his soup into his mouth from a half-inch distance . . . If you've got the right accent and are in command of the geography of the dinner-table, the true mark of the aristocracy is to eat like a pig.'[15]

This sort of *aperçu* is the bonus of the genre. The incidentals of the novel – the Byrnes' cramped London flat, the dusty Labour Rooms – are what count. Byrne's repulsion and self-disgust when confronted with the ageing membership and pointless rituals of a party adrift in the television age go a long way to explain Labour's identity crisis in the early 1960s.

Another prospective Labour candidate, David Marquand, advised his contemporaries that *Look Back in Anger* (1956) was the key political document of the decade.[16] He was not alone; the sense of living 'in an old building' was palpable, even among Conservative writers, whether represented by Eliot in *The Elder Statesman* (1959) – Edelman rendered in blank verse – or in David Walder's *The Short List* (1964), an engagingly disenchanted glance at election rituals. Much less respectable, but reviving Disraeli's 'paranoid style', was Simon Raven's *Alms for Oblivion* sequence, begun as Macmillan neared his Ides of March and likely, as a *New Statesman* reviewer feared, to hack itself a niche as a sociological document. Raven intended 'to cover the English upper middle class scene since the war', in its vulnerability to 'the malice of time, chance, and the rest of the human race'.[17] Only a few of the books were political, the rest reworking Raven's odd autobiography. Yet they had more political life than Snow's, casting back to the slang and impudence of *Coningsby* and the loucher elements of the Palliser novels, which Raven would later adapt for television. When Crossman spluttered about 'social seediness and some fairly scabrous security background' at the time of the Profumo affair, he described Raven's world, and when Raven plunged a Cambridge college into radical ferment in *Places Where They Sing* (1972) he echoed Crossman's panic at *les événements* of 1968.[18]

The expectation of continuity which the *roman fleuve* creates is illusory. Authors write them because politics is so indeterminate that only a 'long view' can make sense of it. Hence the coincidence with more theoretical attempts to explain and reform: Trollope and Bagehot in the 1860s, Wells and Wallas in the 1900s. Following Suez, a spate of books insisted – usually from a social-democratic angle – that the national culture was to blame for an economy lagging behind the rest of Europe. Hugh Thomas's symposium *The Establishment* (1958) was followed by Snow on the Two Cultures (1961), Martin Green's *A Mirror for Anglo-Saxons* and Arthur Koestler's 'Suicide of a Nation' autopsy in *Encounter* (1963). Although the sociologist Michael Young had warned against this sort of thing in his Wellsian-dystopia-cum-pamphlet *The Rise of the Meritocracy* (1958), such prescriptions were élitist, centralist and (given that 'literary bias' was their major grievance) largely the work of the *literati*. If this was, in a sense, an attack on the fetish that wartime success had made of British practices, it coincided queerly with the results of a remarkable inquest that intellectuals connected with the small and Stalinist Communist Party – Arnold Kettle, Francis Klingender, E. P. Thompson, Raymond Williams, Eric Hobsbawm, Jack Lindsay – had made into British civil society, partly as a result of Popular Front policies, partly to get away from the *diktats* of the party bureaucracy. On the Continent revisionism of this sort contributed to the 'modernization' of social democracy, but in Britain the Cold War continued to defer a dialogue which might have restructured British politics.

Instead, the Wilson years showed an élitism grown paranoid and impulsive. The white heat of technology gave way to an obsession with by-elections and opinion polls as two-party stability collapsed. Snow's Fabian corporatism melted; in his penultimate volume, *The Sleep of Reason* (1970), Eliot, now a university chancellor, encounters student radicalism and child-murderers, both stemming from the 'liberal' Bohemia in which he matured. Raven fortified his cynicism with a quixotic restatement of public-school values, along with a Disraelian confidence that ascriptive authority and imagination would win out over bourgeois morality. His world was in no way an improving one, but it was still alive, long after Disraeli's empire had vanished.

IV

This relapse into a cyclic pattern may help explain the popularity in the 1970s of Snow's 'conservative' rival Anthony Powell's *A Dance to the Music of Time*. Powell's skill in characterization, his re-creation of a slightly fusty London life, centred on the Court and retired military men, and well-born but impecunious and young men making their way between the grand and powerful and Bohemia, bring him close enough to the French realists to be faulted for the absence of any serious self-examination by his semi-autobiographical narrator Nick Jenkins. But Jenkins is, throughout the sequence, juxtaposed with the intensely political figure of his school contemporary, Kenneth Widmerpool, and the latter's fate summons up myth and religious tradition. At one level,

Widmerpool is a traditional comic-sinister figure of the Mrs Proudie or Vincent MacMaster type. At another, he represents what Powell's friend Orwell had excoriated: the abasement of the 'new' intelligentsia before the power-ethic of communism. Powell rarely foregrounds any political issue, but his unlikeable left-wingers – Erridge, Mark Members, J. G. Quiggin – contrasted with the amiability of his gentry and army people, suggest the unyielding Toryism articulated in the contrast between the obsequies paid Erridge, 'the socialist peer', and his brother George, who dies of war wounds:

> Musing on the brothers, it looked a bit as if, in an oblique manner, Erridge, at least by implication, had been given the credit for paying the debt that had in fact been irrefutably settled by George. The same was true, if it came to that, of Stringham, Templer, Barnby – to name a few casualties known personally to one – all equally indifferent to putting right the world.[19]

Widmerpool is Fabian man (with odd parallels in appearance and mannerisms to Snow himself), whose paganism exposes him to the cult which destroys him, in circumstances akin to the end of Bunyan's *Pilgrim's Progress*. In *Hearing Secret Harmonies* (1974) Widmerpool appears at Stourwater Castle, the symbol of the success he has consistently sought. He is turned away and made off with by Scorpio Murtlock, 'reincarnation' of the occultist Dr Trelawney, whose appearances in the sequence usually coincide with social disruption – notably the outbreak of the two world wars. It's evident from his own autobiography that Powell finds a place for the occult and irrational as 'anima', while distrusting the materialism that motivates Widmerpool. As with Ford Madox Ford and T. S. Eliot, the historical point of balance he refers to is the 'undivided sensibility' of the first half of the seventeenth century, which could comprehend the metaphysical poets, the occultism of Poussin, and the straightforward transcendentalism of Bunyan.

Powell, *au fait* with this period through his work on John Aubrey, ignored its unstable revolutionary aspect. His notion of manners and conventions could never comprehend the political community of puritan dissent. Instead, like Disraeli, he creates a pattern in which history turns back on itself. The sequence ends with Jenkins's landed Britain on an upswing. The old families have moved into computers and international finance, and land anyhow has recovered its value. The dance has completed its various figures, with little of the social change that the Widmerpools would have expected. The denouement, set in an English gothic castle, is *Sibyl*-like in its restatement of conservatism. At the same time, Nick Jenkins's *accidie*, his absence of interest in the future of his own family, suggests that all is not quite right with his world –

although we still don't know enough about him to assess such feelings. Where it should be profound, *A Dance to the Music of Time* ends up merely ingenious.

Powell at least had some interest in European literature – visible in the influence on him of Amiel, Proust and Conrad – and the politics of *A Dance* took place in a recognizable, if somewhat eccentric, social *milieu*. Compared with him, all the other *fleuves* showed a literary taste grown hopelessly insular. But, though Powell endorsed, Schumpeter-like, the continuity of aristocratic political skills, this did more than subvert Marxian causality; it also discounted any bourgeois takeover. In Powell's tolerance and his uncondescending view of the working class – where it appears – we are back in a sense with T. S. Eliot's concept of culture. But Powell's world – I use the word deliberately – doesn't share his British stasis. In the latter volumes the representatives of organization and activity are American, from a bourgeoisie with which Britain has failed to catch up.[20]

V

The ruling political ideology stressed competition between parliamentary élites; party members – and Labour as a mass-membership party really only dated from the 1940s – supplied constituency horsepower and were otherwise ignored. Despite his libertarianism, Orwell concurred in this; 'democratic Socialism' somehow belongs more to Catalonian anarchists than to activists in dingy halls. Empathy with them required a distinctly nonconformist sense of the value of discussion and self-government – ironically, more evident in the communist Edward Upward's *The Rotten Elements* (1962) than in writers who took parliamentarianism as given.

In the late fifties the working-class world suddenly became interesting – to be evaluated on its own terms, not on those of middle-class self-improvement or Marxian proletarian consciousness. Labour's crisis over nuclear weapons and nationalization and the discrediting of communism after Hungary in 1956 stimulated this quest for class as community – not least by releasing many communists from subjection to the party line. The *leitmotifs* were sounded by two 'academic' but highly subjective works, published in 1958: Richard Hoggart's *The Uses of Literacy* and Raymond Williams's *Culture and Society* – bridges between Marxism and the 'great tradition' of English literature as social criticism. They were shortly followed by attempts to re-create the 'soul' of local radicalism, by Walter Allen in *All in a Lifetime* and Raymond Williams in *Border Country*.

Both books are, effectively, fictional biographies of the writers' fathers – something of a break with an English literary tradition of the divided family and the early plunge into institutional life, in the shape of the boarding school – and ripostes to Gissing/Orwell's dismissal of any working-class 'enlightenment'. The central figures are dignified and serene manual workers – Allen's William Ewart Ashsted is a Birmingham engraver, Williams's Harry Price a railway signalman. The problematic fringes are provided by the meritocracy they, literally, father. Two of Ashsted's sons are technocrats, Harry Price's Matthew has become an economic historian. The plots represent, in imaginative literature, that dialogue – between Williams's Marxism and Allen's humanist sensibility – which orthodox cultural politics had failed to provide.

Will Ashsted, trying while his mind lasts to write down his memories, echoes Mark Rutherford and Tom Wilsher in *To Be a Pilgrim*. Free will and its frustrations count for much in his story. He could have stayed in the United States; he could have risen out of his class, but chose to remain with it. The co-operation involved in class solidarity is both instinctual – passages of *All in a Lifetime* strongly recall the Wordsworth of the *Lyrical Ballads* – and learned. But this balance of thought and feeling only persists in Will's generation. To his successful sons he is a social curiosity, like the aged prole Winston Smith interrogates in *Nineteen Eight-Four*. The third, a thief and a liar, has the imagination, now grown pathological, his brothers lack. Will grinds his lenses – Allen knew Mark Rutherford's veneration for Spinoza, and Edmund Wilson in *To the Finland Station* on Marx 'grinding the lens' – until he is stopped by his well-meaning daughter-in-law. The metaphor is plain enough: his socialist Utopia will never be achieved. Will represents craftsmanship and regional radicalism, both dying; his friend George Thompson, who becomes a Labour MP, is felled by a sexual scandal. There is a parallel with the Wilsher brothers and the fall of Edward, but Allen has not Cary's confidence in the radical tradition. One rather fears for a country with Phil and Will Ashsted – embodiments of William Cooper's clever uncommitted civil servants – in charge.[21]

Border Country started a sequence of novels in which the autobiographical Matthew Price involved himself in the politics of Britain in the 1960s and 1970s. The later books seem ponderous and oddly restricted in their range – of the day-to-day work of politics scarcely anything is heard – and the complexity of Williams's diction almost throttles *Loyalties* (1985). But *Border Country*, which Williams rewrote seven times between 1947 and 1958, is a novel of great perceptivity and moral force, at once *Bildungsroman* and a study of frontiers – of class, nature, country, religion, sex – as they impinge on independent individuals. Williams's affection for his people could have distorted but, as with Flora Thompson's *Lark Rise to Candleford* (1945), the constraints of class and employment are always visible in his tiny *polis* of a railway station on the Herefordshire border.

This is that image of 'felt community' for which Orwell sought haphazardly. When politics impinges, in the shape of the General Strike, its decencies are demonstrated. The stationmaster comes out with his men; Harry is sacked but reinstated when the station's one blackleg, Jack Meredith, stages his own one-man strike. Politics is decided in the intimate humane circle of the railwaymen. Williams, however, pushes in a further problematic. Harry's friend Morgan Rosser, blacklisted on the railway, moves into the jam-making business and does a deal with the local landowner which evicts Meredith from his smallholding to make way for fruit-bushes. Community seems to give way to enterprise and the cash-nexus; yet Rosser also uses his independence to move into Labour politics. Harry's signal-box, his three gardens, his bees, his intellectual agility could almost fit into Marx's picture of a socialist Utopia, yet Rosser and his van represent the new organization and technology which will complicate or postpone it.

Matthew Price shows here a self-awareness less apparent in the later novels. The articulate rationalizing Marxist intellectual, he is almost alienated by Harry and his friends' sense of community, which extends to the 'capitalist' Rosser (who, we later find out, has been bought out by a bigger firm). More than industrial, this has to do with land, religion and love, bonds between railwaymen and Welsh hill farmers. When the gentle withdrawn vicar comes to Glynmawr, he finds its identity is expressed in the chapels; he is 'an outpost'.[22] Nevertheless he recruits Matthew to his own civilization; the Hardyian image of the two surveying the heavens from the church tower contrasts with Harry's view, constricted by the slopes of the Holy Mountain and the signals on the railway.

Matthew leaves Glynmawr for Cambridge, and undertakes research into the migrations which created industrial Wales. Here, as in *All in a Lifetime*, is the 'lens-grinding' symbol, but the outcome is more positive: returning to Glynmawr when his father falls ill, he first feels smothered by the community, but is ultimately reconciled to it – 'by measuring the distance, we come home'. He now knows that his research matters. He has seen his statistics 'get up and walk' and his own life and ambitions interweave with theirs.[23] Williams held fast to such loyalties. But the very effectiveness of *Border Country* raises more awkward issues. Community functions because Glynmawr is Welsh, and Glynmawr is religious: both elements which the materialist in Williams would have to discount in 'British' left-wing politics. His next novel, *Second Generation* (1964), set among academics and car-workers – emigrant Welsh – in Oxford, tries to do so, and fails.[24]

If both books are sparing in irony, this is probably because the step-ladder from the working class to the élite of the welfare state had been hard-won. The Ashsted boys and Matthew Price were part of a new corporatist managerial class. But suppose – as Richard Hoggart feared – this process didn't reinforce social democracy but provoked the clash of cultures?[28] Two other writers, Welsh and English, returned verdicts which were much less respectful – in fact wildly funny – and deeply subversive.

It was only towards the end of his career, when he resumed a Welsh identification, that Raymond Williams discovered the novels and stories of Gwyn Thomas, someone much more damaged by the split between Oxbridge high culture and South Wales. Thomas won a scholarship from the Rhondda to Oxford, hated it and got out as soon as he could. He shared Williams's communism and added to this a ferocious exhilarating language, mastered with the flair of a first-generation English-speaker. Thomas makes no attempt to render phonetically any local dialect, delivering sentences baroque with metaphor and wordplay. 'In odd corners, in the unemployed clubs of our great land, I preached the gospel of dignity and brotherliness', Thomas wrote to his sister in 1940. 'But the corners were too odd and too dark and my voice and the voices like mine were as whispers compared with the roar of the tool-makers and the lie-makers who were fusing the new instruments of force and injustice.'[26] This ambition was out of Lewis Jones – whom he knew – but the tone and imagery capture a perpetual tragi-comedy whereby ideals are undermined – often literally – by the rickety geology and unreliable fauna of the valleys. Dark grudges, repressed appetites, a faulted history lie in wait for the bringer of sweetness and light. This diligent attender of Worker's Education Association classes, his millenarianism thawed into social democracy and graft by Labour *mafiosi*, will be racked by his townsfolk's complaints and vendettas; his ambitions for social betterment will collapse with spectacular ignominy while the reader laughs himself stupid.[27]

Thomas was a 'tragic comedian' in Meredith's sense: his socialism lapped over by 'soft, sinister laughter'. Ultimately the comedy had to pay the bills, and a great novelist was lost. In no way did he celebrate a local *polis*, where the houses could slither down the hill and individuals were dehumanized into 'voters' or 'elements'. Thomas's ambitions were revolutionary and internationalist. The moment of possibility had been in 1926. But his realization of that year in *Gazooka* (1957) is quite *sui generis*. The locked-out miners organize gazooka bands to keep their morale up, and the Meadow Prospect Matadors' epic contest with the Ferndale Dervishes, as brilliantly organized as anything in P. G. Wodehouse, presents a crazy ironic comedy. Miners were taking up D. H. Lawrence's silly suggestion and dressing up in tight red pants. Men were drilling and marching who a decade before had been drilling, marching and falling in France, and a decade hence would be doing the same thing in Spain. Yet, in the middle of a bitter lockout, all this was harmless: the conflicts were within the community, not, as Thomas had hoped, between a united community and its masters. When the defeated bands in their dusty uniforms walk over the mountain between the valleys on an autumn evening, the winter of real defeat, and real betrayal, will soon be upon them.

The engagement with deranged intellectual systems, the retreat into gnomic utterance and verbal bravado recall another bar-room desperado of the Celtic fringe, Flann O'Brien. But Thomas's qualities – of loyalty, wit, and pessimism of the intellect – were reflected by a much younger man on the educational escalator. Dennis Potter, a miner's son from the Forest of Dean, became President of the Oxford Union and a guinea-pig of the new media, holding forth about class in a television programme of the 'Suicide of a Nation' sort, writing a polemic, *The Glittering Coffin* (1963), against Macmillanite materialism, and in 1964 standing for Labour in an unwinnable rural seat. This experience gave rise to his two Nigel Barton plays, which marked the start not only of a remarkable career as a television dramatist but also of television as a channel for fictive politics.

Potter showed a subtle understanding of the medium and respect for his audience: the television set was a disorderly alien, a burglar holding the home to ransom; it could stultify, but it could also bring into people's daily lives events – riots, assassinations, war – which could expel the triviality of panel games and variety shows.[28] Nigel Barton's career and its problems are not just presented on television – television is part of them. His parents *see* their son complaining about the social tightrope that he must walk between home and Oxford; television both inflates the importance of his by-election and has long since weaned the voters away from the old rituals he has to endure.

Class united all four writers. Behind them stood D. H. Lawrence, now let out of the locked library cupboard and about to be the sensation of 1961, with the trial of *Lady Chatterley's Lover*. To them Lawrence mattered more on class than on sex; Hoggart had written the introduction to the Penguin edition, and the quote of the trial was the prosecuting QC asking the jury whether they would allow their family – 'or their servants' – to read the book. Allen, Williams, Thomas and Potter were trying to follow Lawrence in *Sons and Lovers* (1913): to rehabilitate Walter Morel, and a class consciousness which could be emotional as well as political. Will Ashsted's sympathy for his drunken father and his worthless son Tom, the inarticulate decency of Harry Price and Harry Barton, the flamboyance of the gazooka men, all hinted at something missing on the educational escalator. Might the aspirant sons bring their communities only incomprehension and deceit? In his study of his own district, the Forest of Dean, Potter wrote in 1962 of the danger mass culture posed to 'the communal strengths we shall have to protect and expand': 'Describe it how you will, excuse what you will, talk of mobility, opportunity, "post-capitalism", and "we are all workers now", I still think that my father's generation has had its dearest hopes and most deserved ambitions betrayed.'[29]

VI

Towards the close of the Snow and Powell sequences sensationalism increases, characterizations are more forced. Lord Snow viewed the world sourly. Labour leaders had 'lost their confidence . . . shouted down by stupid intellectuals', says a Snow-like peer in *In Their Wisdom* (1974).[30] Even in his civilized and tolerant Toryism, Powell showed that the conventions of politics as well as of fiction had become badly worn, something emphasized by the results when 'insiders' turned novelists. The tranquillity of the 1950s departed. Fictive Britains reeled from crisis to crisis, MPs took to crime and sexual perversion, premiers were kidnapped and/or shot, monarchs seduced, Parliament besieged and – in one apocalyptic production – blown to pieces . . . The overall tone – with menaces offered by students, strikers, the IRA, the KGB – suggested Edgar Wallace, but the perpetrators of the above were, among others, a couple of senior government ministers, a leading American conservative editor, a senior scientist and the Queen's former press secretary.[31] Politics when acted or filmed was equally disconcerting, though ideologically quite different, particularly after the 'generation of 1968' had got to work. The scenarios of Howard Brenton, David Hare and Trevor Griffiths had MI5, the CIA and the nuclear industry subverting away, with the overthrow of any proper socialist government at the top of their agenda.

This seemed to fit into Tory litanies of 'media bias' – although it provided choice of a sort. Perhaps most disturbing, however, was the civilized ingenuity of Anthony Jay and Jonathan Lynn's 'Yes Minister'. Jay, the author of *Management and Machiavelli* (1967), knew what a *polis* was; and not since Galt had there been so adept a defender of one as Sir Humphrey Appleby. This was satire of the highest order – and played a part in the deliberate demoralization which accompanied the application of 'line management' to the Civil Service in the 1980s. Yet in its lack of irony it confirmed its noisiest enthusiast, the Prime Minister, in a deeply negative concept of politics. Ultimately, *hubris* had to intervene. Following an occasion when Mrs Thatcher laboriously scripted and then enacted some joke about Sir Humphrey being an economist (Good God, he read Greats – that was the whole point!), Jay got a K of his own for 'political and public' services, a few months before the achievement of 'governing least' caused much of the British infrastructure to fall apart, the economy to slip into its worst crisis in decades, and the country to be marginalized in European diplomacy. While a 'paranoid style' beyond Disraeli's imaginings boiled away on the airport bookstalls, the Oxbridge élite had at last managed to gestate a delicate, fully functioning *polis* in Whitehall. The only problem was that it didn't relate to anywhere else.[32]

VII

What caused this subversion of the old consensus? I could cite six main factors: publishing economics, media technology, populism, sex, regionalism and violence. As to the first: political fiction, always commercial, was in the 1950s mainly written for hardback readers – over 90 per cent of them public-library borrowers. Authors might be lucky and make something from a paperback at very low royalties, but by the 1970s such rewards were well below National Assistance level.[33] Current issues and politicians, however, have 'high profiles' which *could* take them from the small and shrinking 'quality circuit' of publishing into the expanding 'popular circuit'.[34] The mechanism which gives us Edward Heath on yachts and Roy Hattersley on everything else regards anything churned out by a politician as saleable, even – or especially – if it's only fit to while away the tired businessman's hours on the transatlantic jumbo. Publishing also followed American commercial patterns; the notion of the novel as a seed-bed out of which would grow a few bestsellers was replaced by planning the latter at the 'idea' stage, when the timing, launch, television or film adaptation and associated spin-offs could efficiently be co-ordinated.

John Sutherland has summed up the potency of the product:

> The best-seller expresses and feeds certain needs in the reading public. It consolidates prejudice, provides comfort, is therapy, offers vicarious reward or stimulus. In some socially controlled circumstances it may also indoctrinate or control a population's ideas on politically sensitive subjects.[35]

Added to this was the desire for instruction. The blurb that claimed that '90% of this book is fact!' was meant to be taken seriously by readers guilty at indulging in escapism, and the methods of the whodunit can in fact be quite an effective guide to the more labyrinthine bureaucracies.[36] The Watergate scandal in 1973 provoked 'Washington from the inside' novels in which those not actually involved, but wanting to muscle in on the scandal, broke into fiction of a lurid sort with a politics which massaged the views of the readership. This was Le Queux's formula, but in the transatlantic market British politics *per se* was no longer a draw. In the 1950s Edelman and Snow, like Trollope before them, sold well in the United States; by the 1980s European politics created little impression there unless beefed up with the usual literary steroids. Jeffrey Archer had to give *First among Equals* an 'American' ending (the Tory won), but 'action' became the West's real lingua franca.

VIII

There were alternatives. Until the mid-1950s politics had still constrained drama, film and television. The Lord Chamberlain confined politics in the theatre to the drolleries of William Douglas-Home, little different from Pinero's 'political farces' of the 1890s. The cinema, socially critical in the 1940s, lapsed back into the routine of stiff-upper-lip war movies, dissipating its most corrosive talents. The revived television service continued the deference of Reithian sound broadcasting. But after 1955 things changed, largely through interaction between the media. The seasons of new drama which George Devine launched from the Royal Court theatre had a metropolitan impact as drastic as that of the Vedrenne–Barker management a century earlier. The visit of Bertolt Brecht's Berliner Ensemble in 1955 had been a harbinger, but the new 'angry' drama was also due to the settlement in London of provincial initiatives under way since the prewar years. The communist-influenced workers' theatres of Glasgow and Manchester provided many of the actors and production techniques for Theatre Workshop. Arnold Wesker learned his craft among Jewish theatre groups connected with the Communist Party in the East End. John Arden was converted to the open stage and the ritual quality of public drama by Lyndesay's *Thrie Estaitis* at the Edinburgh Festival in 1948. When he encountered Brecht, therefore, 'I immediately realised what he was talking about'.[37]

Devine wanted novelists to write for the theatre; but playwrights were soon scripting for television and cinema, after the BBC's monopoly – strongly defended by the Establishment – was breached by commercial television. The Conservatives who converted their unwilling party thought little about cultural pluralism; neither did the newspaper – and cinema-owners who had seen – in America - the writing on the screen, but the settlement in which two publicly but not directly state-controlled bodies competed transformed the media.[38] Dissidents at Broadcasting House who had once been sent to Orwell's Room 101 could now hit back from the commercial channels, some of whose most active programme-makers, like Sidney Bernstein of Granada and Sydney Newman of ATV, had started in radical journalism, film-making and theatre. Finally, under the threat of television, the cinema tapped new talent and new freedom to portray social issues and personal relationships. Woodfall Films, set up by John Osborne in the wake of his Royal Court successes, filmed many of the novels of the 'angry' generation, and other producers responded, realizing that only in the cinema could 'adult' themes – sex, mainly – be box office.

The most considerable talent of the period, John Arden, regarded the social purpose of the theatre as 'to bring men together in a kind of secular Eucharist, so that they can leave the building feeling that they *are* a society'.[39] He built on the nonconformist radicalism so vividly present in Cary's novels, demanding a theatre which would fuse the language of pulpit and conventicle with the older rites of folklore and the mystery plays. Further developed by Wesker and John McGrath, this became important to radical theatre in the late 1960s. But individual creativity was constrained by the politics of cultural production. The novel was the writer's dialogue with society, producing a text to be consulted by other individuals: a lasting component of the social structure. A play, television play or film was a specific *event*, to be scheduled and carefully and expensively prepared, its writer integrating with many other people. Its creation was a sequence of political acts, which might not issue in any final production, and in which the 'success' of the writer need not accord with his talent or insight – as Wesker and Arden were to find out.

IX

While this new *polis* was evolving, a traditional one was being destroyed. The literary radicalism provoked by Suez, the exodus from the Communist Party after Hungary, and the Campaign for Nuclear Disarmament, was followed by a general backsliding, not wholly the result of the impact of taxation on suddenly rising incomes. The shift in values which such writers registered implied a populism subversive of much of civil society.

John Braine's novel *Room at the Top* (1957) earned him £300,000 and was later one of the most successful films of the 'new British cinema'. The rise of the local government officer Joe Lampton isn't political in any interactive sense, but Braine set it as firmly in an English industrial town as Stendhal's *Scarlet and Black* is set in Restoration France. Like Julien Sorel, Joe uses sex to break into the élite, and like Julien he is wounded by an affair with an older woman. But only emotionally: where Julien is destroyed on realizing that the power structure he is trying to climb is illusory, Joe's values remain intact – they mythicize not power but material wealth.[40] *Room at the Top* takes the values of English nonconformity, the 'call' of Bunyan's pilgrim, and secularizes it. Joe sees an upper-class young man with a girl and a sports-car:

I saw myself, compared with him, as the Town Hall clerk, the subordinate pen-pusher, half-way to being a zombie, and I tasted the sourness of envy. Then I rejected it. Not on moral grounds; but because I felt then, and still do, that envy's a small and squalid vice – the convict sulking because a fellow-prisoner's been given a bigger helping of skilly. This didn't abate the fierceness of my longing. I wanted an Aston-Martin, I wanted a three-guinea linen shirt, I wanted a girl with a Riviera sun-tan – these were my rights, I felt, a signed and sealed legacy.[41]

The language has biblical and political elements, but the goal is purely material, subversive of the old élite but also quite devoid of any notion of community. Although Braine and others of his contemporaries were seen as giving a voice to the working class, they denoted the dissolution of the structures celebrated by *The Uses of Literacy*, measurable in shuttered chapels and half-empty Labour meetings.

Braine's subsequent career was dismal, but in his fixation with 'positional goods', and in Lampton's evolution into the amoral hero of a television series, he anticipated the 'clan' formula of the late-capitalist 'soap', whereby the *polis* shrinks to the extended – and expensive – family. The reflex of this, an embattled attitude against the outside world, contributed to 'radical right' populist support for the anti-immigrant position of Enoch Powell in 1968. In its turn this threat brought radical theatre 'to the streets'. Agitprop in its battered minibus symbolized literary politics as students and actors, Narodnik-like, invaded canteens and factories to spread the gospel of revolution.

The year 1968 shocked the political élite as much as it had de Gaulle. In Carlyleian terms Crossman saw volcanic fire and lava spilling over the familiar landscape.[42] Radicals believed that drama could enlighten and thus inoculate the masses against Powellite contagion; they were aided by the inflamed imaginations of orthodox politicians, as the 'scientific revolution' gave way to intrigues in Downing Street which outdid anything in *Private Eye*'s 'Mrs Wilson's Diary'. Playwrights who wanted politicians to embody cartoon stereotypes, whether as would-be dictators or as putty in the hands of international capital, found the professionals enthusiastically collaborating, although the 'British sickness' was more to do with a malfunctioning corporatism, inept management and archaic unions. If there are few British business novels, there are no contemporary novels about the politics of union power.

Getting away from such intractability, 1968 offered public spectacle and sexual liberation. Simon Raven could be counted on to play these for all they were worth. In *Places Where They Sing* he had sinister left-wing forces manoeuvring behind a front of student hedonism to take over a Cambridge college. The new order would be ushered in by the ritual copulation of the most fetching student pair on the high altar of the chapel. Perhaps Lancaster College was meant as a metaphor of Britain, perhaps not. On the whole the right was less worried about the state of the nation - and its young critics - than the left. Trevor Griffiths's wordy *The Party* (1973), commissioned by Kenneth Tynan for the National Theatre, began with another couple failing to achieve a symbolic orgasm, and required Lawrence Olivier go on about socialist theory at great length, but the real action - such as it was - centred on the complicated arrangements for televising *les événements* live from Paris.

The Narodnik spirit was put to the test. David Edgar, of the General Will company, observed gloomily that their plays went down well with white-collar well-educated workers, and flopped where they were really poor and oppressed.[43] Yet the commitment was understandable. Suppose racialism became as potent as nationalism in Wales, Scotland and Northern Ireland? Edgar himself recognized this in the play which he wrote when he abandoned the minibus, *Destiny* (1975), a compelling analysis of the links between declining imperialism, economic change and the stifled politics of the English petty bourgeoisie.[44] *Destiny* was researched with the detail of a doctoral thesis, and much of Edgar's subsequent work came close to the 'people's remembrancing' of History Workshop. Others, perhaps not so talented, used the contacts of the collective phase to launch themselves successfully in main-line theatre - by this time largely subsidized where not publicly owned.

X

The Royal Shakespeare Company, one of its directors told a sceptical John Arden, 'is a form of socialist organisation'. Not a line likely to be reassuring to a bourgeoisie experiencing the upsets of the mid-1970s: 25 per cent inflation, union indiscipline, the intervention of the International Monetary Fund. Not surprisingly, the right-wing political thriller staged a recovery, seizing some of the attitudes of more reputable conservative novelists - think of Widmerpool's rôle as, perhaps, a Soviet spy - exaggerating them, throwing in a lot of 'action', hardware and sex, and usually expounding on the unreliability of left-wing governments of any description. Constantine Fitzgibbon's *When the Kissing Had to Stop* (1961) was the prototype, with a CND-supporting Labour government subverted by the Russians and by dissident English conservatives. It was quite clever, with a believable Michael Foot/Victor Gollancz Labour premier and an inept bunch of right-wingers whose intrigues bring about the fate that they want to forestall. Most subsequent efforts followed this formula. What was new and sinister was that politics moved forward to meet them.

The year 1968 left one permanent lesion in the shape of Northern Ireland, the same issue that the conservative consensus had side-tracked in 1886 and 1916–22. One margin of British politics crossed the divide between opposition and civil war. Violence, kidnapping and assassination moved on to the agenda; so, too, did the uncontrolled and secretive response of state agencies. Instead of the parliamentary 'rules of the game', thrillers saw strong individuals taking on terrorists *and* a fainéant establishment. In part prompted by the brutalization of American society which accompanied the Vietnam war, as respect for the State decreased, this also reflected the readership's own position: management transferring its frustrations with bureaucracy and unions into the international politics sphere.[45]

The liberal herbivores looked on in dismay, conscious of a narrowing influence. Several – Margaret Drabble, Melvyn Bragg and Mervyn Jones among others – attempted political themes, particularly around 1978 when a crisis on an 1848 scale seemed imminent.[46] An unreassuring tone owed as much to their unsure political footing as to gloomy plots. *Angst* was back on an Early Victorian scale, with the well-meaning, trapped between predatory capitalism and revolutionary youth, trying to present a moral politics, while the economic machinery that preserved the BBC and the Arts Council was seizing up and far below political society something very atavistic was going on. Repelled by the young Narodniks, they tried to find out what made capitalism tick – or, in Britain, not tick. Beatrice Webb's 'sense of guilt', detached from its usual Fabian moorings, led to some changes of political allegiance in 1979 and to the foundation of the Social Democrat Party in 1981. The result smashed the two-party system to pieces. Some of these novels betrayed by their structure that their authors aimed at television serialization. The novel, as such, was a *pis aller*. More systematic leftists straightforwardly took on politics–media relations. Raymond Williams's *The Volunteers* and David Craig and Nigel Gray's *The Rebels and the Hostage* (both 1978) tried – like Heinrich Böll in *The Lost Honour of Katherina Blum* (1973) – to explain why individuals could choose, or at least sanction, terrorism, in an environment where the media – state or commercial – were everywhere intrusive. David Hare and Ian McEwen presented in film some of the most vivid political criticism of the period, in *Licking Hitler* (1978), *The Imitation Game* (1979) and *The Ploughman's Lunch* (1985), which treated the manipulations of 'black' propaganda. Their very effectiveness showed what, in a metropolitan, post-industrial society, were the *real* politics. The great distraction from the ideologies of 1968 had become the new main line. Yet it was a main line without a British terminus. The cosmopolis of media, its international networks of interest and authority swamping legislatures, represented an uncompromising new capitalism. In one of the better novels by an MP, Joe Ashton's *Grassroots* (1978), a working-class socialist from a heavy industrial centre threatened with works closures is baffled and all but destroyed – not by 'the rules of the game' but by the fact that these no longer apply. Drunkenly intervening in a set-up parliamentary debate, stood up by the female television interviewer whom he fancies, he staggers back through a nightmarish London to the night train to Gritnall. His people sustain him, but their industry is still doomed.

XI

To aim political fiction at the mass media – and succeed – meant that the product had also to entertain. Enthusiasts for Trevor Griffiths's television series 'Bill Brand', a ponderous left-wing analysis of the Labour Party in the late 1970s, alleged that it got high viewing-figures, considering . . . Others, including the *Guardian*'s television critic, believed that this was because Brand's girl-friend rarely had any clothes on.[47] Even in quite serious political serials – perhaps especially in them, where the boredom threshold was low – naked girls tended to be brought on to stop the plot seizing up, rather as Disraeli switched to some palatial country house or summoned up the Secret Societies.

D. H. Lawrence – *the* author of the early 1960s – had played his part in this; not the class-and-culture man who had brooded over Williams, Allen and Hoggart, but the apostle of what *Lady Chatterley's Lover* – in its 1961 version – had largely been about. 'The word' was seen as liberating and demotic, connected with being Orwell's 'rebel from the waist down', while 'sex' still suggested Freudianism and the neuroses of the élite. That Parkin changed from the communist of *The First Lady Chatterley* into the phallocrat Mellors of the Penguin text implied a political deterioration, but the radicals of 1961 were content to 'recover' the working-class male – at the expense of the working-class female.

Exploited both by capital and by men in the 1960s, women became civic individuals with a new and pungent political critique, while 'permissiveness' reinforced the old images of MPs betraying wives and constituents. Remington in *The New Machiavelli* required a lot of extra-marital cuddling to compensate for the idiocies of Westminster, and the tradition was faithfully – if that's the word – carried on by Fienburgh, Edelman, Brian Sedgemore, Chris Mullin, Douglas Hurd and Michael Spicer, and so on. While one particular woman was smashing through British conventions like a tank, the position of women in orthodox political fiction can only be summed up in one word: prone.[48]

But consider British politics from the point of view of a sex-maniac. Jock MacLeish, the hero of Alasdair Gray's 'sado-masochistic fantasy' *1982 Janine* (1984) gives himself up to thoughts of women in skin-tight denim in a hotel in Greenock, a situation so depressing that, after bouts of masturbation and drinking, he tries to end it all. The result, however, is a rediscovery of his history – as theatrical-lighting wizard turned security adviser to a group of multinational firms – in which he finds himself in a bondage which is as much political as sexual:

> 'If you win the race by a short head you will have lost it,' we were told, so we won by a short head and lost the race. Then came cuts in public spending, loss of business and increased unemployment and now Westminster has decided to spend the North Sea oil revenues building a fucking tunnel under the English Channel. If we ran that race again we would win by a head and a neck so we won't be allowed to run it again, cool down you are goading yourself into a FRENZY my friend, think about fucking Superb, think about fucking Janine, don't think about fucking POLITICS![49]

The novel is set in Galt's 'west' but could almost be in Oceania. Orwell on sex has been inverted. Men are dictators from the waist down. *1982 Janine* is uncomfortable in examining the incursion of politics into the personal sphere, and in linking sexual domination to political authoritarianism. MacLeish, the perfervidly ingenious Scot, has lived off the women in his life – rather as the culture of Clydeside radicalism was set in shipyard, engineering shop, pub, union meeting and football ground, and simply assumed that some lesser breed was there to mind the bairns. Gray doesn't so much parallel Hugh MacDiarmid's *A Drunk Man Looks at the Thistle* (1926) as expand it into areas where MacDiarmid's touch was weak. What begins as a pathological case-study ends as a report on the state of the nation.

Gray's nation is not Britain. By inverting the stereotype and seeing sex – as an ideal of decent human relationships – not as a disturber of politics but as its victim, Gray ends up with a smaller *polis*. He has written that Scotland's failure in 1979 to secure a measure of self-goverment overcame a writer's block and made him finish his first novel, *Lanark*. The combination of realism and surrealism in this huge work has caused it to be compared with that other great city-novel, James Joyce's *Ulysses*, but Gray's Unthank is much more a political–social construct, a nightmarish dehumanized product of unrestricted industrialism and individualistic economics, whose peculiarities are paralleled by the organization of the novel itself, its pseudo-academic schemes of references and footnotes, its black-and-white drawings, its 'complags' and 'difplags' – its conscious debts to the Scottish Enlightenment, Carlyle, MacDiarmid and Joyce Cary. It is no coincidence that the presiding figure on the title-page is the 'multiple man' of the frontispiece of Hobbes's *Leviathan*.[50]

If the exhausted formulas of the political novel 'commodify' personal relations into sex, to reverse this brings into question the basis of metropolitan politics. This critique, from feminist writers or those who have taken a woman's point of view, was evident in Joyce Cary's second trilogy, in which the marriage of Nina Slapton and Chester Nimmo is seen as 'micropolitical' as well as sexual. If unsatisfactory in both respects, it still follows rules which produce a general social benefit, whereas the sexual satisfaction Nina derives from her affairs with Jim Latter doesn't socialize Latter at all. Cary challenges Orwell's view of sex as a barrier against totalitarianism; the wilfully private man can be an insensitive menace in politics.[51]

Not that this was news to feminist writers! Yet the same criticism can be made of Doris Lessing in *The Golden Notebook* (1962). Lessing's concern with individuality rather than with institutions moves her closer to the European 'metropolitan' novel of personal psychology and society. But her heroine Anna Wulf, as a woman, a colonial and a communist in the 1950s, is so marginal within British politics that her individuation imprisons rather than liberates. Outside the ghetto of the communist party, her search for psychological harmony inevitably centres on personal relationships. That the only satisfactory one of these is with a well-socialized American businessman undermines her ostensible radicalism. She lacks both the technical and symbolic means of describing the 'real' political world outside.

Lessing was, however, right to regard herself as the precursor of a much more politicized women's writing, even if this initially meant plays rather than novels. The feminist drama which came with the radicalization of 1968 took up where the productions of the suffragettes had left off – moving from propaganda to more complex studies of the politics of the voiceless and disregarded – and coincided with the reprinting, by Virago and other publishers, of the political fiction of Storm Jameson, Naomi Mitchison and Vera Brittain.[52] The more reflective literature which followed both interrogated these traditions and drew on them. If the Disraelian political novel has roots in fairy-story, epic and pantomime – and the extremities of twentieth-century history still fuelled fantasies of the Tolkien/C. S. Lewis sort – then these qualities have been stunningly resumed in Fay Weldon's *The President's Child* (1982), whose heroine, a London-based Australian journalist, is trapped and all but destroyed by the agents of an American presidential hopeful. The appeal of the paraphernalia of the fairy story – enchanters, magic mirrors, and so on – is not diminished when their effects can be replicated by technology, and to this Weldon adds a symbolism which makes her heroine emblematic of a Britain modulating into Airstrip One. A writer hitherto concerned with the 'micropolitics' of marriage and sex – and their systematic exploitation of the female partner – could almost by definition add an original world-view to international politics. If other roots lie in dystopic communities, riven by anti-social ideas and forces, as in Peacock and Wells, then Weldon, too, has been there in *The Shrapnel Academy* (1986). While Margaret Drabble, earnestly trying to adapt a private discourse to comment on wide social themes, while maintaining the metropolitan structure, tended to produce confused herbivores whose attempts at intervention ended in gentle ineffectuality, Weldon and Zoë Fairbairns, in *Benefits* (1979), profited by annexing the traditional (and anyway fairly outlandish) impedimenta of the political tale, and transferring it into fable or science fiction. *Because* women have been so rigidly excluded from the parliamentary structure, it is easier for them to create a new dialectical community.

XII

The sort of cocksure leftist that women – and nearly everyone else – complained about was Howard Kirk in Malcolm Bradbury's *The History Man* (1975); televised in 1981, his amoral determinism did its bit to discredit the Labour left. 'Campus novels' – of which there were soon many – had their resemblances to Galt, and 'Yes Minister', in the manoeuvrings of power-brokers, committees and students, but seemed custom-built for a literate and still transatlantic market, with a formulaic content dominated by shop-talk, intrigue and sex. As the breakthrough from 'quality' to 'popular' had much to do with publishing contacts and literary prizes, campus politics flowed effortlessly into literary politics. Where *The Masters* had related to the secular issues of the 1930s, the campus novel now seemed as complacently hermetic as the parliamentary novel.

The obverse of this was unwonted literary activity in non-metropolitan Britain. *1982 Janine* is only one novel about life in Glasgow and the west of Scotland from an output which has, against the general trend of publishing, been steadily growing, in a complex reaction to over-centralization and unsuccessful modernization.[53] As in the 1880s, a 'popular' regional novel had developed as a museum of comforting social archaisms, like the 'heritage industry' which transformed 'backwardness' into commercial profit and social placebo. This sub-genre stemmed from successful television adaptations, notably of Galsworthy's *Forsyte Saga* in the early 1960s. A. J. Cronin's 'Doctor Finlay's Casebook', set in Scotland in the 1920s, and 'Upstairs Downstairs', set in the town house of an Edwardian Tory MP, incorporated enough radical impulses – feminism, Ibsenite social criticism – to make their formula long-lasting.[54] 'House-party' novels such as those of Isabel Colegate – *The Orlando Trilogy*, *The Shooting Party* (1982) – retained the commercial clout Mrs

Humphry Ward had once enjoyed, while 'romance-and-regionalism' of the Catherine Cookson sort took over from 'Regencies', foregrounding ports and mill-towns. While this tended to reduce politics to the family, and issues settled by love or death, it also stressed themes such as class, single parenthood and female solidarity – even if this only restored the situation in Winifred Holtby's day.

Raymond Williams wrote in 1982 of the 'limited "regional" novel . . . passing out of serious consideration and possibility, in advanced capitalist societies', but noted that it was still effective in a post-colonial *milieu*.[55] Much of Britain, however, considered itself colonized; and, as the Glasgow example showed, regionality could persist when a 'British' class solidarity broke up. The asocial individualism of Thatcherism, foreboded by John Braine, was unaccompanied by propaganda fiction of the Nevil Shute kind in which small entrepreneurs took on unions and big players. Maggieolatry seemed to suffice. Nor was there the *embourgeoisement* that critics of the old class system had noted in the 1960s. The key cultural document of the 1980s was the British tabloid press – right-wing, trivial, insular – and while there were some *Tono-Bungay*-like inquests by Julian Rathbone and John Mortimer into Thatcherland, those home counties on which the *Sun* never set, there was little suggestion of ways forward or out.

In Rathbone's *Nasty, Very* (1986) sleazy Charlie Bosham creeps from his property-developer chrysalis to become a Tory MP, to the accompaniment of Mrs Thatcher proclaiming a Britain reborn after the Falklands War. But the Falklands saw Scotland and Wales distance themselves from English enthusiasm. Once substantial, imperial loyalties had given way to regional cultures which were seen as historical as well as political. This affected more than one form of communication: in Wales the campaign for a Welsh-medium television service; in Ireland the drama. But overall there was a common stress on the political perceptions and actions of ordinary people, and on the 'normality' of such regional identity in Europe.

Scots explored the relation between Scottish and British pathology. Gray probed the dislocations of the Enlightenment and industrialization; George Mackay Brown went further back to the Reformation, and the imposition of a deterministic Calvinism. In *Fergus Lamont* (1979), Robin Jenkins analysed the soldier stereotype and, in *The Temptation of George Darroch* (1984), the last great purely Scottish political issue – the struggle of the Church for freedom from state and landlord control which climaxed in the Disruption of 1843. Is Jenkins's parish minister, Darroch, to side with his wealthier parishioners, or face eviction for his basic beliefs? Darroch is a weak well-meaning man who prevaricates until the last minute, knowing that the religious issue is delusive, with little to offer a society riven by industry and inequality. Like Alexander's Johnny

Gibb, he asserts his independence, and 'goes out' with the men who were to form the Free Church: but this was a tepid gesture in a situation all too close to the mishandled outcome of devolution in 1979.[56]

Is there, in fact, a satisfactory Scottish *polis*? Alan Massie, in whose work politics bulks as large as in Buchan's, is unconvinced. Scotland, like Lampedusa's Sicily in *The Leopard*, is too small and backward to be more than a passive spectator of a world of large-scale units. Nationalism is an atavistic destructive response. In *A Night in Winter* (1984) his most sympathetic characters seem paralysed by the retreat of history from Scotland, capable only of sentimental retrospection. With William Boyd's *The New Confessions* (1986) we have a hero who leaps right out of Scotland into the cosmopolis of the film world to confront the great dialectics of the twentieth century. However tragic John James Todd's career may be, he is never history's victim. Perhaps the significant thing was that in a 'post-industrial' economy, where culture had become an industry, such confrontations *were* politics, their dialectic spread by the peripatetic theatre started by John McGrath's 7:84 company, and the growth of distinctively Scottish media and publishing, their effects visible in an increasingly independent political and cultural life.

Welsh literary politics was, because of the language issue, *sui generis*, but shared the Scots fear that, without self-government, partial causes (nonconformity, temperance) would become distorting. Gwyn Thomas reacted against the language, the conservatism of its cultural leader, Saunders Lewis, and the power that Welsh-speakers exerted within the Welsh establishment. Lewis's ideas, oversimplified and sentimentalized, figured in the success of Richard Llewellyn's *How Green Was My Valley* (1939) and its projection of an arcadian reactionary community which contrived to be industrial *and* picturesque. But, while Welsh Kailyard was as prehensile as its Scottish counterpart, the European orientation of Welsh nationalism informed Lewis's plays and Richard Hughes's *Human Predicament* (1961, 1973) in which the juxtaposition of Wales, England, New England, Africa and Bavaria underlay an exploration of the breakdown of the humanist political ethic in the interwar years: an enterprise akin to Carlyle on the French Revolution, which ultimately defeated him. That said, the torso of the work, the skilful delineation of fading English Liberals, wild American teenagers or the *schickeria* of Munich, fits into a convincing intellectual history, perhaps easier to grasp in fractured Wales than in comfortable England:

. . . suppose that in the name of emergent Reason the very we-they line itself within us had been deliberately so blurred and denied that the huge countervailing charges it once carried were themselves dissipated or suppressed? The normal penumbra of the self would then become a no-man's land: the whole self-conscious being has lost its footing

. . . In such a state the solipsist malgré-lui may well turn to mad remedies, to pathological dreaming; for his struggles to regain his footing would indeed be an upheaval from being's very roots . . . gurgling up hot lava suddenly on to the green grass.[57]

What affected post-1918 Germany hit, with lessened force, a Wales in which *Border Country*'s linkages between class and nation – railwaymen and miners – were decaying. Raymond Williams's *Loyalties* (1985) ends in the miners' strike, which virtually destroyed the élite of the Welsh labour force, yet despite his intellectual awareness of traditional community Williams seemed uncertain about what must follow it. Even in the history of the Principality, myth and argument shifted facts around. The writer had to establish 'when', as Gwyn A. Williams put it, the country was.[58]

For Emyr Humphreys, in *The Taliesin Tradition* (1983) the roots of Welsh identity lay in the epics of the language. Accepting Saunders Lewis's leadership but restating the liberal nonconformity that Lewis rejected, Humphreys in his *Land of the Living* sequence created an epic for twentieth-century Wales, which despite an uncertain start with *National Winner* in 1971 has created in Amy Parry a Welsh sister to Chris Guthrie. From the point in *Flesh and Blood* (1974) when Lucas Parry, Amy's lay-preacher uncle, spurns a lift from the manager of the local slate quarry as he takes the orphaned child home, politics is viewed from a Welsh eye: through a prism of language, class, religious dissent. From then until *Open Conspirators* (1988), Humphreys vividly renders the politics and culture of interwar Wales. Some characters plainly represent figures like Lewis Jones, Saunders Lewis or Lady Rhondda; others, such as Lloyd George, appear only in chiaroscuro. The weight of the description is with the local polity: the professors, deacons, political organizers, poets and shopkeepers are described with a subtle sympathetic irony reminiscent of Greene or Powell, yet are also *literally* interpreted to us, their dialogue and feelings being translated from the Welsh. Amy's shift from Plaid Cymru into the Labour Party makes a powerful symbolic commentary on a troubled national identity. 'The central figure', Humphreys has said, 'had to be a woman: Wales would have disappeared long ago if it had depended on men.'[59] If 'Amy Cymru' is flawed, will this unsentimental realism help overcome the setback that Welsh nationality suffered in the referendum of 1979, or is it the *mirage* of consciousness: 'What we think, we can', as Louis MacNeice wrote, 'the old idealist lie'?

In Ireland engagement with politics has mattered less than the need to set its pathology in a historical context and, if need be, to escape from it into a life of individual fulfilment and moral action. Thus the grand-scale historical novel survives in good health in James Plunkett's

Strumpet City (1969), restating the O'Caseyite humanist socialism that had succumbed to the heroics of Easter 1916, and Thomas Flanagan's meticulous historical reconstructions of 1898 and Fenianism, *The Year of the French* (1979) and *The Tenants of Time* (1988). In the 1960s the Ulsterman Sam Thompson followed up O'Casey's critique in plays – *Over the Bridge* (1960) and *Cemented with Love* (1965) – which were to prove the forerunners of a remarkable dramatic movement.[60] Nationalism and radical nonconformity were corrupted into bigotry and violence – Ian Paisley a caricature Bunyan; Bobby Sands establishing his ascendancy in the Maze by his ability to 'tell' the story of Leon Uris's pro-IRA potboiler *Trinity* (1973) – by a North simultaneously 'industrialized' and depressed, and the weakness of any democratic socialist ideal able to create a decentralized polity embracing the entirety of the British Isles.[61] This agenda continued to obsess John Arden, in further attempts to reconcile the puritan radicalism and ritualistic folk-community themes which had always marked his drama. The metropolis – and even the leftish agitprop-derived theatre – not being interested, he kept more and more to his Irish base and, in plays like *The Island of the Mighty* (1972), *The Non-Stop Connolly Show* (1977), *Pearl* (1979), and the novel *Books of Bale* (1988), continued a project of cultural explanation and synthesis which must bear comparison with the programmes of Carlyle or MacDiarmid.[62]

Arden's idea of the drama as 'social eucharist' was badly needed in Ireland in the 1970s and 1980s; the public arts took over the dialectics which political institutions were ill-fitted to perform. Novels served as reconnaissance and diagnosis. In Bernard Maclaverty's *Cal* (1983) an unemployed Londonderry boy drifts into a terrorist group, and then, through a relationship with the young widow of a policeman, is gradually driven to question his conduct and to make moral choices through the qualities of reason and feeling that she opens up to him. He tips off the police, to try to prevent the IRA blowing up the library where his lover works. The bomb is placed inside a hollowed-out copy of *Middlemarch*. There could be a parallel with *The Princess Casamassima*, written during the Anglo-Irish crisis of the 1880s. But where James sanctions the *status quo* Cal's moral choice – which will destroy his love and his future – confronts the terrorists *and* the moral decline of the 'forces of law and order'.

Cal returns to the radical tradition of regarding tragic dignity as the entitlement of ordinary people. More positively, the renaissance of Ulster literature has concentrated much of its strength in the theatre not just as a commentary on the problems of the province, but as a collective political act which could potentially overcome the tragic isolation depicted in *Cal*. Not surprisingly, its subject has been social action – strikes or labour organization. Following the precedent of the Larkinite labour movement, and the rôles women have played, both in the family and as breadwinners, it has advanced a politics radically critical of existing rigid divisions. This owed something to the agitprop of the late 1960s, but the work of Brian Friel and Frank McGuinness gained a remarkable following, particularly in Catholic urban areas, and when playwrights like Martin Lynch moved into the professional theatre from companies like Charabanc their working-class audience followed.[63]

Theatre requires a lively host community, which can exist independently of metropolitan print-capitalism, just as in the 1930s Grassic Gibbon, Storm Jameson and Winifred Holtby were matched by radical theatre, stronger in Manchester and in Glasgow than in London. But promising developments in the 1950s and 1960s were never really sustained outside the Celtic fringe. In the over-centralization of publishing and politics, the real losers continue to be the English provinces – rarely featuring, despite the work of Sid Chaplin, Alan Plater and Tom Haddaway, in more than a supporting rôle. In the 1930s, in *Shabby Tiger*, Howard Spring concluded his usual 'No resemblance is intended . . .' bit with the line 'There is no such city as Manchester'. If this is now the conventional wisdom of the metropolitan publisher, the reason is not simply the self-satisfaction of London literary cliques. The intellectual life of immigrant-created English provincial cities was always to a great extent created by Irish, Welsh or Scots incomers – like the Irish leader-writer who, in C. E. Montague's *A Hind Let Loose* (1910), steers the destinies of both the Tory and the Liberal parties in Hallam (a thinly disguised Manchester). As the economic springs run down, the old loyalties compel.

XIII

Sensationalism may be in order, given the frantic gyrations of metropolitan politics, economics and literary life. 'Globalization' has destroyed the ethical basis of political economy, producing individuals wielding power and incurring debt, on a scale beyond that of many nation states. This has, not least, affected publishing and the media, detaching its operations from any 'national' community, but giving it an almost alarming political salience. The London literary world, after a sequence of giant takeovers, found itself in 1988–9 plunged into fearsome political crises by *Spycatcher* and later by *The Satanic Verses*, as a result of which Salman Rushdie may be forced to play a rôle out of John Buchan for the rest of his days. Nerve and constitutional manipulation beyond anything permissible elsewhere in Europe kept Mrs Thatcher in Downing Street; while her luck held, Edgar Wallace was better than Trollope, let alone Bagehot, at describing this sort of thing.

It's difficult to conceive of a British *Staatsphilosophie* since the British have never thought in terms of a state. As written constitutions and corpuses of administrative law don't invite one to be very imaginative about them, the commitment and personal psychology of the European political novel have been related to ideology and (usually revolutionary) change, taking wing when political society is in crisis. The British canvas has been the narrower but hitherto more 'realistic' dialectic between the conventions of institutions and those of 'personal relationships'; and although the period when the two fused, the epoch of Trollope, Meredith and George Eliot, was only a brief one, roughly from the mid-1860s to the mid-1880s, its influence lasted. But it didn't find crises easy to cope with.

Wells's *The New Machiavelli*, a genuine attempt to mediate between ideas, praxis *and* the personal life, elided these so 'tastelessly' that it was disowned by its author, but such value-judgements were less likely on the British periphery, or in those parts of the state apparatus where surpassing patriotism had traditionally justified murky ethics. From the days of Le Queux the political thriller had been the disreputable relative of the political novel; now, as sensationalism overwhelmed the political novel, and authoritarianism the State, the thriller began to resume the ethical and ideological seriousness of Conrad and Greene. In the hands of John le Carré – particularly in *A Perfect Spy* – it has become something like the European metropolitan novel (even involving the heavily symbolic appearance of Thomas Mann himself), a novel of argument about civil society but one set in a collapsing *polis*.

It was, as Leslie Stephen wrote, at the edge of normality that normal behaviour was defined. Le Carré, while a critic of the constricting conservatism of post-1945 British society, regarded it as worth defending.[64] *A Small Town in Germany* (1968) could still contrast some British decencies with the febrile quality of a restored European democracy. In *A Perfect Spy* this no longer seems the case. The quasi-autobiographical Magnus Pym (a name itself echoing the radicalism of the English Civil War) inhabits an embassy world of social and sexual betrayal in a serious, if dull, Europe. A spy in the Russian service, his communist ideals seem no more significant, so he calls off, disappears. He retreats to a boarding-house in a small Devon resort and, as 'Mr Canterbury', writes his recollections.

A Perfect Spy has strong subliminal echoes of Bunyan and Carlyle: the quest for conviction, the notion of civil society as a crust over a void which is personal as much as social. Pym is also employed by the post-Disraelian, and consequently post-Carlyleian British state, but finds it dissolving. The moral composition of Magnus Pym's 'soul' is, like that of Carlyle, heavily impregnated by German romanticism; his response is a pilgrimage like that undertaken by Tancred, or Hannay in

Buchan, but his Paraclete, or Mr Standfast, turns out to be his fellow German romantic, Otto, his Czech control.[65]

Several things about *A Perfect Spy* recall the last great English political novel, Joyce Cary's Chester Nimmo trilogy, completed in 1955 – the provincial setting (in Devon), the experimental quality of the narration, shifting between first and third person, the hints of myth and epic, the ambiguous relationship of the hero to his country and his con-man father. Nimmo, the Devon cottager's son – and palpably a near-relative of Lloyd George – is a fantasist, a sexual predator, at once hero and betrayer of radicalism. On the other hand he has the ability to make the system work, and a loyalty to ordinary people. When in *Not Honour More* Nimmo is hunted by Latter, the 'man of honour', to a humiliating death, while trying to bring the two sides in the General Strike together, one sees fanaticism destroying the germ of politics and of patriotism, the capacity to settle problems through discussion. Not a promising augury for the period after 1955. The loyalty to a nation or a community which can appeal to Jock MacLeish or Amy Parry – and which still motivated the strong English radicalism of Nimmo and of Cary himself – seems, in *A Perfect Spy*, to have atrophied. And no amount of strident appeals from Downing Street, or the dump-bucket patriotism of those who have been winners in the Thatcher years, is likely to bring it back.

NOTES

1   See in particular Robert Mckenzie, *British Political Parties* (London: Heinemann, 1953), pp. 1–5.
2   Paul Johnson, 'No sex for Johnnie', *New Statesman*, 28 July 1961; his own novel was *Left of Centre* (London: MacGibbon & Kee, 1958).
3   See Noel Annan's review in the *London Review of Books*, 17 October 1985.
4   See Philip Snow, *Stranger and Brother* (London: Macmillan, 1982), pp. 166 ff.
5   ibid, p. 35.
6   See Blake Morrison, *The Movement* (Oxford: Oxford University Press, 1980), pp. 52, 63, 158 ff.
7   Cooper, *Memoirs of a New Man* (Harmondsworth: Penguin, 1968), p. 37.
8   John Halperin, *C. P. Snow: An Oral Biography* (Brighton: Harvester Press, 1983), p. xiii.
9   Philip Snow, *Stranger and Brother*, p. 157.
10 Richard Crossman, *The Diaries of a Cabinet Minister* (London: Hamish Hamilton/Jonathan Cape, 1975), entry for 10 October 1964.
11 Maurice Edelman, *The Prime Minister's Daughter* (London: Hamish Hamilton, 1964), p. 79.
12 Statement from 'Maurice Edelman' in *Contemporary Novelists* (London: Macmillan, 1969).
13 William Clark, *From Three Worlds* (London: Sidgwick & Jackson, 1987), pp. 208–9.

14   Entry for 9 February 1959, in *The Backbench Diaries of Richard Crossman*, ed. Janet Morgan (London: Hamish Hamilton/Jonathan Cape, 1981), pp. 734–5.

15   Wilfred Fienburgh, *No Love for Johnnie* (London: Hutchinson, 1959), pp. 50–1.

16   Quoted in Robert Hewison, *In Anger: Culture and the Cold War, 1945–60* (London: Weidenfeld & Nicholson, 1981), pp. 177 ff.

17   The blurb for *The Rich Pay Late* (London: Anthony Blond, 1964), and see Robert Taubman in *New Statesman*, 15 October 1965.

18   Entry of 2–9 June, 1963, in Crossman, *Backbench Diaries*, p. 1000; and see also Crossman, *Diaries of a Cabinet Minister*, Vol. 2 (London: Hamish Hamilton/Jonathan Cape, 1976), pp. 779–80.

19   Anthony Powell, *Books Do Furnish a Room* (London: Heinemann, 1971), p. 51.

20   Graham Martin, 'Anthony Powell and Angus Wilson', in Boris Ford (ed.), *The New Pelican Guide to English Literature* (Harmondsworth: Penguin, 1985), pp. 193–200.

21   Walter Allen, op.cit., (Harmondsworth: Penguin, 1962); see also Walter Allen, *As I Walked Down New Grub Street* (London: Heinemann, 1981), pp. 1–5.

22   Raymond Williams, *Border Country* (Harmondsworth: Penguin, 1964), p. 214.

23   ibid., p. 333.

24   See J. P. Ward, *Raymond Williams* (Cardiff: University of Wales Press, 1981).

25   Richard Hoggart, *The Uses of Literacy* (Harmondsworth: Penguin, 1960), ch. 10.

26   Quoted in Michael Parnell, *Laughter from the Dark: A Life of Gwyn Thomas* (London: John Murray, 1988), p. 74.

27   See Dai Smith, 'A novel history', in Tony Curtis (ed.), *Wales: The Imagined Nation* (Bridgend: Poetry Wales Press, 1986), pp. 146 ff.

28   Dennis Potter, *The Nigel Barton Plays* (Harmondsworth: Penguin, 1966), pp. 7–22.

29   Dennis Potter, *The Changing Forest* (London: Secker & Warburg, 1962), p. 105.

30   C. P. Snow, *In Their Wisdom* (London: Macmillan, 1974), p. 28.

31   See Douglas Hurd and Andrew Osmond, *Send Him Victorious* (London: Collins, 1968), and *Scotch on the Rocks* (London: Collins, 1969); Michael Spicer, *Final Act* (London: Severn House, 1981); Hardiman Scott, *Operation 10* (London: Bodley Head, 1982), 1981; Fred and Geoffrey Hoyle, *The Westminster Disaster* (London: Heinemann, 1979); William F. Buckley, *Saving the Queen* (New York: Warner, 1976); Michael Shea, *Tomorrow's Men* (London: Weidenfeld & Nicholson, 1982), 1981. And see Joan Smith, 'Who's afraid of Frederick Forsyth', *New Statesman*, 15 January 1988.

32   See Jonathan Lynn and Antony Jay (eds), *Yes Minister: The Diaries of a Cabinet Minister*, 3 vols, BBC, 1981–3.

33   See Mervyn Jones, *Chances* (London: Verso, 1988), for the economics of an author of hardback political fiction.

34   Per Gedin, 'The book market', in Ford, *New Pelican Guide*, pp. 406 ff.

35   John Sutherland, *Bestsellers: Popular Fiction of the 1970s* (London: Routledge, 1981), p. 34.

36   See, for example, Ruth Dudley Edwards's, *Corridors of Death* (London:

Quartet, 1981), set in the Department of Trade and Industry, and Stanley Johnson's *The Commissioner* (London: Pan, 1987), in the EEC in Brussels.

37 Ronald Hayman, *Arnold Wesker* (London: Heinemann, 1970), pp. 8–9; Howard Goorney, *The Theatre Workshop Story* (London: Eyre Methuen, 1981), pp. 2–18; Malcolm Page, *Arden on File* (London: Methuen, 1985), p. 78.

38 See H. H. Wilson, *Pressure Group: the Campaign for Commercial Television* (New Brunswick, NJ: Rutgers University Press, 1961), pp. 206–15.

39 Page, *Arden on File*, p. 74.

40 See Arthur Marwick, 'The filming of *Room at the Top*', in Arthur Marwick (ed.), *Literature and Society* (London: Routledge, 1990). This interpretation is substantially derived from the research of my friend Walter Greiner, to whom I am deeply indebted.

41 John Braine, *Room at the Top* (London: Eyre & Spottiswoode, 1957), p. 31.

42 Crossman, *Diaries of a Cabinet Minister*, Vol. 2, pp. 779–80.

43 Quoted in Catherine Itzin, *Stages in the Revolution* (London: Methuen, 1979), pp. 106–7.

44 George Bull, *Modern British Political Dramatists* (London: Macmillan, 1985), pp. 169 ff.

45 This is discussed at length in the present writer's 'Political thrillers and the Condition of England', in Arthur Marwick (ed.), *Literature and Society* (London: Routledge, 1990).

46 Margaret Drabble, *The Ice Age* (London: Weidenfeld, 1979); Melvyn Bragg, *Autumn Manoeuvres* (London: Secker & Warburg, 1978); Mervyn Jones, *Today the Struggle* (London: Quartet, 1978).

47 See Mike Poole and John Wyver, *Powerplays: Trevor Griffiths and Television* (London: British Film Institute, 1984), pp. 1–10.

48 John Sweeney, 'Lashings of HP Sauce', *Guardian*, 24 December 1988, says all, and more than all, that may be said about this theme.

49 Alasdair Gray, *Lanark* (Edinburgh: Canongate, 1983), p. 66; and see C. Harvie, 'Drunk men looking at thistles', *Cencrastus*, no. 19 (Winter 1984), pp. 7–9.

50 See in particular Douglas Gifford's essay on Gray in *Chapman*, no. 50–1 (1989), and Gray's afterword to Agnes Owens, *Gentlemen of the West* (Harmondsworth: Penguin, 1986), pp. 129–41.

51 Cornelia Cook, *Joyce Cary: Liberal Principles* (London: Vision, 1981), pp. 217 ff.

52 See Elizabeth Wilson, *Only Halfway to Paradise* (London: Tavistock, 1980), pp. 156 ff.

53 See Moira Burgess, *The Glasgow Novel*, 2nd edn (Glasgow: Scottish Library Association, 1986), pp. 64 ff.

54 See Colin McArthur, *Television and History* (London: British Film Institute, 1978), pp. 40 ff.

55 Raymond Williams, 'Region and class in the novel' in Martin and Jefferson, *The Uses of Fiction* (Milton Keynes: Open University Press, n.d.), p. 67.

56 Robin Jenkins, 'Speaking as a Scot', *Scottish Review*, no. 27 (August 1982), pp. 18–19.

57 Richard Hughes, *The Fox in the Attic* (Harmondsworth: Penguin, 1964), p. 100.

58 See Gwyn A. Williams, *When Was Wales?* (Harmondsworth: Penguin, 1985), pp. 278 ff.

59 Humphreys, interview in *New Welsh Review*, no. 2 (Autumn 1988), p. 9.
60 See Hagal Mengel, *Sam Thompson and Modern Drama in Ulster* (Frankfurt: Peter Lang, 1986).
61 See Tom Paulin on Paisley in *Ireland and the English Crisis* (Newcastle: Bloodaxe, 1984), and Ruth Dudley Edwards, 'Irish historical novels', paper delivered at the Irish Studies Seminar, Brighton, April 1982.
62 See Page, *Arden on File*, pp. 81 ff.
63 See John Osmond, *Divided Kingdom* (London: Constable, 1988), on drama in Northern Ireland; I am also deeply grateful to Eberhard Bort for his expertise in this area.
64 Quoted in John Atkins, *The British Spy Novel* (London: Calder, 1984), pp. 144–5.
65 For Le Carré's interest in German romanticism, see David Monaghan, *The Novels of John Le Carré* (Oxford: Blackwell, 1985), pp. 2–5.

Index

(For reasons of space, only authors with many works cited have these displayed in the index. Otherwise look up the page references for those names marked with a ★.)